FOUNDATIONS OF THE REPUBLIC

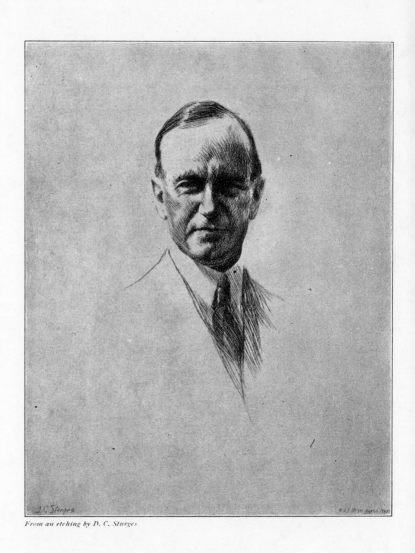

From an etching by D. C. Sturges

Calvin Coolidge

FOUNDATIONS
OF THE REPUBLIC

SPEECHES AND ADDRESSES

BY

CALVIN COOLIDGE

Essay Index Reprint Series

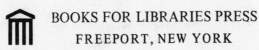

BOOKS FOR LIBRARIES PRESS
FREEPORT, NEW YORK

First Published 1926
Reprinted 1968

LIBRARY OF CONGRESS CATALOG CARD NUMBER:
68-8450

PRINTED IN THE UNITED STATES OF AMERICA

CONTENTS

I

He gave utterance to the aspiration of humanity with an eloquence which held the attention of all the earth and made America a new and enlarged influence in the destiny of mankind.

PROCLAMATION UPON THE DEATH OF WOODROW WILSON, FEBRUARY 3, 1924

To the People of the United States:

The death of Woodrow Wilson, President of the United States from March 4, 1913, to March 4, 1921, which occurred at 11:15 o'clock today at his home at Washington, District of Columbia, deprives the country of a most distinguished citizen, and is an event which causes universal and genuine sorrow. To many of us it brings the sense of a profound personal bereavement.

His early profession as a lawyer was abandoned to enter academic life. In this chosen field he attained the highest rank as an educator, and has left his impress upon the intellectual thought of the country. From the Presidency of Princeton University he was called by his fellow citizens to be the Chief Executive of the State of New Jersey. The duties of this high office he so conducted as to win the confidence of the people of the United States, who twice elected him to the Chief Magistracy of the Republic. As President of the United States he was moved by an earnest desire to promote the best interests of the country as he conceived them. His acts were prompted by high motives and his sincerity of purpose can not be questioned. He led the nation through the terrific struggle of the world war with a lofty idealism which never failed him. He gave utterance to the aspiration of humanity with an eloquence which held the attention of all the earth and made America a new and enlarged influence in the destiny of mankind.

In testimony of the respect in which his memory is held

by the Government and people of the United States, I do hereby direct that the flags of the White House and of the several Departmental buildings be displayed at half staff for a period of thirty days, and that suitable military and naval honors under orders of the Secretary of War and of the Secretary of the Navy may be rendered on the day of the funeral.

II

In the case of a people which represents many nations, cultures and races, as does our own, a unification of interests and ideals in recreations is bound to wield a telling influence for solidarity of the entire population. No more truly democratic force can be set off against the tendency to class and caste than the democracy of individual parts and prowess in sport.

THE DEMOCRACY OF SPORTS

This conference has been called to encourage Americans to make more of their opportunities and appropriate more of the advantages of America. For a long time one of the ideals of perfection has been that of a sound mind in a sound body. When most of our original educational institutions were founded, they at first served a race of pioneers. They were attended by those whose very existence depended on an active outdoor life in the open country. The most universal custom among all the people was bodily exercise. Those days long ago passed away for most of the people of this country.

There is still and must ever be a tremendous amount of manual labor, but to a large extent this has become specialized and too often would be designated correctly as drudgery. The opportunity for education of the mind, however, has greatly increased until it has become well-nigh universal. School and college athletics have become necessary. With the development of our industrial and commercial life, there are more and more those who are engaged in purely clerical activities. All of this makes it more necessary than ever that we should stimulate every possible interest in out of door health-giving recreation.

I am hopeful that the conference can coordinate our national resources and opportunities in a way better to serve this purpose. It is by no means intended that there should be any suggestion of Federal domination in these activities. Necessarily they are largely local and individual, and to be helpful they must always be spontaneous. But

At the National Conference on Outdoor Recreation, Washington, D. C., May 22, 1924.

7

this conference can be of great aid by making something
of an inventory of our national resources and opportunities
and determining how these may best be put to the most
desirable use, and, further, by exchanging ideas, create new
interests and open to view new fields.

Nearly every city is making large appropriations for laying out spacious parks and playgrounds. These are providing recreation fields for the playing of outdoor games
by both old and young. Golf courses and tennis courts
abound. Too much emphasis can not be placed on the
effort to get the children out of the alleys and off the streets
into spacious open places where there is good sunlight
and plenty of fresh air. Such an opportunity has both a
physical and mental effect. It restores the natural balance
of life and nourishes the moral fiber of youth.

Another activity which is being encouraged is that of
gardening. This is necessarily somewhat limited, but the
opportunity for engaging in it has never been anywhere near
exhausted. It makes its appeal alike to youth and age.
It is extremely practical on the one hand, and lends itself
to the artistic on the other.

A form of recreation not so accesible to many as games,
but one which has in it a peculiar hold on that which is
elemental in human nature, is hunting and fishing. These
are true outdoor sports in the highest sense, and must be
pursued in a way that develops energy, perseverance, skill,
and courage of the individual. They call for personal direction, and can not be taken up vicariously. There is a great
wealth of life and experience in this field which is never
exhausted, and always fresh and new. It is accompanied by
traits of character which make a universal appeal. A
knowledge of these arts may well be cultivated and cherished
like a knowledge of the humanities and the sciences.
Around hunting and fishing is gathered a great wealth of
prose and poetry, which testifies to the enduring interest

which these sports have held all through the development of the race.

A certain type of outdoor activity has been much developed in recent years and calls great throngs together, which may properly be designated as exhibition games. Under this head comes first in importance baseball, which is often known as the national game. Football and polo come in the same class. These activities require such long and intensive training that participation in them is necessarily confined to a class and can not be said to be open to the general public. But for creating an interest which extends to every age and every class, for giving an opportunity for a few hours in the open air which will provide a change of scene, a new trend of thought, and the arousing of new enthusiasm for the great multitude of our people, these have no superior.

But it is unnecessary for me to do more than mention a few of the representative forms of recreation. We all know that their name is legion, and that different tastes require different activities. I am not trying to recommend one above another, but I am trying to point out the national value which would accrue if there were an organized, instructed, and persistent effort to bring these benefits to the people at large. It can not be that our country is making a great outlay for playgrounds in our schools, for athletic fields in our colleges, for baseball fields in our cities, for recreation parks in our metropolitan districts, for State and national forest reservations, unless these all represent an opportunity for a real betterment of the life of the people. These are typically American in all their aspects. They minister directly to the welfare of all our inhabitants.

Civilization is measured in no small part by these standards. The famous beauty and symmetry of the Greek race in its prime was due in no small part to their general participation in athletic games. This meant development.

We can see in the gladiatorial shows of Rome, which degenerated into the butchery alike of beasts and men, the sure sign of moral decay which ended in the destruction of the empire and the breaking up of the great influence it had cast over the world. It is altogether necessary that we keep our own amusements and recreations within that field which will be prophetic, not of destruction, but of development. It is characteristic of almost the entire American life that it has a most worthy regard for clean and manly sports. It has little appetite for that which is unwholesome or brutal.

We have at hand these great resources and great opportunities. They can not be utilized to their fullest extent without careful organization and methodical purpose. Our youth need instruction in how to play as much as they do in how to work. There are those who are engaged in our industries who need an opportunity for outdoor life and recreation no less than they need opportunity of employment. Side by side with the industrial plant should be the gymnasium and the athletic field. Along with the learning of a trade by which a livelihood is to be earned should go the learning of how to participate in the activities of recreation, by which life is made not only more enjoyable, but more rounded out and complete. The country needs instruction in order that we may better secure these results.

A special consideration suggests the value of a development of national interest in recreation and sports. There is no better common denominator of a people. In the case of a people which represents many nations, cultures and races, as does our own, a unification of interests and ideals in recreations is bound to wield a telling influence for solidarity of the entire population. No more truly democratic force can be set off against the tendency to class and caste than the democracy of individual parts and prowess in sport.

Out of this conference I trust there may come a better appreciation of the necessary development of our life along these directions. They should be made to contribute to health, to broader appreciation of nature and her works, to a truer insight into the whole affair of existence. They should be the means to acquainting all of us with the wonders and delights of this world in which we live, and of this country of which we are the joint inheritors. Through them we may teach our children true sportsmanship, right living, the love of being square, the sincere purpose to make our lives genuinely useful and helpful to our fellows. All of these may be implanted through a wise use of recreational opportunities.

I want to see all Americans have a reasonable amount of leisure. Then I want to see them educated to use such leisure for their own enjoyment and betterment, and the strengthening of the quality of their citizenship. We can go a long way in that direction by getting them out of doors and really interested in nature. We can make still further progress by engaging them in games and sports. Our country is a land of cultured men and women. It is a land of agriculture, of industries, of schools, and of places of religious worship. It is a land of varied climes and scenery, of mountain and plain, of lake and river. It is the American heritage. We must make it a land of vision, a land of work, of sincere striving for the good, but we must add to all these, in order to round out the full stature of the people, an ample effort to make it a land of wholesome enjoyment and perennial gladness.

III

A mightier force than ever followed Grant or Lee has leveled both their hosts, raised up an united Nation, and made us all partakers of a new glory. It is not for us to forget the past but to remember it, that we may profit by it. But it is gone; we can not change it. We must put our emphasis on the present and put into effect the lessons the past has taught us.

THE UNITED NATION.

If I am correctly informed by history, it is fitting that the Sabbath should be your Memorial Day. This follows from the belief that except for the forces of Oliver Cromwell no army was ever more thoroughly religious than that which followed General Lee. Moreover, these ceremonies necessarily are expressive of a hope and a belief that rise above the things of this life. It was Lincoln who pointed out that both sides prayed to the same God. When that is the case, it is only a matter of time when each will seek a common end. We can now see clearly what that end is. It is the maintenance of our American form of government, of our American institutions, of our American ideals, beneath a common flag, under the blessings of Almighty God.

It was for this purpose that our Nation was brought forth. Our whole course of history has been proceeding in that direction. Out of a common experience, made more enduring by a common sacrifice, we have reached a common conviction. On this day we pause in memory of those who made their sacrifice in one way. In a few days we shall pause again in memory of those who made their sacrifice in another way. They were all Americans, all contending for what they believed were their rights. On many a battlefield they sleep side by side. Here, in a place set aside for the resting place of those who have performed military duty, both make a final bivouac. But their country lives.

The bitterness of conflict is passed. Time has softened it; discretion has changed it. Your country respects you for cherishing the memory of those who wore the gray. You respect others who cherish the memory of those who wore the blue. In that mutual respect may there be a firmer friendship, a stronger and more glorious Union.

When I delivered the address dedicating the great monument to General Grant in the city of Washington, General Carr was present, with others of his comrades, and responded for the Confederacy with a most appropriate tribute. He has lately passed away, one of the last of a talented and gallant corps of officers. To the memory of him whom I had seen and heard and knew as the representative of that now silent throng, whom I did not know, I offer my tribute. We know that Providence would have it so. We see and we obey. A mightier force than ever followed Grant or Lee has leveled both their hosts, raised up an united Nation, and made us all partakers of a new glory. It is not for us to forget the past but to remember it, that we may profit by it. But it is gone; we cannot change it. We must put our emphasis on the present and put into effect the lessons the past has taught us. All about us sleep those of many different beliefs and many divergent actions. But America claims them all. Her flag floats over them all. Her Government protects them all. They all rest in the same divine peace.

At the Confederate Memorial, Arlington National Cemetery, Virginia, Sunday, May 25, 1924.

IV

American citizenship is a high estate. He who holds it is the peer of kings. It has been secured only by untold toil and effort. It will be maintained by no other method. It demands the best that men and women have to give. But it likewise awards to its partakers the best that there is on earth. To attempt to turn it into a thing of ease and inaction would be only to debase it. To cease to struggle and toil and sacrifice for it is not only to cease to be worthy of it but is to start a retreat toward barbarism. No matter what others may say, no matter what others may do, this is the stand that those must maintain who are worthy to be called Americans.

FREEDOM AND ITS OBLIGATIONS.

We meet again upon this hallowed ground to commemorate those who played their part in a particular outbreak of an age-old conflict. Many men have many theories about the struggle that went on from 1861 to 1865. Some say it had for its purpose the abolition of slavery. President Lincoln did not so consider it. There were those in the South who would have been willing to wage war for its continuation, but I very much doubt if the South as a whole could have been persuaded to take up arms for that purpose. There were those in the North who would have been willing to wage war for its abolition, but the North as a whole could not have been persuaded to take up arms for that purpose. President Lincoln made it perfectly clear that his effort was to save the Union—with slavery if he could save it that way; without slavery if he could save it that way. But he would save the Union. The South stood for the principle of the sovereignty of the States. The North stood for the principle of the supremacy of the Union.

This was an age-old conflict. At its foundation lies the question of how can the Government govern and the people be free? How can organized society make and enforce laws and the individual remain independent? There is no short sighted answer to these inquiries. Whatever may have been the ambiguity in the Federal Constitution, of course the Union had to be supreme within its sphere or cease to be a Union. It was also certain and obvious that each State had to be sovereign within its sphere or cease to be a State.

At Arlington National Cemetery, May 30, 1924.

19

It is equally clear that a government must govern, must prescribe and enforce laws within its sphere or cease to be a government. Moreover, the individual must be independent and free within his own sphere or cease to be an individual. The fundamental question was then, is now, and always will be through what adjustments, by what actions, these principles may be applied.

It needs but very little consideration to reach the conclusion that all of these terms are relative, not absolute, in their application to the affairs of this earth. There is no absolute and complete sovereignty for a State, nor absolute and complete independence and freedom for an individual. It happened in 1861 that the States of the North and the South were so fully agreed among themselves that they were able to combine against each other. But supposing each State of the Union should undertake to make its own decisions upon all questions, and that all held divergent views. If such a condition were carried to its logical conclusion, each would come into conflict with all the others, and a condition would arise which could only result in mutual destruction. It is evident that this would be the antithesis of State sovereignty. Or suppose that each individual in the assertion of his own independence and freedom undertook to act in entire disregard of the rights of others. The end would be likewise mutual destruction, and no one would be independent and no one would be free. Yet these are conflicts which have gone on ever since the organization of society into government, and they are going on now. To my mind this was fundamental of the conflict which broke out in 1861.

The thirteen Colonies were not unaware of the difficulties which these problems presented. We shall find a great deal of wisdom in the method by which they dealt with them. When they were finally separated from Great Britain, the allegiance of their citizens was not to the Nation, for there was none. It was to the States. For the conduct of the war there had been a voluntary confederacy loosely constructed and practically impotent. Continuing after peace was made, when the common peril which had been its chief motive no longer existed, it grew weaker and weaker. Each of the States could have insisted on an entirely separate and independent existence, having full authority over both their internal and external affairs, sovereign in every way. But such sovereignty would have been a vain and empty thing. It would have been unsupported by adequate resources either of property or population, without a real national spirit, ready to fall prey to foreign intrigue or foreign conquest. That kind of sovereignty meant but little. It had no substance in it. The people and their leaders naturally sought for a larger, more inspiring ideal. They realized that while to be a citizen of a State meant something, it meant a great deal more if that State were a part of a national union. The establishment of a Federal Constitution giving power and authority to create a real National Government did not in the end mean a detriment, but rather an increment to the sovereignty of the several States. Under the Constitution there was brought into being a new relationship, which did not detract from but added to the power and the position of each State. It is true that they surrendered the privilege of performing certain acts for themselves, like the regulation of commerce and the maintenance of foreign relations, but in becoming a part of the Union they received more than they gave.

The same thing applies to the individual in organized society. When each citizen submits himself to the authority of law he does not thereby decrease his independence or freedom, but rather increases it. By recognizing that he is a part of a larger body which is banded together for a common purpose, he becomes more than an individual, he rises to a new dignity of citizenship. Instead of finding himself restricted and confined by rendering obedience to public law, he finds himself protected and defended and in the exercise of increased and increasing rights. It is true that as civilization becomes more complex it is necessary to surrender more and more of the freedom of action and live more and more according to the rule of public regulation, but it is also true that the rewards and the privileges which come to a member of organized society increase in a still greater proportion. Primitive life has its freedom and its attraction, but the observance of the restrictions of modern civilization enhances the privileges of living a thousandfold.

Perhaps I have said enough to indicate the great advantages that accrue to all of us by the support and maintenance of our Government, the continuation of the functions of legislation, the administration of justice, and the execution of the laws. There can be no substitute for these, no securing of greater freedom by their downfall and failure, but only disorganization, suffering and want, and final destruction. All that we have of rights accrue from the Government under which we live.

In these days little need exists for extolling the blessings of our Federal Union. Its benefits are known and recognized by all its citizens who are worthy of serious attention. No one thinks now of attempting to destroy the Union by armed force. No one seriously considers withdrawing from it. But it is not enough that it should be free from attack— it must be approved and supported by a national spirit. Our prime allegiance must be to the whole country. A sentiment of sectionalism is not harmless because it is unarmed. Resistance to the righteous authority of Federal law is not innocent because it is not accompanied by secession. We need a more definite realization that all of our country must stand or fall together, and that it is the duty of the Government to promote the welfare of each part and the duty of the citizen to remember that he must be first of all an American.

Only one conclusion appears to me possible. We shall not promote our welfare by a narrow and shortsighted policy. We can gain nothing by any destruction of government or society. That action which in the long run is for the advantage of the individual, as it is for the support of our Union, is best summed up in a single word—renunciation. It is only by surrendering a certain amount of our liberty, only by taking on new duties and assuming new obligations, that we make that progress which we characterize as civilization. It is only in like manner that the citizens and the States can maintain our Federal Union and become partakers of its glory. That is the answer to every herald of discontent and to every preacher of destruction. While this is understood, American institutions and the Amercian Union are secure.

This principle can not be too definitely or emphatically proclaimed. American citizenship is a high estate. He who holds it is the peer of kings. It has been secured only by untold toil and effort. It will be maintained by no other method. It demands the best that men and women have to give. But it likewise awards to its partakers the best that there is on earth. To attempt to turn it into a thing of ease and inaction would be only to debase it. To cease to struggle and toil and sacrifice for it is not only to cease to be worthy of it but is to start a retreat toward barbarism. No matter what others may say, no matter what others may do, this is the stand that those must maintain who are worthy to be called Americans.

But that great struggle was carried on by those whom this day is set apart to commemorate, not only for the preservation of the Union. The authority of the Federal Government had been resisted by armed force. They were also striving to restore peace. It must be remembered that our Republic was organized to avoid and discourage war, and to promote and establish peace. It is the leading characteristic of our national holidays that they are days of peace. The ways of our people are the ways of peace. They naturally seek ways to make peace more secure.

It is not to be inferred that it would be anything less than courting national disaster to leave our country barren of defense. Human nature is a very constant quality. While there is justification for hoping and believing that we are moving toward perfection, it would be idle and absurd to assume that we have already reached it. We can not disregard history. There have been and will be domestic disorders. There have been and will be tendencies of one nation to encroach on another. I believe in the maintenance of an Army and Navy, not for aggression but for defense. Security and order are our most valuable possessions. They are cheap at any price. But I am opposed to every kind of military aggrandizement and to all forms of competitive armament. The ideal would be for nations to become parties to mutual covenants limiting their military establishments, and making it obvious that they are not maintained to menace each other. This ideal should be made practical as fast as possible.

Our Nation has associated itself with other great powers for the purpose of promoting peace in the regions of the Pacific Ocean. It has steadily refused to accept the covenant of the League of Nations, but long before that was thought of, before the opening of the present century, we were foremost in promoting the calling of a conference at The Hague to provide for a tribunal of arbitration for the settlement of international disputes. We have made many treaties on that basis with other nations.

But we have an opportunity before us to reassert our desire and to lend the force of our example for the peaceful adjudication of differences between nations. Such action would be in entire harmony with the policy which we have long advocated. I do not look upon it as a certain guaranty against war, but it would be a method of disposing of troublesome questions, an accumulation of which leads to irritating conditions and results in mutually hostile sentiments. More than a year ago President Harding proposed that the Senate should authorize our adherence to the protocol of the Permanent Court of International Justice, with certain conditions. His suggestion has already had my approval. On that I stand. I should not oppose other reservations, but any material changes which would not probably receive the consent of the many other nations would be impracticable. We can not take a step in advance of this kind without assuming certain obligations. Here again if we receive anything we must surrender something. We may as well face the question candidly, and if we are willing to assume these new duties in exchange for the benefits which would accrue to us, let us say so. If we are not willing, let us say that. We can accomplish nothing by taking a doubtful or ambiguous position. We are not going to be able to avoid meeting the world and bearing our part of the burdens of the world. We must meet those burdens and overcome them or they will meet us and overcome us. For my part I desire my country to meet them without evasion and without fear in an upright, downright, square, American way.

While there are those who think we would be exposed to peril by adhering to this court, I am unable to attach great weight to their arguments. Whatever differences, whatever perils exist for us in the world, will come anyway, whether we oppose or support the court. I am one of those who believe we would be safer and that we would be meeting our duties better by supporting it and making every possible use of it. I feel confident that such action would make a greater America, that it would be productive of a higher and finer national spirit, and of a more complete national life.

It is these two thoughts of union and peace which appear to me to be especially appropriate for our consideration on this day. Like all else in human experience, they are not things which can be set apart and have an independent existence. They exist by reason of the concrete actions of men and women. It is the men and women whose actions between 1861 and 1865 gave us union and peace that we are met here this day to commemorate. When we seek for the chief characteristic of those actions, we come back to the word which I have already uttered—renunciation. They gave up ease and home and safety and braved every impending danger and mortal peril that they might accomplish these ends. They thereby became in this Republic a body of citizens set apart and marked for every honor so long as our Nation shall endure. Here on this wooded eminence, overlooking the Capital of the country for which they fought, many of them repose, officers of high rank and privates mingling in a common dust, holding the common veneration of a grateful people. The heroes of other wars lie with them, and in a place of great preëminence lies one whose identity is unknown, save that he was a soldier of this Republic who fought that its ideals, its institutions, its liberties, might be perpetuated among men. A grateful country holds all these services as her most priceless heritage, to be cherished forevermore.

We can testify to these opinions, not by our words but by our actions. Our country can not exist on the renunciation of the heroic souls of the past. Public service, from the action of the humblest voter to the most exalted office, can not be made a mere matter of hire and salary. The supporters of our institutions must be inspired by a more dominent motive than a conviction that their actions are going to be profitable. We can not lower our standards to what we think will pay, but we must raise them to what we think is right. It is only in that direction that we shall find true patriotism. It is only by that method that we can maintain the rights of the individual, the sovereignty of the States, the integrity of the Union, the permanency of peace, and the welfare of mankind. You soldiers of the Republic enrolled under her banner that through your sacrifices there might be an atonement for the evils of your day. That is the standard of citizenship for all time. It is the requirement which must be met by those who hold public place. That must be the ideal of those who are worthy to share in the glory which you have given to the name of America, the ideal of those who hold fellowship with Washington and Lincoln.

V

The progress of the colored people on this continent is one of the marvels of modern history. We are perhaps even yet too near to this phenomenon to be able fully to appreciate its significance. That can be impressed on us only as we study and contrast the rapid advancement of the colored people in America with the slow and painful upward movement of humanity as a whole throughout the long human story.

THE PROGRESS OF A PEOPLE

Iᴛ has come to be a legend, and I believe with more foundation of fact than most legends, that Howard University was the outgrowth of the inspiration of a prayer meeting. I hope it is true, and I shall choose to believe it, for it makes of this scene and this occasion a new testimony that prayers are answered. Here has been established a great university, a sort of educational laboratory for the production of intellectual and spiritual leadership among a people whose history, if you will examine it as it deserves, is one of the striking evidences of a soundness of our civilization.

The accomplishments of the colored people in the United States, in the brief historic period since they were brought here from the restrictions of their native continent, can not but make us realize that there is something essential in our civilization which gives it a special power. I think we shall be able to agree that this particular element is the Christian religion, whose influence always and everywhere has been a force for the illumination and advancement of the peoples who have come under its sway.

The progress of the colored people on this continent is one of the marvels of modern history. We are perhaps even yet too near to this phenomenon to be able fully to appreciate its significance. That can be impressed on us only as we study and contrast the rapid advancement of the colored people in America with the slow and painful upward movement of humanity as a whole throughout the long human story.

At Howard University, June 6, 1924.

An occasion such as this which has brought us here can not but direct our consideration to these things. It has been a painful and difficult experience, this by which another race has been recruited to the standard of civilization and enlightenment; for that is really what has been going on; and the episodes of Negro slavery in America, of civil war, and emancipation, and, following that, the rapid advancement of the American colored people both materially and spiritually, must be recognized as parts of a long evolution by which all mankind is gradually being led to higher levels, expanding its understanding of its mission here, approaching nearer and nearer to the realization of its full and perfected destiny.

In such a view of the history of the Negro race in America, we may find the evidences that the black man's probation on this continent was a necessary part in a great plan by which the race was to be saved to the world for a service which we are now able to vision and, even if yet somewhat dimly, to appreciate. The destiny of the great African Continent, to be added at length—and in a future not now far beyond us—to the realms of the highest civilization, has become apparent within a very few decades. But for the strange and long inscrutable purpose which in the ordering of human affairs subjected a part of the black race to the ordeal of slavery, that race might have been assigned to the tragic fate which has befallen many aboriginal peoples when brought into conflict with more advanced communities. Instead, we are able now to be confident that this race is to be preserved for a great and useful work. If some of its members have suffered, if some have been denied, if some have been sacrificed, we are able at last to realize that their sacrifices were borne in a great cause. They gave vicariously, that a vastly greater number might be preserved and benefited through them. The salvation of a race, the destiny of a continent, were bought at the price of these sacrifices.

Howard University is but one of the many institutions which have grown up in this country, dedicated to this purpose of preserving one of the races of men and fitting it for its largest usefulness. Here is a people adapted, as most people are not, to life in the tropics. They are capable of redeeming vast luxuriant areas of unexampled productivity, and of reclaiming them for the sustenance of mankind and the increasing security of the human community. It is a great destiny, to which we may now look forward with confidence that it will be fully realized.

Looking back only a few years, we appreciate how rapid has been the progress of the colored people on this continent. Emancipation brought them the opportunity of which they have availed themselves. It has been calculated that in the first year following the acceptance of their status as a free people, there were approximately 4,000,000 members of the race in this country, and that among these only 12,000 were the owners of their homes; only 20,000 among them conducted their own farms, and the aggregate wealth of these 4,000,000 people hardly exceeded $20,000,000. In a little over a half century since, the number of business enterprises operated by colored people had grown to near 50,000, while the wealth of the Negro community has grown to more than $1,100,000,000. And these figures convey a most inadequate suggestion of the material progress. The 2,000 business enterprises which were in the hands of colored people immediately following emancipation were almost without exception small and rudimentary. Among the 50,000 business operations now in the hands of colored people may be found every type of present-day affairs. There are more than 70 banks conducted by thoroughly competent colored business men. More than 80 per cent of all American Negroes are now able to read and write. When they achieved their freedom not 10 per cent were literate. There are nearly 2,000,000 Negro pupils in the public schools; well-nigh 40,000 Negro teachers are listed, more than 3,000 following their profession in normal schools and colleges. The list of educational institutions devoting themselves to the race includes 50 colleges, 13 colleges for women, 26 theological schools, a standard school of law, and 2 high-grade institutions of medicine. Through the work of these institutions the Negro race is equipping men and women from its own ranks to provide its leadership in business, the professions, in all relations of life.

This, of course, is the special field of usefulness for colored men and women who find the opportunity to get adequate education. Their own people need their help, guidance, leadership, and inspiration. Those of you who are fortunate enough to equip yourselves for these tasks have a special responsibility to make the best use of great opportunities. In a very special way it is incumbent upon those who are prepared to help their people to maintain the truest standards of character and unselfish purpose. The Negro community of America has already so far progressed that its members can be assured that their future is in their own hands. Racial hostility, ancient tradition, and social prejudice are not to be eliminated immediately or easily   But they will be lessened as the colored people by their own efforts and under their own leaders shall prove worthy of the fullest measure of opportunity.

The Nation has need of all that can be contributed to it through the best efforts of all its citizens. The colored people have repeatedly proved their devotion to the high ideals of our country. They gave their services in the war with the same patriotism and readiness that other citizens did. The records of the selective draft show that somewhat more than 2,250,000 colored men were registered. The records further prove that, far from seeking to avoid participation in the national defense, they showed that they wished to enlist before the selective service act was put into operation, and they did not attempt to evade that act afterwards. The propaganda of prejudice and hatred which sought to keep the colored men from supporting the national cause completely failed. The black man showed himself the same kind of citizen, moved by the same kind of patriotism, as the white man. They were tempted, but not one betrayed his country. Among well-nigh 400,000 colored men who were taken into the military service, about one-half had overseas experience. They came home with many decorations and their conduct repeatedly won high commendation from both American and European commanders.

The armies in the field could not have done their part in the war if they had not been sustained and supported by the far greater civilian forces at home, which through unremitting toil made it possible to sustain our war effort. No part of the community responded more willingly, more generously, more unqualifiedly, to the demand for special extraordinary exertion, than did the members of the Negro race. Whether in the military service, or in the vast mobilization of industrial resources which the war required, the Negro did his part precisely as did the white man. He drew no color line when patriotism made its call upon him. He gave precisely as his white fellow citizens gave, to the limit of resources and abilities, to help the general cause. Thus the American Negro established his right to the gratitude and appreciation which the Nation has been glad to accord.

We are not all permitted the privilege of a university training. We can not all enter the professions. What is the great need of American citienship? To my mind it is this, that each should take up the burden where he is. "Do the day's work," I have said, and it should be done in the remembrance that all work is dignified. Your race is entitled to great praise for the contribution it makes in doing the work of the world.

There will be other crises in the national history which will make other demands for the fullest and most unselfish contribution to the national interest. No generation will be denied its opportunity, will be spared its duty, to put forth its best efforts. We devoutly hope that these contributions will not be demanded upon the field of battle. But they will be just as truly needed, just as urgently summoned, in the activities of peace, the efforts of industry, the performance of all the obligations of citizenship. We can not go out from this place and occasion without refreshment of faith and renewal of confidence that in every exigency our Negro fellow citizens will render the best and fullest measure of service whereof they are capable.

VI

With us economy is imperative. It is a full test of our national character. Bound up in it is the true cause, not of the property interests, not of any privilege, but of all the people. It is pre-eminently the source of popular rights. It is always the people who toil that pay. It seems to me, therefore, worthy of our highest endeavor.

ECONOMY IN THE INTEREST OF ALL.

THIS is the seventh regular meeting of the Business Organization of the Government. The first of these meetings was held three years ago. This marks the close of three years of action under the Budget system. At the first meeting was commenced an intensive campaign in behalf of the people who pay the taxes in our country. The foes of that campaign were extravagance and inefficiency in the public service. For three years we have waged this intensive campaign. It has been a united effort, and united effort never fails of accomplishment. The people of this Nation are beginning to win. In that short space of time we have accomplished the unbelievable. Uncoördinated procedures of official action have been coördinated. Departmental interests have been made subservient to the common interests of the Government as a whole. The business of Government has been established on an efficient basis. You have done this, and for doing it you are entitled to the thanks of the American people. This has been and is their fight.

We are often told that we are a rich country, and we are. We are often reminded that we are in the best financial condition of any of the great powers, and we are. But we must remember that we also have a broader scale of existence and a higher standard of living. We have a freer Government and a more flexible organization of society. Where more is given, more is required. A tropical state of savagery almost maintains itself. American civilization is the product of a constant and mighty effort. One of the greatest perils to an extensive republic is the disregard of individual rights.

At the Seventh Regular Meeting of the Business Organization of the Government at Memorial Contenental Hall, June 30, 1924.

In our own country such rights do not appear to be in immediate danger from direct attack, but they are always in jeopardy through indirect action.

One of the rights which the freeman has always guarded with most jealous care is that of enjoying the rewards of his own industry. Realizing that the power to tax is the power to destroy, and that the power to take a certain amount of property or of income is only another way of saying that for a certain proportion of his time a citizen must work for the Government, the authority to impose a tax on the people has been most carefully guarded. Our own Constitution requires that revenue bills should originate in the House, because that body is supposed to be more representative of the people. These precautions have been taken because of the full realization that any oppression laid upon the people by excessive taxation, any disregard of their right to hold and enjoy the property which they have rightfully acquired, would be fatal to freedom. A government which lays taxes on the people not required by urgent public necessity and sound public policy is not a protector of liberty, but an instrument of tyranny. It condemns the citizen to servitude. One of the first signs of the breaking down of free government is a disregard by the taxing power of the right of the people to their own property. It makes little difference whether such a condition is brought about through the will of a dictator, through the power of a military force, or through the pressure of an organized minority. The result is the same. Unless the people can enjoy that reasonable security in the possession of their property, which is guaranteed by the Constitution, against unreasonable taxation, freedom is at an end. The common man is restrained and hampered in his ability to secure food and clothing and shelter. His wages are decreased, his hours of labor are lengthened. Against the recurring tendency in this direction there must be interposed the constant effort of an informed electorate and of patriotic public servants. The importance of a constant reiteration of these principles can not be overestimated. They can not be denied. They must not be ignored.

There is a most urgent necessity for those who are charged with the responsibility of government administration to realize that the people of our country can not maintain their own high standards, they can not compete against the lower standards of the rest of the world, unless we are free from excessive taxes. With us economy is imperative. It is a full test of our national character. Bound up in it is the true cause, not of the property interests, not of any privilege, but of all the people. It is preëminently the source of popular rights. It is always the people who toil that pay. It seems to me, therefore, worthy of our highest endeavor. It is this which gives the real importance to this meeting.

I would not be misunderstood. I am not advocating parsimony, I want to be liberal. Public service is entitled to a suitable reward. But there is a distinct limit to the amount of public service we can profitably employ. We require national defense, but it must be limited. We need public improvements, but they must be gradual. We have to make some capital investments, but they must be certain to give fair returns. Every dollar expended must be made in the light of all our national resources, and all our national needs. It is here that the Budget system gets its strength as a method of fiscal administration.

What progress we have made in ordering the national finances is easily shown. A comparison of our receipts and expenditures for the last four years illustrates conclusively what has been accomplished during the three years of the Budget system.

For the fiscal year ending June 30, 1921, the last pre-Budget year, our expenditures were $5,538,000,000 and our receipts $5,624,000,000. For the succeeding three years, which include the year which ends to-day, our expenditures were $3,795,000,000, $3,697,000,000 and $3,497,000,000 respectively. Here we show a progressive and consistent reduction in expenditures. On the other side of the ledger our receipts for 1922 were $4,109,000,000; 1923, $4,007,-000,000; and 1924, $3,995,000,000. An analysis of these figures shows that in the face of a progressive reduction in receipts we have still achieved a substantial surplus at the end of each of the fiscal years—$314,000,000 for 1922, $310,000,000 for 1923, and in excess of $500,000,000 for 1924. The amounts which I have stated as being the expenditures, receipts and surplus for the fiscal year 1924, which ends to-day, are only approximate. We will not have the actual figures until the books are finally balanced. The surplus accumulated at the end of each of the last three fiscal years has been applied to the reduction of the public debt in addition to the reductions required by law under the sinking fund and other acts. Without the aid of this recurring surplus the public debt would be $1,100,000,000 more than it now stands, and the interest charges would be some $45,000,000 greater next year than we shall now have to pay.

Along with this reduction in expenditures has gone a progressive reduction of the public debt with its attendant relief from the burden of interest. On June 30, 1921, the public debt was $23,976,000,000. In 1922 it had been reduced more than $1,000,000,000 to $22,964,000,000. In 1923 it had been reduced more than $600,000,000 to $22,-349,000,000. In 1924 it has been reduced again by more than $1,000,000,000, and stands at an estimated amount of $21,254,000,000, which is a reduction in three years of $2,-722,000,000, and means a saving of interest of more than $120,000,000 each year.

This shows that the intensive campaign which was commenced three years ago has been waged unrelentingly. In this campaign we have had the active coöperation and support of the Congress. The three budgets presented by the Chief Executive to the Congress have carried drastic, progressive reductions in their estimates for funds. Congress has adhered to Budget procedure in passing upon these estimates. The appropriations granted have been in harmony with the financial program of the Chief Executive.

When we met six months ago I stated to you that this fight for economy had but one purpose—that its benefits would accrue to the whole people through reduction in taxes. Taxes have now been reduced. Under the new tax law, tax receipts, as now estimated, will be approximately $6,000,000 per day less for 1925 than they were in 1921. While our immediate need is for tax reform, as distinguished from tax reduction, we must continue this campaign for economy so as to make possible further tax reduction. We owe this to the people of our Nation, to the people who must pay with their toil. The relief which has recently been afforded must be only the beginning. So in all your efforts, in all your sacrifices, you must bear in mind that you are making them for the people of our country. There could be no nobler cause or one showing higher patriotism. Bear in mind always that we are here as the servants of the people and that only as we serve them well and faithfully shall we succeed.

This insistent demand for economy and reduction in expenditures necessarily requires increasing efficiency of administration. I realize that it is making an ever-increasing call upon the administrative ability of responsible officials. But this is a call for real service. It demands a most searching inquiry into the field of your activities so as to remove entirely from them all elements which are not essential and so as to curtail all those which may be reduced without prejudice to the welfare of the Nation. If there is any question as to the authority of heads of departments or establishments to discontinue or reduce any phase of existing work, it is my desire that they report the matter to me. The duty and the opportunity to-day of the Government's administrators is not to enter upon new fields of enterprise. On the other hand, it is their duty and opportunity to carry on approved and necessary activities with the smallest possible expenditure. In the past twenty years the Government's activities have developed and multiplied in a most extraordinary way. Certainly the initiation of new activities should be discouraged unless essential to the well-being of the Nation. We, the administrators of the Government's great business interests, should have at this time only one thought and policy—to perform efficiently the functions devolving upon us under the law. And we should accomplish this with the smallest possible demand upon the Treasury. We have made real progress in this direction. Our responsibility to the taxpayers demands further progress.

To-morrow we commence a new fiscal year. We will have a smaller revenue by reason of the lessening of the burden of the taxpayer under the new tax law. On the other hand, we will have an increase in our fixed charges. The World War adjusted compensation act alone adds approximately $132,000,000 to our fixed charges for 1925. A real battle faces us, but we are organized for the fight. The best estimate to-day indicates a surplus of approximately $25,000,000 for the next fiscal year. This estimate is predicated on an expenditure program which, exclusive of the redemption of the public debt, amounts to $3,083,000,000. I desire that this expenditure program be reduced by $83,-000,000. I do not contemplate total expenditures for the next fiscal year which will exceed $3,000,000,000, exclusive of the redemption of the public debt. This will give us a surplus at the end of 1925 of $108,000,000. This, or a greater surplus, should be our aim. The people have faith in us. We must preserve this faith. Our efforts and our accomplishments are also serving as inspiration to the other nations of the world. We are setting the example for reduction in the cost of government and for return to ordinary peace-time conditions. There can be no faltering. Our duty is plain. As we have progressed in these last three years, so we must continue.

You, with your intimate knowledge of the details of your work, know where further practical economies can be effected. I desire, however, that you give especial attention to the matter of personnel. This is by far the most costly item in our expenditures. We must reduce the Government payroll. I am satisfied that it will lead to greater efficiency. And in this same connection I desire careful scrutiny of travel orders. Our travel expense item is too great. An order for travel should be given only when absolutely necessary. You can effect economy in this item. A further fertile field for economy is the item of printing and binding. I am sometimes startled at the number of Government publications which come to my attention. It can not be that all are necessary.

In this effort for economy and efficiency in the Federal service the coördinating agencies created by Executive order have played a most important part. The necessity and value of coördination have been clearly demonstrated. It has brought the departments and establishments into intimate contact. Contradictory plans, conflicting procedures, have been supplanted by common plans and harmonious procedures. It is essential that this work go on. I realize the heavy demands upon the members of the several coördinating boards. They have also their departmental work to perform. This calls again for a real sacrifice, but for a sacrifice in the interest of the taxpayers.

You are now preparing your preliminary estimates for

the fiscal year 1926. For that fiscal year it will be my purpose to transmit to Congress estimates of appropriations which, excluding the interest on and reduction in the public debt, and the Postal Service, will not exceed a total of $1,800,000,000. This tentative limitation is in furtherance of my program for a progressive reduction in the cost of government.

I regret that there are still some officials who apparently feel that the estimates transmitted to the Bureau of the Budget are the estimates which they are authorized to advocate before the committees of the Congress. Let me say here that under the budget and accounting act the only lawful estimates are those which the Chief Executive transmits to the Congress. It is these estimates that call for your loyal support. Unless such support be given, you are not fulfilling your obligations to your office. I trust that neither the Chief Executive nor the Appropriations Committees of Congress again will have occasion to call your attention to the provisions of the budget and accounting act. This law must be observed not only in its letter but in its spirit. I herewith serve notice again as Chief Executive that I propose to protect the integrity of my budget.

We must have no carelessness in our dealings with public property or the expenditure of public money. Such a condition is characteristic either of an undeveloped people, or of a decadent civilization. America is neither. It stands out strong and vigorous and mature. We must have an administration which is marked, not by the inexperience of youth, or the futility of age, but by the character and ability of maturity. We have had the self-control to put into effect the Budget system, to live under it and in accordance with it. It is an accomplishment in the art of self-government of the very highest importance. It means that the American Government is not a spendthrift, and that it is not lacking in the force or disposition to organize and administer its finances in a scientific way. To maintain this condition puts us constantly on trial. It requires us to demonstrate whether we are weaklings, or whether we have strength of character. It is not too much to say that it is a measure of the power and integrity of the civilization which we represent. I have a firm faith in your ability to maintain this position, and in the will of the American people to support you in that determination. In that faith in you and them, I propose to persevere. I am for economy. After that I am for more economy. At this time and under present conditions that is my conception of serving all the people.

I will now turn this meeting over to General Lord, the Director of the Bureau of the Budget. He is human. He hates to say no. But he is a brave man, and he does his duty without fear or favor. This Nation is his debtor. He will tell you more in detail of the things which have been accomplished and of the work which lies before you under the financial program which I have outlined to you. But let me leave this final word with you. So far as it is within my power I will not permit increases in expenditures that threaten to prevent further tax reduction or that contemplate such an unthinkable thing as increase in taxes. If with increasing business our revenues increase, such increase should not be absorbed in new ways of spending. They should be applied to the lowering of taxes. In that direction lies the public welfare.

VII

It needed but little contemplation to determine that the greatest obstacle to freedom was ignorance. If there was to be self-government, if there was to be popular sovereignty, if there was to be an almost unlimited privilege to vote and hold office, if the people were going to maintain themselves and administer their own political and social affairs, it was necessary as a purely practical matter that they should have a sufficiently trained and enlightened intelligence to accomplish that end. Popular government could only be predicated on popular education.

EDUCATION: THE CORNERSTONE OF SELF-GOVERNMENT

FOR almost a century and a half the Fourth of July has been marked as Independence Day. It has been given over to the contemplation of those principles and those institutions which America peculiarly represents. In times gone by the exuberance of youth and the consciousness of power recently gained has often made it an occasion for boastfulness. Long orations have been made, which consisted for the most part of a reassurance to ourselves and a notice to the world that we were a great Nation. Those days are past. Our own people need no reassurance, the world needs no notice, of this long self-evident conclusion. Our country has not ceased to glory in its strength, but it has come to a realization that it must have something more than numbers and wealth, something more than a fleet and an army, to satisfy the longing of the soul. It knows that to power must be added wisdom, and to greatness must be added morality. It is no longer so solicitous to catalogue the powers which it possesses, as to direct those great forces for the spiritual advancement of the American people at home and the discharge of the obligations to humanity abroad. America is turning from the things that are seen to the things that are unseen.

By this I do not mean that there is in contemplation, or required, any change in our fundamental institutions. I mean, rather, that we are beginning to reap the rewards which accrue from the existence of those institutions and

At the Convention of the National Education Association, Washington, D. C., July 4, 1924.

our devotion and loyalty to them. Some principles are so constant and so obvious that we do not need to change them, but we need rather to observe them. The world is fairly well agreed on the probable permanence of the first four tables of the arithmetic with which I struggled when I attended the district school. It is not thought that they need to be changed, or that we can make any progress by refusing to apply them. Those who seek to evade them in the ordinary business and procedure of life would undoubtedly find that such action would work either to the ruin of any commercial enterprise, or if it did not, the beneficiaries of such a disregard of the commonly accepted rules of addition would undoubtedly find that a very large majority of people would be old-fashioned enough to charge them with fraud. The institutions of the Government and society may not always be susceptible of a demonstration which is as exact as those of mathematics, but nevertheless political relationship is a very old science which has been set out in theory and wrought out in practice through very many centuries. Its fundamental principles are fairly well established. That there could have been gathered together a body of men so learned in that science, so experienced in its application, so talented and so wise in its statement and demonstration, as those who prepared, formulated, and secured the adoption of the American Constitution, will never cease to be the wonder and admiration of the profoundest students of Government. After making every allowance for a fortunate combination of circumstances and the accomplishments of human ingenuity, they have been nearly all forced to come to the belief that it can be accounted for only by the addition of another element, which we must recognize as the guiding hand of Providence. As we can make progress in science not by the disregard, but by the application of the laws of mathematics, so in my firm conviction we can make progress politically and socially, not by a disregard of those fundamental principles which are the recognized, ratified and established American institutions, but by their scrupulous support and observance. American ideals do not require to be changed so much as they require to be understood and applied.

The return of this day quite naturally invites us to a reconsideration of those principles set out in the Declaration of Independence, which were for the first time fully established in a form of government by the adoption of the American Constitution. Such a consideration presents many angles, for it touches the entire life of the Nation. To deal with so large a subject adequately, it is obvious would require extensive treatment. On this occasion it is possible only to touch on one phase of it.

It can not be too often pointed out that the fundamental conception of American institutions is regard for the individual. The rights which are so clearly asserted in the Declaration of Independence are the rights of the individual. The wrongs of which that instrument complains, and which it asserts it is the purpose of its signers to redress, are the wrongs of the individual. Through it all runs the recognition of the dignity and worth of the individual, because of his possession of those qualities which are revealed to us by religion. It is this conception alone which warrants the assertion of the universal right to freedom. America has been the working out of the modern effort to provide a system of government and society which would give to the individual that freedom which his nature requires.

It is easy to appreciate both the soundness and the grandeur of such a vision. Its magnitude implies that it was a conception not to be accomplished in a day or a year, but by the slow and toilsome experience of generations. The foundations of the structure have been laid, the rules of action have been stated. It is for us to make such contri-

bution as we are able toward its completion and adoption.
The end sought has been to create a nation wherein the individual might rise to the full stature of manhood and
womanhood.

It needed but little contemplation to determine that
the greatest obstacle to freedom was ignorance. If there
was to be self-government, if there was to be popular sovereignty, if there was to be an almost unlimited privilege
to vote and hold office, if the people were going to maintain
themselves and administer their own political and social
affairs, it was necessary as a purely practical matter that
they should have a sufficiently trained and enlightened intelligence to accomplish that end. Popular government
could only be predicated on popular education. In addition to this, the very conception of the value and responsibility of the individual, which made him worthy to be en-
trusted with this high estate, required that he should be
furnished the opportunity to develop the spiritual nature,
with which he was endowed, through adequate education.

Merely to state the American ideal is to perceive not
only how far we still are from its realization, but to comprehend with what patience we must view many seeming
failures, while we contemplate with great satisfaction much
assured success.

We can see the early beginnings of our country and understand the situation in those days better than it was
understood by its own contemporaries. It was a time of
great toil and hardship. The entire settled area could be
described as little more than a frontier. Everything in the
way of modern convenience was wanting, and save where a
sea-going commerce was beginning, there was an entire ab-
sence of wealth. The America which we know had yet to
be made. But the land was blessed with a great people
and with great leaders. Washington and Jefferson, Franklin and Mason, Hamilton and Madison, Adams and Mar-

shall, suggest a type of citizenship and leadership, of scholarship and statesmanship, of wisdom and character, of ability and patriotism, unsurpassed by any group of men ever brought together to direct the political destinies of a nation. They did what they could in their time for the advancement of the public welfare, and they were not discontented because they could not immediately secure perfection. They had a vision and they worked toward it. They knew that in their day it was not to be fully realized. They did not lack the courage to have faith in the future.

They started the country on that long road of stupendous achievement with which you are all so familiar. To provide for that human welfare which was the cherished hope of the Declaration of Independence and the well-wrought-out plan of the Federal Constitution, it was necessary to develop the material resources of our country. There had to be created the instruments with which to minister to the well-being of the people. National poverty had to be replaced with national possessions. Transportation had to be provided by land and water. Manufacturing plants had to be erected. Great agricultural resources had to be brought under cultivation. The news service of the press had to be established. The schoolhouse, the university, the place of religious worship, all had to be built. All of these mighty agencies had to be created, that they might contribute to a unified national life where freedom might reign and where the citizen might be his own sovereign.

It was only as this work was accomplished, as these instruments were provided, these properties built, and these possessions accumulated, that there could be a reduction in the hours of labor, an increase in the rewards of employment, and a general betterment in those material conditions which result in a higher standard of living. The leisure for culture had to be secured in this way. Servitude of all kinds is scarcely ever abolished unless there is created economic opportunity for freedom. We are beginning to see that the economic development of our country was not only necessary for advancing the welfare of the people, but that we must maintain an expanding power of production if that welfare is to be increased. Business makes a most valuable contribution to human progress.

As we look back upon all this development, while we know that it was absolutely dependent upon a reign of law, nevertheless some of us can not help thinking how little of it has been dependent on acts of legislation. Given their institutions, the people themselves have in the past, as they must in the future, to a very large degree worked out their own salvation without the interposition of the Government. It is always possible to regulate and supervise by legislation what has already been created, but while legislation can stimulate and encourage, the real creative ability which builds up and develops the country, and in general makes human existence more tolerable and life more complete, has to be supplied by the genius of the people themselves. The Government can supply no substitute for enterprise.

As a result of the activity of all these forces, our country has developed enormous resources. It has likewise to be admitted that its requirements are very large, but the fact remains that it has come into a position where it has the accumulations of wealth and means of production more adequately to provide for the welfare of its people, and more securely to establish their physical, mental, and moral well-being. You are making your contribution to this great work in the field of education. It is here especially that the growth and progress of our country can be most easily understood. You can realize what an opportunity for securing the higher things of life they have provided when you recall that it is claimed that one out of every four persons in this Nation, either as pupil, administrator, or teacher, is now in some capacity directly concerned in education.

In the year 1921-22, the latest time for which complete statistics have been compiled, the students in the elementary and secondary schools, in the colleges and universities, had reached the unprecedented number of 26,206,756, and the total number of teachers and administrators approximately 882,500. If to this number one should add the parents, the members of school boards, and the taxpayers who maintain them, it becomes clear at once how universal is the direct or indirect concern of our citizens with the schools.

Another indication, both of our increasing resources and of the tremendous importance of education in the life of the Nation, is the great amount of money which we are able to spend for it. Twelve years ago the total money expended for all educational purposes amounted approximate to $705,781,900. In 10 years this had increased to $2,144,651,000. Even when one takes into account the depreciation of the dollar, due to the economic changes caused by the World War, it becomes clear that the American people have demonstrated their faith in education and their determination to use the wealth of the Nation for the creation of the highest type of manhood and womanhood.

While I believe that educators are under obligation to expend public funds economically, it seems obvious that the recent increase in expenses for this purpose is a most wise investment. It is impossible to conceive that there should be any increase in agricultural products, in the production of manufactures, or any other increase in our material wealth, through ignorance. The reaction to using the resources of the country to develop the brains of the country through education has always been greatly to stimulate and increase the power of the people to produce.

As already indicated, America is turning from the mere thought of the material advantage to a greater appreciation of the cultural advantage of learning. It is coming to be valued more and more for its own sake. People desire not only the intelligence to comprehend economic and social problems, but they are finding increased leisure is little more than time wasted in indulgence, unless an opportunity for self-development and self-expression has been provided in youth by the cultivation of a taste for literature, history, and the fine arts.

It is necessary also that education should be the hand-maid of citizenship. Our institutions are constantly and very properly the subject of critical inquiry. Unless their nature is comprehended, and their origin is understood, unless their value be properly assessed, the citizen falls ready prey to those selfish agitators who would exploit his prejudices to promote their own advantage. On this day, of all days, it ought to be made clear that America has had its revolution and placed the power of Government square-ly, securely, and entirely in the hands of the people. For all changes which they may desire, for all grievances which they may suffer, the ballot box furnishes a complete method and remedy. Into their hands has been committed com-plete jurisdiction and control over all the functions of Gov-ernment. For the most part our institutions are attacked in the name of social and economic reform. Unless there be some teaching of sound economics in the schools, the voter and taxpayer are in danger of accepting vague theories which lead only to social discontent and public disaster. The body politic has little chance of choosing patriotic of-ficials who can administer its financial affairs with wisdom and safety, unless there is a general diffusion of knowledge and information on elementary economic subjects sufficient to create and adequately to support public opinion. Every-one ought to realize that the sole source of national wealth is thrift and industry, and that the sole supply of the pub-lic treasury is the toil of the people. Of course, patriotism is always to be taught. National defense is a necessity and

a virtue, but peace with honor is the normal, natural condition of mankind, and must be made the chief end to be
sought in human relationship.

Another element must be secured in the training of citizenship, or all else will be in vain. All of our learning and
science, our culture and our arts, will be of little avail, unless they are supported by high character, unless there be
honor, truth, and justice. Unless our material resources are
supported by moral and spiritual resources, there is no
foundation for progress. A trained intelligence can do
much, but there is no substitute for morality, character, and
religious convictions. Unless these abide, American citizenship will be found unequal to its task.

It is with some diffidence that I speak of the required
facilities of the school in this presence. We are able to
give more attention to the schoolhouse than formerly. It
ought to be not only convenient, commodious, and sanitary,
but it ought to be a work of art which would appeal to the
love of the beautiful. The schoolhouse itself ought to impress the scholar with an ideal, it ought to serve as an inspiration.

But the main factor of every school is the teacher. Teaching is one of the noblest of professions. It requires an
adequate preparation and training, patience, devotion, and
a deep sense of responsibility. Those who mold the human
mind have wrought not for time, but for eternity. The
obligation which we all owe to those devoted men and
women who have given of their lives to the education of the
youth of our country that they might have freedom through
coming into a knowledge of the truth is one which can never
be discharged. They are entitled not only to adequate rewards for their service, but to the veneration and honor of
a grateful people.

It is not alone the youth of the land which needs and
seeks education, but we have a large adult population re-

quiring assistance in this direction. Our last census showed nearly 14,000,000 foreign-born white persons residing among us, made up largely of those beyond school age, many of whom nevertheless need the opportunity to learn to read and write the English language, that they may come into more direct contact with the ideals and standards of our life, political and social. There are likewise over 3,000,-000 native illiterates. When it is remembered that ignorance is the most fruitful source of poverty, vice, and crime, it is easy to realize the necessity for removing what is a menace, not only to our social well-being, but to the very existence of the Republic. A failure to meet this obligation registers a serious and inexcusable defect in our Government. Such a condition not only works to a national disadvantage, but directly contradicts all our assertions regarding human rights. One of the chief rights of an American citizen is the right to an education. The opportunity to secure it must not only be provided, but if necessary made compulsory.

It is in this connection that we are coming to give more attention to rural and small village schools, which serve 47 per cent of the children of the Nation. It is significant that less than 70 per cent of these children average to be in attendance on any school day, and that there is a tendency to leave them in charge of undertrained and underpaid teachers. The advent of good roads should do much to improve these conditions. The old one-room country school, such as I attended, ought to give way to the consolidated school, with a modern building, and an adequate teaching force, commensurate with the best advantages that are provided for our urban population. While life in the open country has many advantages that are denied to those reared on the pavements and among crowded buildings, it ought no longer to be handicapped by poor school facilities. The resources exist with which they can be provided, if they are but adequately marshalled and employed.

The encouragement and support of education is peculiarly the function of the several States. While the political units of the district, the township, and the county should not fail to make whatever contribution they are able, nevertheless since the wealth and resources of the different communities vary, while the needs of the youth for education in the rich city and in the poor country are exactly the same, and the obligations of society toward them are exactly the same, it is proper that the State treasury should be called on to supply the needed deficiency. The State must contribute, set the standard, and provide supervision if society is to discharge its full duty not only to the youth of the country, but even to itself.

The cause of education has long had the thoughtful solicitude of the National Government. While it is realized that it is a State affair, rather than a national affair, nevertheless it has provided by law a Bureau of Education. It has not been thought wise to undertake to collect money from the various States into the National Treasury and distribute it again among the various States for the direct support of education. It has seemed a better policy to leave their taxable resources to the States, and permit them to make their own assessments for the support of their own schools in their own way. But for a long time the cause of education has been regarded as so important and so preëminently an American cause, that the National Government has sought to encourage it, scientifically to investigate its needs, and furnish information and advice for its constant advancement. Pending before the Congress is the report of a committee which proposes to establish a Department of Education and Relief, to be presided over by a Cabinet officer. Bearing in mind that this does not mean any interference with the local control, but is rather an attempt to recognize and dignify the importance of educational effort, such proposal has my hearty indorsement and support.

It is thus that our educational system has been and is ministering to our national life. Our country is in process of development. Its physical elements are incomplete. Its institutions have been declared, but they are very far from being adopted and applied. We have not yet arrived at perfection. A scientific investigation of child life has been begun, but yet remains to be finished. There is a vast amount of ignorance and misunderstanding, of envy, hatred, and jealousy, with their attendant train of vice and crime. We are not yet free, but we are struggling to become free economically, socially, politically, spiritually. We have limited our amount of immigration in order that the people who live here, whether of native or foreign origin, might continue to enjoy the economic advantages of our country, and that there might not be any lowering of the standards of our existence, that America might remain American. We have submitted an amendment to the national Constitution designed to protect the child life of the Nation from the unwarranted imposition of toil, that it might have greater opportunity for enlightenment. All of these movements are in the direction of increased national freedom, and an advance toward the realization of the vision of Washington and Lincoln.

A new importance is attaching to the cause of education. A new realization of its urgent necessity is taking hold of the Nation. A new comprehension that the problem is only beginning to be solved is upon the people. A new determination to meet the requirements of the situation is everywhere apparent. The economic and moral waste of ignorance will little longer be tolerated. This awakening is one of the most significant developments of the times. It indicates that our national spirit is reasserting itself. It is a most reassuring evidence that the country is recovering from the natural exhaustion of the war, and that it is rising to a new life and starting on a new course. It is intent, as never before, upon listening to the word of the teacher, whether it comes from the platform, the schoolhouse, or the pulpit. The power of evil is being broken. The power of the truth is reasserting itself. The Declaration of Independence is continuing to justify itself.

VIII

Doubters do not achieve; skeptics do not contribute; cynics do not create. Faith is the great motive power, and no man realizes his full possibilities unless he has the deep conviction that life is eternally important, and that his work, well done, is a part of an unending plan.

WHAT IT MEANS TO BE A BOY SCOUT

THERE was no Boy Scout organization in my boyhood, but every boy who has the privilege of growing up on a farm learns instinctively the three fundamentals of scouthood.

The first is a reverence for nature. Boys should never lose their love of the fields and the streams, the mountains and the plains, the open places and the forests. That love will be a priceless possession as your years lengthen out. There is an instructive myth about the giant Antæus. Whenever in a contest he was thrown down, he drew fresh strength from his mother, the earth, and so was thought invincible. But Hercules lifted him away from the earth and so destroyed him. There is new life in the soil for every man. There is healing in the trees for tired minds and for our overburdened spirits, there is strength in the hills, if only we will lift up our eyes. Remember that nature is your great restorer.

The second is a reverence for law. I remember the town meetings of my boyhood, when the citizens of our little town met to levy taxes on themselves, and to choose from their own number those who should be their officers. There is something in every town meeting, in every election, that approaches very near to the sublime. I am thrilled at the thought of my audience tonight, for I never address boys without thinking, among them may be a boy who will sit in this White House. Somewhere there are boys who will be presidents of our railroads, presidents of colleges, of

Address delivered at the White House July 25, 1924, and transmitted by telephone to a farewell meeting in New York for a group of Boy Scouts who were to sail July 26 to attend an international gathering of the organization in Copenhagen.

banks, owners of splendid farms and useful industries, members of Congress, representatives of our people in foreign lands. That is the heritage of the American boy.

It was an act of magnificent courage when our ancestors set up a nation wherein any boy may aspire to anything. That great achievement was not wrought without blood and sacrifice. Make firm your resolution to carry on nobly what has been so nobly begun. Let this nation, under your influence, be a finer nation. Resolve that the sacrifices by which your great opportunities have been purchased will be matched by a sacrifice, on your part, that will give your children even a better chance.

The third is a reverence for God. It is hard to see how a great man can be an atheist. Without the sustaining influence of faith in a divine power we could have little faith in ourselves. We need to feel that behind us is intelligence and love. Doubters do not achieve; skeptics do not contribute; cynics do not create. Faith is the great motive power, and no man realizes his full possibilities unless he has the deep conviction that life is eternally important, and that his work, well done, is a part of an unending plan.

These are not only some of the fundamentals of the teachings of the Boy Scouts, they are the fundamentals of our American institutions. If you will take them with you, if you will be living examples of them abroad, you will make a great contribution toward a better understanding of our country, and receive in return a better understanding of other countries; for you will find in foreign lands, to a very large extent, exactly what you carry there yourselves. I trust that you can show to your foreign associates in the great scout movement that you have a deep reverence for the truth and are determined to live by it; that you wish to protect and cherish your own country and contribute to the well being, right thinking and true living of the whole world.

IX

Our Constitution guarantees equal rights to all our citizens, without discrimination on account of race or color. I have taken my oath to support that Constitution. It is the source of your rights and my rights. I propose to regard it, and administer it, as the source of the rights of all the people, whatever their belief or race.

EQUALITY OF RIGHTS

My dear Sir:

Your letter is received, accompanied by a newspaper clipping which discusses the possibility that a colored man may be the Republican nominee for Congress from one of the New York districts. Referring to this newspaper statement, you say:

"It is of some concern whether a Negro is allowed to run for Congress anywhere, at any time, in any party, in this, a white man's country. Repeated ignoring of the growing race problem does not excuse us for allowing encroachments. Temporizing with the Negro whether he will or will not vote either a Democratic or a Republican ticket, as evidenced by the recent turnover in Oklahoma, is contemptible."

Leaving out of consideration the manifest impropriety of the President intruding himself in a local contest for nomination, I was amazed to receive such a letter. During the war 500,000 colored men and boys were called up under the draft, not one of whom sought to evade it. They took their places wherever assigned in defense of the nation of which they are just as truly citizens as are any others. The suggestion of denying any measure of their full political rights to such a great group of our population as the colored people is one which, however it might be received in some other quarters, could not possibly be permitted by one who feels a responsibility for living up to the traditions and

Letter to Mr. Charles F. Gardner, Fort Hamilton, New York, dated August 9, 1924.

maintaining the principles of the Republican Party. Our Constitution guarantees equal rights to all our citizens, without discrimination on account of race or color. I have taken my oath to support that Constitution. It is the source of your rights and my rights. I propose to regard it, and administer it, as the source of the rights of all the people, whatever their belief or race. A colored man is precisely as much entitled to submit his candidacy in a party primary, as is any other citizen. The decision must be made by the constituents to whom he offers himself, and by nobody else. You have suggested that in some fashion I should bring influence to bear to prevent the possibility of a colored man being nominated for Congress. In reply, I quote my great predecessor, Theodore Roosevelt:

"* * * I cannot consent to take the position that the door of hope—the door of opportunity—is to be shut upon any man, no matter how worthy, purely upon the grounds of race or color."

Yours very truly, etc.

X

We perform different tasks, but the spirit is the same. We are proud of work and ashamed of idleness. With us there is no task which is menial, no service which is degrading. All work is ennobling and all workers are ennobled.

THE HIGH PLACE OF LABOR

LABOR DAY is more entitled than any other to be called a national holiday. Other holidays had their origin in state legislative action. Labor Day had its origin in national legislative action. After Congress had taken the lead the states followed. It is moreover a peculiarly American holiday. It is a most characteristic representation of our ideals. No other country, I am told, makes a like observance. But in America this high tribute is paid in recognition of the worth and dignity of the men and women who toil.

You come here as representative Americans. You are true representatives. I cannot think of anything characteristically American that was not produced by toil. I cannot think of any American man or woman preëminent in the history of our Nation who did not reach their place through toil. I cannot think of anything that represents the American people as a whole so adequately as honest work. We perform different tasks, but the spirit is the same. We are proud of work and ashamed of idleness. With us there is no task which is menial, no servcie which is degrading. All work is ennobling and all workers are ennobled.

To my mind America has but one main problem, the character of the men and women it shall produce. It is not fundamentally a Government problem, although the Government can be of a great influence in its solution. It is the real problem of the people themselves. They control its property, they have determined its government, they

Address delivered to a Group of Labor Leaders, who called on the President, Sept. 1, 1924.

manage its business. In all things they are the masters of their own destiny. What they are, their intelligence, their fidelity, their courage, their faith, will determine our material prosperity, our successes and happiness at home, and our place in the world abroad.

If anything is to be done then, by the Government, for the people who toil, for the cause of labor, which is the sum of all other causes, it will be by continuing its efforts to provide healthful surroundings, education, reasonable conditions of employment, fair wages for fair work, stable business prosperity, and the encouragement of religious worship. This is the general American policy which is working out with a success more complete for humanity, with its finite limitations, than was ever accomplished anywhere else in the world. The door of opportunity swings wide open in our country. Through it, in constant flow, go those who toil. America recognizes no aristocracy save those who work. The badge of service is the sole requirement for admission to the ranks of our nobility.

These American policies should be continued. We have outlawed all artificial privilege. We have had our revolution and our reforms. I do not favor a corporation government, a bank government, a farm government or a labor government. I am for a common-sense government by all the people according to the American policy and under the American Constitution. I want all the people to continue to be partakers in self government. We never had a government under our Constitution that was not put into office by the votes of the toilers.

It is only necessary to look about you to observe the practical effect of this policy. It is somewhat difficult to find men in important Government positions who did not in their beginnings live by the work of their hands. Of those who sit at the Cabinet table of the Nation none were born to the purple, save only as they were born to become

American citizens, and nearly all in early life earned their living by actual manual labor. The Secretary of Labor comes from union labor ranks. In each important national conference in which labor is interested, labor has been represented. On several occasions under this administration that has been the practice. It was so at the Conference on Unemployment, on Transportation, on Agriculture, on the Business Cycle, on Intermittent Employment in Construction Industries, and on the great Washington Conference for the Limitation of Armaments. The same policy prevails in the membership of many of our important commissions. The Chairman of the United States Sh'pping Board, one of the most important places of business administration in the Government, is filled by a man who was prominent in organized labor. The St. Lawrence River, the Interstate Commerce, and the United States Employees' Compensation Commissions, the Vocational Education and the Railway Labor Boards, are examples of this policy and are results of the open door of opportunity. Those who have been identified with toil are now, and will continue to be, in important places of government authority. The wage earners of America have been mixing their work with brains ever since the day of George Washington.

But the Government of the United States is not for the gratification of the people who happen to hold office. It is established to promote the general welfare of all the people. That is the American ideal. No matter how many officeholders there may be, or what their origin, our institutions are a failure unless they serve all the citizens in their own homes. It is always necessary to find out what effect the institutions of Government and society have on the wage earner, in order to judge of the desirability of their continuation.

One of the outstanding features of the present day is

that American wage earners are living better than at any other time in our history. They have not only retained, but actually increased, the gains they made during the war. The cost of living has been high, but the increase in wages has been greater. Compilations of the Department of Labor demonstrate that the wages of an hour, or a day, buy more now than it ever did before. Not only are the American wage earners now receiving more money, and more of the things that money will buy, for their work, than any other wage earners in the world, but more than was ever before received by any community of wage earners. We have here in the United States not only the best paid workers in the world, but the best paid workers that ever lived in this world.

All this has been accomplished in spite of a general shortening of the hours of labor in the industries. The case of the iron and steel, and the box board industry, are particularly notable in this regard. As a direct result of President Harding's initiative the iron and steel manufacturers were brought together, and an agreement was reached under which the 12-hour day and the 7-day week have been eliminated. Secretary Davis did the same for the box board workers.

Yet this has been done without any loss in wages. On the other hand, there has been actual gain. The Department of Labor statistics show that in 1924 the customary working time per week in blast furnaces has been reduced to 75 per cent of the customary working time per week in 1913. But earnings per hour in 1924 are more than two and one-half times the earnings per hour in 1913. Despite the great reduction in hours, weekly earnings in this industry stand 90% above weekly earnings of 1913.

In the open-hearth furnace department of the iron and steel industry, working hours are now only 74% of the working hours of 1913. But earnings per hour are more than two and two-thirds times the earnings per hour of 1913. Earnings per week are 99% above the weekly earnings of 1913. All other departments of the iron and steel industry have enjoyed large increases in earnings per hour and per week.

I know that figures are sometimes tiresome. But these I am quoting are so eloquent that I am sure you will pardon other illustrations. In the shoe industry regular working hours are now 11% lower than in 1913, hourly wages are two and one-seventh times those of 1913, and full-time weekly earnings are 92% above those of 1913.

In cotton manufacturing hourly earnings are more than two and one-half times those of 1913. Working hours have been reduced 8%, and wages by the week are almost two and one-third times what they were in 1913.

The figures I have quoted apply to workers in these industries, regardless of whether they are organized or unorganized. A study of wages in organized trades shows that in 1923 the average wage per hour was two and one-ninth times that in 1913, and two and one-third times that of 1907. Taking the entire body of union men, working hours have been reduced 6% as against 1913 and 8% as against 1907. But their weekly pay in 1923 was 99% higher than in 1913, and two and one-sixth times as high as in 1907. And let it be added, the figures show that average wages of organized workers in 1924, are higher than in 1923.

But increased wages, in terms of money, mean little if they are entirely absorbed by higher prices of the necessaries of life. In order to know whether an increase in the money wage is also an increase in the real wage, we must know how much the prices have advanced. On that point, I find that the cost of living of the average family for the same standard of living has been falling since the high point was reached in 1920, and is now, in terms of money, only 69% above the level of 1913. That is, the increase in wages has far outrun the advance in the cost of living. Real wages, as determined by the things that money wages will buy, are higher today than ever before in our history.

A moment ago I said that the American workman is now not only better paid than he was ever before, but better paid than any other workman in the world's history. I want to give one or two illustrations to show his advantage over wage earners of other countries. Some very recent figures have made it possible to compare British and American earnings. They show that the average British cotton mill worker earned $7.85 per week in June this year, while the average American cotton mill worker earned $14.95. The British woolen mill operative earned $9.56 per week; the American $26.21. The British potter earned $8.34, compared to the American potter's $26.70.

But once more, we must inquire about the comparative buying power of money in the two countries before we can be assured that the actual earnings of the Americans are higher than those of the British wage earner. It happens that the British Government has made a study of wages and living costs in the principal cities of several countries, as of 1923. It was found that a bricklayer in Madrid receives a wage which buys only 50% as much as the London bricklayer can buy with his wage. The Vienna bricklayer has a wage whose purchasing power is 57% of that of the London bricklayer. The Berlin bricklayer's wage has 61% of the buying power of the London bricklayer; while the Paris bricklayer's wage will purchase 71% as much as will the wage of the London bricklayer.

These figures show that the British working man is easily the aristocrat of all Europe. He earns much higher wages, measured in buying power, than any working man on the continent. And yet, this same British authority shows that the New York bricklayer earns a wage whose effective buying power is two and three-fourths times that of the London bricklayer.

In other trades and occupations the comparisons lead to similar conclusions. Wherever you turn, the statistics of wages and living costs show that the American wage earner enjoys a buying power enormously greater than that of any other wage earner in the world.

We do not need to import any foreign economic ideas or any foreign government. We had better stick to the American brand of government, the American brand of equality, and the American brand of wages. America had better stay American.

These are some of the material results of present American policies. We have enacted many laws to protect the health of those who are employed in the industries. Especial efforts have been made in this direction in behalf of women and children. We are attempting at the present time to secure a constitutional amendment giving Congress jurisdiction over child labor. The efforts of the states and Nation to provide and encourage education have been such that it is fair to claim that any youth, no matter how humble his circumstances, can unaided secure a college education by the exercise of his own efforts. We have achieved an equality of opportunity which has opened up the avenues of a more abundant life to all the people.

There are two sides to every bargain. It is not only human nature, but necessary to progress, that each side should desire to secure a good trade. This is the case in contracts for employment. In order to give wage earners reasonable advantages, their right has been established to organize, to bargain collectively, and to negotiate through their own chosen agents. The principle also of voluntary arbitration has come to exist almost as a right. Compulsory arbitration has sometimes been proposed, but to my mind it cannot be reconciled with the right of individual freedom. Along with the right to organize goes the right to strike, which is recognized in all private employment. The establishment of all these principles has no doubt been productive of industrial peace, which we are at the present time enjoying to a most unusual degree. This has been brought about by the general recognition that on the whole labor leaders are square, and on the whole employers intend to be fair. When this is the case, mutual conference is the best method of adjusting differences in private industry. Of course employment affecting public safety or public necessity is not private employment, and requires somewhat different treatment. In this field we have been making an interesting experiment in relation to railroad labor. This has no doubt been a step in advance. It could probably be modified, through mutual agreement, to the benefit of all concerned.

Soon after the close of the war the policy of deflation was adopted, which no doubt some though might be used to secure a reduction in wages and the dissolution of labor organizations. This administration refused to lend itself to any such program, and at once adopted a policy, which it has steadily pursued, of helpfulness to business, industry and labor. The Federal Reserve System has constantly reduced discount rates, business has revived, and the millions who were without employment have found plenty of work at an increasing rate of wages. It is my belief that this policy represents one of the most important and helpful services on the part of the United States Government which was ever performed for the benefit of the wage earners of this Nation. When almost everything else went crashing down, a change of front took place in time to save them from almost certain destruction.

As a result of all these fortunate circumstances, organized labor is fast becoming one of the powers of capital in this country. Its coöperative enterprises and its entrance into the field of banking and investment have given it not only a new power of influence, but a new point of view. It is learning the problems of enterprise and management by actual experience. This again is the working out of the American ideal in industry. It is the beginning of a more complete economic equality among all the people. I believe it to be the beginning of an era of better understanding, more sympathy, and more fellowship, among those who serve the common welfare through investment and management, and those who serve as wage earners. We have yet a long way to go, but progress has begun and the way lies open to a more complete understanding that will mark the end of industrial strife.

It is my policy to continue these conditions in so far as it is possible and to continue this march of progress. There are two important domestic factors in this situation. One is restrictive immigration. This has been adopted by this administration chiefly for the purpose of maintaining American standards. It undoubtedly has a very great economic effect. We want the people who live in America, no matter what their origin, to be able to continue in the enjoyment of their present unprecedented advantages. This opportunity would certainly be destroyed by the tremendous influx of foreign peoples, if immigration were not restricted. Unemployment would become a menace, and there would follow an almost certain reduction of wages, with all the attendant distress and despair which is now suffered in so many parts of Europe. Our first duty is to our own people. The second important factor is that of a tariff for protection. I have already given you some examples of the wages paid in Europe. Such a scale means that goods can be produced much cheaper there than they can here. If our policy of protection is to be abandoned, the goods which are now made by the wage earners of America will be made by the wage earners of Europe.

Our own people will be out of employment. Our entire business system will be thrown into confusion with the want and misery which always accompany the hard times of attempted economic readjustment. Under free trade the only way we could meet European competition would be by approaching the European standard of wages. I want to see the American standard of living maintained. We shall not be misled by any appeal for cheap goods, if we remember that this was completely answered by President McKinley when he stated that cheap goods make cheap men. By restrictive immigration, by adequate protection, I want to prevent America from producing cheap men.

To these must be added economy of expenditure by the local and national governments. There are about 24,-000,000 heads of families in the United States. It takes 5,000,000 of these working at $5.00 a day to pay the present cost of governments. This gives us some idea of what public expense takes out of the productive power of the Nation. No matter what anyone may say about making the rich and the corporations pay the taxes, in the end they come out of the people who toil. It is your fellow workers who are ordered to work for the Government, every time an appropriation bill is passed. The people pay the expense of government, often many times over, in the increased cost of living. I want taxes to be less, that the people may have more.

I am for peace and against aggressive war. I am opposed to warlike preparations. But I am in favor of an adequate Army and Navy to insure our citizens against any interference with domestic tranquillity at home or any imposition abroad. It is only in peaceful conditions that there is a real hope of progress. I want to have America co-operate in securing speedy settlement of European differences, and assist in financing a revival of business which would be of world-wide benefit to wage earners. I am in favor of continuing and extending the policy of covenants between nations for further disarmament and more extensive guarantees of permanent peace.

These are some of the policies which I believe we should support, in order that our country may not fail in the character of the men and women which it produces. I want to see our institutions more and more humane. But I do not want to see any of the people cringing suppliants for the favor of the Government, when they should all be independent masters of their own destiny. I want to encourage business, that it may provide profitable employment. I want to see jobs hunting for men, rather than men hunting for jobs. I want the factory able to consume at a fair price the products of the farm. I want every individual, no matter how humble, to know that over him is the protection of public law. I want to raise the economic condition and increase the moral and spiritual well-being of our country. The foundation for a new era is being steadily and surely laid. Whether we shall enter upon it, depends upon the attitude of our fellow countrymen. I have an abiding faith in the American people.

XI

The cause of freedom has been triumphant. We believe it to be, likewise, the cause of peace.

ORDERED LIBERTY AND WORLD PEACE.

THIS occasion is dedicated to freedom. The people of Baltimore, and of Maryland, are gathered here in that spirit. Because Americans cherish that sentiment they cherish the name of Lafayette. On the anniversary of his birth, we are gathered about his statue in this proud city which we know he loved, almost in the shadow of the stately monument reared to his great friend Washington, to rededicate ourselves to the inspiring memory of a true son of world freedom.

This is not only his birthday, but the anniversary of the farewell reception extended to him at the White House by President Adams during his last visit to our country. This day not only recalls his youth and his dashing figure in our Revolution, but it reminds us of the venerable man, half a century later, held in love and admiration by two countries for the sacrifices he had made in the service of liberty.

His picture to me seems always to have the enthusiasm and freshness of youth, moved with the high-minded and patriotic purpose of maturity. He displayed the same ambition for faithful service, whether he was leading his soldiers in the last charge for American liberty at Yorktown or rebuking the mob at Paris for its proposal to make him king. His part in the French Revolution is well known. He served the cause of ordered liberty in America; he was unwilling to serve any other cause in France. His admirers might say of him on the first anniversary of Bastile Day, "He is galloping through the ages." But he refused to be

Address delivered at the dedication of a monument to Lafayette, at Baltimore, Md., Saturday, September 6, 1924.

a man on horseback. He knew that the welfare of his country lay in moderation. The people trusted him, but the extremists, whether Jacobin or Royalist, feared him. He urged the National Assembly to establish by constitutional guarantees what the Revolution had gained.

As Commander of the National Guard, again he might have made himself dictator. Instead he was pleading with the Assembly to adopt the preamble of the American Constitution as the foundation of its declaration of rights. When alien armies were brought to France to crush her liberties he was put at the head of the Army of the North, but treachery and suspicion overcame him. He was retired from his command and was seeking to leave the country when he was captured and held for five years in imprisonment. Tradition has it that he was released through the joint efforts of Washington and Napoleon.

He had a deep appreciation of this action, but always refused to support the Napoleonic regime. After Waterloo he insisted that Napoleon must abdicate and that the nation must guarantee his life and liberty. When the Bourbons were restored he denounced usurpations in the name of royalty, as he had formerly denounced usurpations in the name of liberty. As a consequence he was charged with treason. He defied the Assembly to try him on such a charge. "During the whole of a life devoted entirely to liberty I have constantly been attacked by the enemies of that cause," he declared. "I demand a public inquiry within the walls of this chamber and in the face of this nation." As his enemies dared not meet the challenge, he was acquitted.

After a few years of private retirement he emerged to pay a visit to this country, one hundred years ago. Congress bestowed upon him citizenship and treasure and he was received everywhere with reverence and acclaim. When the Revolution of July occurred in 1830 he once more became Commander of the National Guard, where his influence saved his people from horrible excesses. Again there was an effort to establish a republic and make him President. But he thought a constitutional monarchy best adapted to the needs of his nation. So he refused this most appealing of all honors and returned to his country home. His long career was ended.

He represents a noble and courageous dedication to the service of freedom. He never sought for personal aggrandizement, but under heavy temptation remained loyal to the great Cause. He possessed a character that will abide with us through the generations. He loved his fellowmen, and believed in the ultimate triumph of self-government. But he did not consider France had reached a point where representative democracy would be a success. He was practical. Like Washington, he refused a crown. But while he believed Washington performed a great service in accepting the Presidency of America, he believed he had performed an equally great service in rejecting the Presidency of France. He approved the establishment of our republican institutions, and hoped they would one day be a model for the government of his own country. He recognized the value of native institutions. So, while he was loyal to freedom, he was likewise loyal to the Crown. In moderation, in the gradual evolution of government and society, he perceived the strongest defense against both reaction and revolution, and the greatest hope for permanent progress.

We have come here today to honor the memory of Lafayette, because long ago he came to this country as a private citizen at his own expense and joined us in fighting for the maintenance and extension of our institutions. It was not so much to acquire new rights, as to maintain old rights, that the men of that day put their fortunes to the hazard of war. They were resisting usurpations; they were combating unlawful tyrannies. No doubt they wanted to be Americans, but they wanted most of all to be free. They believed in individual liberty, safeguarded by constitutional guarantees. This principle to them was dearer than life itself. What they fought to preserve and extend, we ought to be ready to fight to maintain.

Very little danger exists of an open and avowed assault upon the principle of individual freedom. It is more likely to be in peril indirectly perhaps from the avowed intention of protecting it or enlarging it. Out of a long experience with many tyrannies abroad and a weak and inefficient government at home, the Constitution of the United States was adopted and ratified. The people who largely contributed to the early settlement of America came to escape the impositions of despotic kings. Many of the early inhabitants were separatists from the established church. They fled under the threat of the English King, that he would make them conform or harry them out of the land. Their descendants fought the Revolutionary war in order that they might escape the impositions of a despotic parliament.

This lesson was firmly in the minds of those who made the American Constitution. They proposed to adopt institutions under which the people should be supreme, and the government should derive its just powers from the consent of the governed. They were determined to be a sovereign people under a government having such powers as they from time to time should confer upon it by a written constitution. They did not propose to be under the tyranny of either the executive or the legislature.

They knew, however, that self-government is still government, and that the authority of the Constitution and the law is still authority. They knew that a government without power is a contradiction in terms. In order that their President and their Congress might not surpass the bounds of the authority granted to them, by the Constitution which the people had made, and so infringe upon the liberties of the people, they established a third independent department of the government, with the power to interpret and declare the Constitution and the law, the inferior courts and the Supreme Court of the United States. No President, however powerful, and no majority of Congress however large, can take from an individual, no matter how humble, that freedom and those rights which are guaranteed to him by the Constitution. The Supreme Court has final authority to determine all questions arising under the Constitution and laws of the United States.

That power and that authority has to reside somewhere in every government. Originally it lay with the king. After limitations began to be placed upon him, it was conferred upon the parliamentary body. One of the great contributions which America made to the science of government was the establishment of an independent judiciary department under which this authority resides in the Supreme Court. That tribunal has been made as independent and impartial as human nature could devise. This action was taken with the sole purpose of protecting the freedom of the individual, of guarding his earnings, his home, his life.

It is frequently charged that this tribunal is tyrannical. If the Constitution of the United States be tyranny; if the rule that no one shall be convicted of a crime save by a jury of his peers; that no orders of nobility shall be granted; that slavery shall not be permitted to exist in any state or territory; that no one shall be deprived of life, liberty or property without due process of law; if these and many other provisions made by the people be tyranny, then the Supreme Court when it makes decisions in accordance with these principles of our fundamental law is tyrannical. Otherwise it is exercising the power of government for the preservation of liberty. The fact is that the Constitution is the source of our freedom. Maintaining it, interpreting it, and declaring it, are the only methods by which the Constitution can be preserved and our liberties guaranteed.

Somewhere must be lodged the power to declare the Constitution. If it be taken away from the Court, it must go either to the executive or the legislative branch of the Government. No one, so far as I know, has thought that it should go to the Executive. All those who advocate changes propose, I believe, that it should be transferred in whole or in part to the Congress. I have a very high regard for legislative assemblies. We have put a very great emphasis upon representative government. It is the only method by which due deliberation can be secured. That is a great safeguard of liberty. But the legislature is not judicial. Along with what are admitted to be the merits of the question, also what is supposed to be the popular demand and the greatest partisan advantage weigh very heavily in making legislative decisions. It is well known that when the House of Representatives sits as a judicial body, to determine contested elections, it has a tendency to decide in a partisan way. It is to be remembered also that under recent political practice there is a strong tendency for legislatures to be very much influenced by the Executive. Whether we like this practice or not, there is no use denying that it exists. With a dominant Executive and a subservient legislature, the opportunity would be very inviting to aggrandizement and very dangerous to liberty. That way leads toward imperialism.

Some people do not seem to understand fully the purpose of our constitutional restraints. They are not for protecting the majority, either in or out of the Congress. They can protect themselves with their votes. We have adopted a written constitution in order that the minority, even down to the most insignificant individual, might have their rights protected. So long as our Constitution remains in force, no majority, no matter how large, can deprive the individual of the right of life, liberty or property, or prohibit the free exercise of religion or the freedom of speech or of the press. If the authority now vested in the Supreme Court were transferred to the Congress, any majority no matter what their motive could vote away any of these most precious rights. Majorities are notoriously irresponsible. After irreparable damage had been done the only remedy that the people would have would be the privilege of trying to defeat such a majority at the next election. Every minority body that may be weak in resources or unpopular in the public estimation, also nearly every race and religious belief, would find themselves practically without protection, if the authority of the Supreme Court should be broken down and its powers lodged with the Congress.

The same reasoning that applies to the individual person applies to the individual state. A very broad twilight zone exists in which it is difficult to distinguish where state right ends and federal right begins. Deprived of the privilege of its day in court, each state would be compelled to submit to the exactions of the Congress or resort to resistance by force. On the other hand, the legislatures of states, and sometimes the people, through the initiative and referendum, may pass laws which are very injurious to the minority residents of that state, by attempting to take away the privilege which they hold under the Federal Constitution. Except for the courts, such a minority would have no remedy for wrong done them. Their ultimate refuge is the Supreme Court of the United States.

At a time when all the world is seeking for the adjudication of differences between nations, not by war, but by reason, the suggestion that we should limit the jurisdiction of our domestic courts is reactionary in the highest degree. It would cast aside the progress of generations to begin again the contest for supremacy between executive and legislature. Whichever side has won in that struggle, the people have always lost.

Our Constitution has raised certain barriers against too hasty change. I believe such provision is wise. I doubt if there has been any change that has ever really been desired by the people which they have not been able to secure. Stability of government is a very important asset. If amendment be made easy, both revolution and reaction, as well as orderly progress, also become easy. The nation has lost little, but has gained much, through the necessity of due deliberation. The pressing need of the present day is not to change our constitutional rights, but to observe our constitutional rights.

A deliberate and determined effort is being made to break down the guarantees of our fundamental law. It has for its purpose the confiscation of property and the destruction of liberty. At the present time the chief obstacle to this effort is the Supreme Court of the United States. In this contest there is but one place for a real American to stand. That is on the side of ordered liberty under constitutional government. This is not the struggle of the rich and powerful. They will be able to survive. It is the struggle of the common run of people. Unless we can maintain our institutions of liberty unimpaired they will see their savings swept away, their homes devastated, and their children perish from want and hunger.

The time to stop those who would loosen and weaken the fabric of our government is before they begin. The time for Americans to range themselves firmly, squarely and uncompromisingly behind American ideals is now. The great body of our people have an abiding faith in their own country. The time has come when they should supplement that faith with action. The question is whether America will allow itself to be degraded into a communistic and socialistic state, or whether it will remain American. Those who want to continue to enjoy the high estate of American citizenship will resist all attempts to encroach upon their liberties by encroachment upon the power of the courts.

The Constitution of the United States has for its almost sole purpose the protection of the freedom of the people. We must combat every attempt to break down or to make it easy, under the pretended guise of legal procedure, to throw open the way to reaction or revolution. To adopt any other course is to put in jeopardy the sacred right to life, liberty, property, and the pursuit of happiness.

Lafayette was always an interested student of our affairs. Though he distrusted the effort to make France a republic, he believed greatly in our Republic and our Constitution. He had fought to establish American independence, in order that these might come into being. That independence to which he contributed has come to be with us a national axiom. We have always guarded it with the utmost jealousy. We have sought to strengthen it with the Monroe Doctrine. We have refrained from treaties of offensive and defensive alliance. We have kept clear from political entanglements with other countries. Under this wise and sound policy America has been a country on the whole dedicated to peace, through honorable and disinterested relations with the other peoples of the earth. We have always been desirous not to participate in controversies, but to compose them. What a success this has brought to us at home, and what a place of respect and moral power it has gained for us abroad, is known of all men.

To continue to be independent we must continue to be whole-hearted American. We must direct our policies and lay our course with the sole consideration of serving our own people. We cannot become the partisans of one nation, or the opponents of another. Our domestic affairs should be entirely free from foreign interference, whether such attempt be made by those who are without or within our own territory. America is a large country. It is a tolerant country. It has room within its borders for many races and many creeds. But it has no room for those who would place the interests of some other nation above the interests of our own nation.

To be independent to my mind does not mean to be isolated, to be the priest or the Levite, but rather to be the good Samaritan. There is no real independence save only as we secure it through the law of service.

The course of our country in recent years has been an example of these principles. We have avoided entanglements by reserving to our own decision when and how we should help. We have not failed to help. We have contributed hundreds of millions of dollars to foreign charities. We have given freely of our counsel to the settlement of difficulties in Latin America and the adjustment of war problems in Europe. We are still pursuing that course. It has been a practical course, and it has secured practical results. One of these most important results is found in the disarmament treaties, which have saved our own country to date about $300,000,000, and likewise relieved other nations. Another important result has been the adoption of the Dawes plan for the settlement of reparations. The effect these will have in averting war and promoting peace cannot possibly be overestimated. They stand out as great monuments, truly directing the course of men along the way to more civilization, more enlightenment, and more righteousness. They appear to me properly to mark the end of the old order, and the beginning of a new era. We hope they are the end of aggressive war and the beginning of permanent peace.

Great changes have come over the world since Lafayette first came here desirous of aiding the cause of freedom.

His efforts in behalf of an American republic have been altogether successful. In no other country in the world was economic opportunity for the people ever so great as it is here. In no other country was it ever possible in a like degree to secure equality and justice for all. Just as he was passing off the stage, the British adopted their reform measures giving them practically representative government. His own France has long since been welcomed into the family of republics. Many others have taken a like course. The cause of freedom has been triumphant. We believe it to be, likewise, the cause of peace.

But peace must have other guarantees than constitutions and covenants. Laws and treaties may help, but peace and war are attitudes of mind. American citizens, with the full sympathy of our Government, have been attempting with apparent success to restore stricken Europe. We have acted in the name of world peace and of humanity. Always the obstacles to be encountered have been distrust, suspicion and hatred. The great effort has been to allay and remove these sentiments. I believe that America can assist the world in this direction by her example. We have never forgotten the service done us by Lafayette, but we have long ago ceased to bear an enmity toward Great Britain by reason of two wars that were fought out between us. We want Europe to compose its difficulties and liquidate its hatreds. Would it not be well if we set the example and liquidated some of our own? The war is over. The militarism of Central Europe which menaced the security of the world has been overthrown. In its place have sprung up peaceful republics. Already we have assisted in refinancing Austria. We are about to assist refinancing Germany. We believe that such action will be helpful to France, but we can give further and perhaps even more valuable assistance both to ourselves and to Europe by bringing to an end our own hatreds. The best way for us who wish all our inhabitants to be single-minded in their Americanism is for us to bestow upon each group of our inhabitants that confidence and fellowship which is due to all Americans. If we want to get the hyphen out of our country, we can best begin by taking it out of our own minds. If we want France paid, we can best work towards that end by assisting in the restoration of the German people, now shorn of militarism, to their full place in the family of peaceful mankind.

I want to see America set the example to the world both in our domestic and foreign relations of magnanimity.

We cannot make over the people of Europe. We must help them as they are, if we are to help them at all. I believe that we should help, not at the sacrifice of our independence, not for the support of imperialism, but to restore to those great peoples a peaceful civilization. In that course lies the best guarantee of freedom. In that course lies the greatest honor which we can bestow upon the memory of Lafayette.

XII

Our conception of authority, of law and liberty, of property and service, ought not to be that they imply rules of action for the mere benefit of someone else, but that they are primarily for the benefit of ourselves. The Government supports them in order that the people may enjoy them.

AUTHORITY AND RELIGIOUS LIBERTY

SOMETHING in all human beings makes them want to do the right thing. Not that this desire always prevails; oftentimes it is overcome and they turn towards evil. But some power is constantly calling them back. Ever there comes a resistance to wrongdoing. When bad conditions begun to accumulate, when the forces of darkness become prevalent, always they are ultimately doomed to fail, as the better angels of human nature are roused to resistance.

Your great demonstration which marks this day in the City of Washington is only representative of many like observances extending over our own country and into other lands, so that it makes a truly world-wide appeal. It is a manifestation of the good in human nature which is of tremendous significance. More than six centuries ago, when in spite of much learning and much piety there was much ignorance, much wickedness and much warfare, when there seemed to be too little light in the world, when the condition of the common people appeared to be sunk in hopelessness, when most of life was rude, harsh and cruel, when the speech of men was too often profane and vulgar, until the earth rang with the tumult of those who took the name of the Lord in vain, the foundation of this day was laid in the formation of the Holy Name Society. It had an inspired purpose. It sought to rededicate the minds of the people to a true conception of the sacredness of the name of the Supreme Being. It was an effort to save all reference to the Deity from curses and blasphemy, and restore

Address before the Holy Name Society, Washington, D. C., September 21, 1924.

the lips of men to reverence and praise. Out of weakness there began to be strength; out of frenzy there began to be self-control; out of confusion there began to be order. This demonstration is a manifestation of the wide extent to which an effort to do the right thing will reach when it is once begun. It is a purpose which makes a universal appeal, an effort in which all may unite.

The importance of the lesson which this Society was formed to teach would be hard to overestimate. Its main purpose is to impress upon the people the necessity for reverence. This is the beginning of a proper conception of ourselves, of our relationship to each other, and our relationship to our Creator. Human nature cannot develop very far without it. The mind does not unfold, the creative faculty does not mature, the spirit does not expand, save under the influence of reverence. It is the chief motive of an obedience. It is only by a correct attitude of mind begun early in youth and carried through maturity that these desired results are likely to be secured. It is along the path of reverence and obedience that the race has reached the goal of freedom, of self-government, of a higher morality, and a more abundant spiritual life.

Out of a desire that there may be a progress in these directions, with all that such progress means, this great Society continues its efforts. It recognizes that whoever has an evil tongue cannot have a pure mind. We read that "out of the abundance of the heart the mouth speaketh." This is a truth which is worthy of much thought. He who gives license to his tongue only discloses the contents of his own mind. By the excess of his words he proclaims his lack of discipline. By his very violence he shows his weakness. The youth or man who by disregarding this principle thinks he is displaying his determination and resolution and emphasizing his statements is in reality only revealing an intellectual poverty, a deficiency in self-control and self-respect, a want of accurate thinking and of spiritual insight, which cannot come save from a reverence for the truth. There are no human actions which are unimportant, none to which we can be indifferent. All of them lead either towards destruction and death, or towards construction and life.

To my mind, the great strength of your Society lies in its recognition of the necessity of discipline. We live in an impatient age. We demand results, and demand them at once. We find a long and laborious process very irksome, and are constantly seeking for a short cut. But there is no easy method of securing discipline. It is axiomatic that there is no royal road to learning. The effort for discipline must be intensive, and to a considerable degree it must be lifelong. But it is absolutely necessary, if there is to be any self-direction or any self-control. The worst evil that could be inflicted upon the youth of the land would be to leave them without restraint and completely at the mercy of their own uncontrolled inclinations. Under such conditions education would be impossible, and all orderly development intellectually or morally would be hopeless. I do not need to picture the result. We know too well what weakness and depravity follow when the ordinary processes of discipline are neglected.

Yet the world has never thoroughly learned this lesson It has never been willing entirely to acknowledge this principle. One of the greatest needs of the present day is the establishment and recognition of standards, and holding ourselves up to their proper observance. This cannot be done without constant effort and it will meet constant opposition. Always there have been those who fail to recognize this necessity. Their opposition to it and their philosophy of life were well expressed by Robert Burns in that poem which describes the carousings of a collection of vagabonds, where one of them gave his views:

"A fig for those by law protected!
Liberty's a glorious feast!
Courts for cowards were erected,
Churches built to please the priest."

That character clearly saw no use for discipline, and just as clearly found his reward in the life of an outcast. The principles which he proclaimed could not lead in any other direction. Vice and misery were their natural and inevitable consequences. He refused to recognize or obey any authority, save his own material inclinations. He never rose above his appetites. Your Society stands as a protest against this attitude of mind.

But there are altogether too many in the world who consciously or unconsciously do hold those views and follow that example. I believe such a position arises from a misconception of the meaning of life. They seem to think that authority means some kind of an attempt to force action upon them which is not for their own benefit, but for the benefit of others. To me they do not appear to understand the nature of law, and therefore refuse obedience. They misinterpret the meaning of individual liberty, and therefore fail to attain it. They do not recognize the right of property, and therefore do not come into its possession. They rebel at the idea of service, and therefore lack the fellowship and coöperation of others. Our conception of authority, of law and liberty, of property and service, ought not to be that they imply rules of action for the mere benefit of someone else, but that they are primarily for the benefit of ourselves. The Government supports them in order that the people may enjoy them.

Our American government was the result of an effort to establish institutions under which the people as a whole should have the largest possible advantages. Class and privilege were outlawed, freedom and opportunity were guaranteed. They undertook to provide conditions under which service would be adequately rewarded, and where the people would own their own property and control their own government. They had no other motive. They were actuated by no other purpose. If we are to maintain what they established, it is important to understand the foundation on which they built, and the claims by which they justified the sovereign rights and royal estate of every American citizen.

They did not deny the existence of authority. They recognized it and undertook to abide by it, and through obedience to it secure their freedom. They made their appeal and rested their cause not merely upon earthly authority, but in the very first paragraph of the Declaration of Independence asserted that they proposed "to assume, among the powers of the earth, the separate and equal station to which the laws of nature and of nature's God entitle them." And as they closed that noble document in which they submitted their claims to the opinions of mankind they again revealed what they believed to be the ultimate source of authority by stating that they were also "appealing to the Supreme Judge of the world for the rectitude of" . . . their "intentions."

When finally our Constitution was adopted, it contained specific provision that the President and members of the Congress and of state legislatures, and all executive and judicial officials, should be qualified for the discharge of their office by oath or affirmation. By the statute law of the United States, and I doubt not by all States, such oaths are administered by a solemn appeal to God for help in the keeping of their covenants. I scarcely need to refer to the fact that the houses of the Congress, and so far as I know the state legislatures, open their daily sessions with prayer. The foundation of our independence and our Government rests upon our basic religious convictions. Back of the authority of our laws is the authority of the Supreme Judge of the World, to whom we still appeal for their final justification.

The Constitution and laws of our country are adopted and enacted through the direct action of the people, or through their duly chosen representatives. They reflect the enlightened conscience of our country. They ought always to speak with the true and conscientious voice of the people. Such voice has from time immemorial had the authority of divine sanction. In their great fundamentals they do not change. As new light arrives they may be altered in their details, but they represent the best that we know at any given time. To support the Constitution, to observe the laws, is to be true to our own higher nature. That is the path, and the only path, towards liberty. To resist them and violate them is to become enemies to ourselves and instruments of our own destruction. That is the path towards servitude. Obedience is not for the protection of someone else, but for the protection of ourselves. It needs to be remembered that it has to be secured not through the action of others, but through our own actions. Liberty is not collective, it is personal. All liberty is individual liberty.

Coincident with the right of individual liberty under the provisions of our Government is the right of individual property. The position which the individual holds in the conception of American institutions is higher than that ever before attained anywhere else on earth. It is acknowledged and proclaimed that he has sovereign powers. It is declared that he is endowed with inalienable rights which no majority, however great, and no power of the Government, however broad, can ever be justified in violating. The principle of equality is recognized. It follows inevitably from belief in the brotherhood of man through the fatherhood of God. When once the right of the individual to liberty and equality is admitted, there is no escape from the conclusion that he alone is entitled to the rewards of his own industry. Any other conclusion would necessarily imply either privilege or servitude. Here again the right of individual property is for the protection of society.

When service is performed, the individual performing it is entitled to the compensation for it. His creation becomes a part of himself. It is his property. To attempt to deal with persons or with property in a communistic or socialistic way is to deny what seems to me to be this plain fact. Liberty and equality require that equal compensation shall be paid for equal service to the individual who performs it. Socialism and communism cannot be reconciled with the principles which our institutions represent. They are entirely foreign, entirely un-American. We stand wholly committed to the policy that what the individual produces belongs entirely to him to be used by him for the benefit of himself, to provide for his own family and to enable him to serve his fellow men.

Of course we are all aware that the recognition of brotherhood brings in the requirement of charity. But it is only on the basis of individual property that there can be any charity. Our very conception of the term means that we deny ourselves of what belongs to us, in order to give it to another. If that which we give is not really our own, but belongs to the person to whom we give it, such an act may rightfully be called justice, but it cannot be regarded as charity.

Our conceptions of liberty under the law are not narrow and cramped, but broad and tolerant. Our Constitution guarantees civil, political and religious liberty; fully, completely and adequately; and provides that "no religious test shall ever be required as a qualification to any office or public trust under the United States." This is the essence of freedom and toleration solemnly declared in the fundamental law of the land.

These are some of our American standards. These principles, in the province to which they relate, bestow upon the people all there is to bestow. They recognize in the people all that there is to recognize. They are the ultimates. There is no beyond. They are solely for the benefit and advantage of all the people. If any change is made in these principles it will not be by giving more to the people, but by taking from them something of that which they now have. It cannot be progress. It must be reaction. I do not say that we, as citizens, have always held ourselves to a proper observance of these standards towards each other, but we have nevertheless established them and declared our duty to be obedience to them. This is the American ideal of ordered liberty under the law. It calls for rigid discipline.

What a wide difference between the American position and that imagined by the vagabond who thought of liberty as a glorious feast unprotected and unregulated by law. This is not civilization, but a plain reversion to the life of the jungle. Without the protection of the law, and the imposition of its authority, equality cannot be maintained, liberty disappears and property vanishes. This is anarchy. The forces of darkness are traveling in that direction. But the spirit of America turns its face towards the light.

That spirit I have faith will prevail. America is not going to abandon its principles or desert its ideals. The foundation on which they are built will remain firm. I believe that the principle which your organization represents is their main support. It seems to me perfectly plain that the authority of law, the right to equality, liberty and property, under American institutions, have for their foundation reverence for God. If we could imagine that to be swept away, these institutions of our American government could not long survive. But that reverence will not fail. It will abide. Unnumbered organizations of which your own is one exist for its promotion. In the inevitable longing of the human soul to do right is the secure guarantee of our American institutions. By maintaining a society to promote reverence for the Holy Name you are performing both a pious and a patriotic service.

We Americans are idealists. We are willing to follow the truth solely because it is the truth. We put our main emphasis on the things which are spiritual. While we possess an unsurpassed skill in marshalling and using the material resources of the world, still the nation has not sought for wealth and power as an end but as a means to a higher life.

Yet Americans are not visionary, they are not sentimentalists. They want idealism, but they want it to be practical, they want it to produce results. It would be little use to try to convince them of the soundness and righteousness of their institutions, if they could not see that they have been justified in the past history and the present condition of the people. They estimate the correctness of the principle by the success which they find in their own experience. They have faith but they want works.

The fame of the advantages which accrue to the inhabitants of our country has spread throughout the world. If we doubt the high estimation in which these opportunities are held by other peoples, it is only necessary to remember that they sought them in such numbers as to require our own protection by restrictive immigration. I am aware that our country and its institutions are often the subject of censure. I grieve to see them misrepresented for selfish and destructive aims. But I welcome candid criticism, which is moved by a purpose to promote the public welfare. But while we should always strive for improvement by living in more complete harmony with out ideals, we should not permit incidental failure or unwarranted blame to obscure the fact that the people of our country have secured the greatest success that was ever before experienced in human history.

The evidence of this is all about us, in our wealth, our educational facilities, our charities, our religious institutions, and in the moral influence which we exert on the world. Most of all, it is apparent in the unexampled place which is held by the people who toil. Our inhabitants are especially free to promote their own welfare. They are unburdened by militarism. They are not called upon to support any imperialistic designs. Every mother can rest in the assurance that her children will find here a land of devotion, prosperity and peace. The tall shaft near which we are gathered and yonder stately memorial remind us that our standards of manhood are revealed in the adoration which we pay to Washington and Lincoln. They are unrivaled and unsurpassed. Above all else, they are Americans. The institutions of our country stand justified both in reason and in experience. I am aware that they will continue to be assailed. But I know they will continue to stand. We may perish, but they will endure. They are founded on the Rock of Ages.

XIII

The governments of the past could fairly be characterized as devices for maintaining in perpetuity the place and position of certain privileged classes, without any ultimate protection for the rights of the people. The Government of the United States is a device for maintaining in perpetuity the rights of the people, with the ultimate extinction of all privileged classes.

A FREE REPUBLIC

No American coming to Philadelphia on this anniversary could escape being thrilled at the thought of what this commemoration means. It brings to mind events, which in the course of the century and a half that has passed since the day we are celebrating, have changed the course of human history. Then was formed the ideal of the American nation. Two years later this was put into practical effect by the Declaration of Independence. Here too was prepared and adopted the Federal Constitution, guaranteeing unity and perpetuation of our national life. The place of this imperial city in history is secure.

Your heritage has that mysterious quality by which it has enriched not only your own citizens, but the people of the earth. Wherever we find a nation which has gained its liberty, which has shaken itself free from despotism and established a republic, there reigns the influence with which the exalted record of your achievements has directed the destiny of the world.

We cannot do justice to the memory of the men and work of the first Continental Congress without recalling events which preceded it and recognizing the consequences which followed it. The first important act of coöperation among the Colonies had resulted from their need for common defense in the French and Indian War two decades earlier. Even prior to that various royal Governors had proposed some union of the Colonies under a viceroy. But this meant a weakening of the local and popular assemblies and

At Philadelphia, Sept. 25th, 1924, on the anniversary of the first Continental Congress.

a broader and more effective control by the Crown. Such proposals were resisted by the inhabitants, who were extremely jealous of their liberties. As far back as 1754 a colonial conference was held at Albany on the initiation of the Governors. Only a minority, however, attended. At that time Benjamin Franklin, with a prophetic vision, proposed a plan of union which bore a remarkable resemblance to our present Constitution. But the people feared this would destroy their local government, leaving them at the mercy of a distant Parliament, while the English authorities feared that by revealing to the Colonies an accurate knowledge of their own power it would inspire ambitions for independence. So the plan of Franklin at that time found no support on either side of the Atlantic.

But the idea grew. When the English Government entered upon a course which threatened the liberties of the Colonies by passing the Stamp Act and the Boston Port Act, by interfering with the local Assemblies, by suspending the writ of habeas corpus, by maintaining a standing army quartered on the people, by denying to the inhabitants the right of trial by a jury of the vicinage, by undertaking to make judicial officers the creatures of the Crown, and other unwarranted tyrannies, the first Continental Congress was assembled to register a solemn protest against these illegal exactions.

They came with various credentials from local Assemblies and voluntary conventions, scarcely representing the people in a legal way but reflecting their spirit in the determination to defend their liberties. It was no ordinary gathering. Among them were Jay and Livingston, Galloway and Mifflin, Biddle and Chase, Harrison, Lee, Randolph, the Rutledges, the Adamses, and finally, George Washington. They were men of faith. They believed in their cause. They trusted the people. They doubted not that a Higher Power would support them in their effort for right and freedom. Judged by the character of the state papers which they produced, and by their later careers in the field or at the council table, after 150 years they still rank as a most remarkable gathering of men. Their deliberations and actions are worthy of the most careful study by the American people. If we could better understand what they said and did to establish our free institutions, we should be less likely to be misled by the misrepresentations and distorted arguments of the hour, and be far better equipped to maintain them.

The Colonists claimed certain rights of self-government. They were determined to maintain that principle. The burdens which resulted from the pretentions of King George and his ministers, and the exactions of Parliament, were not of great consequence and could be borne, but the principle which the people declared was of supreme importance. To acquiesce even in minor violations was to admit that a course of action might be taken which would deprive them of the chartered rights of Englishmen and reduce them to mere subjects. But in their resistance they resorted neither to threats nor extreme measures, but pursued the dignified, stronger and unanswerable course of moderation. The Congress prepared a petition to the King, an address to the people of the Colonies, an address to the people of England, and an address to the people of Quebec. While they protested vigorously against their grievances, they protested also a loyalty to the Crown and a pride in the Empire. They declared they were supporting the common cause of liberty, both of the Colonies and England itself.

"May not a ministry with the same armies enslave you?" they asked the English people. "Do not treat this as chimerical. Know that in less than half a century, the quit-rents reserved to the Crown from the numberless grants of this vast continent, will pour large streams of wealth into the royal coffers, and if to this be added the power of taxing America at pleasure, the Crown will be rendered independent of you for supplies, and will possess more treasure than will be necessary to purchase the remains of liberty in your Island. In a word, take care that you do not fall into the pit that is preparing for us."

No wonder such a statement aroused the sympathy for the Colonial cause of such broad and liberal statesmen as Pitt and Burke.

But to the Crown and to the traditions of English liberty it contained only expressions of loyalty. The address to King George was an explicit and unmistakable document, but it closed with these words of loyal devotion: "That Your Majesty may enjoy every felicity through a long and glorious reign over loyal and happy subjects, and that your descendants may inherit your prosperity and dominions till time shall be no more, is and always will be our sincere and fervent prayer." They indulged in no bluster, no threats, and no departures from the proprieties of a petition to the throne. But they had no hesitation about making a plain statement of the truth, because they politely observed, "as Your Majesty enjoys the signal distinction of reigning over freemen, we apprehend the language of freemen cannot be displeasing."

But the Congress did not confine itself to addresses and petitions. It wished not only to win the approbation of the opinion of the world, but to prove its right to speak for the Colonies. It was necessary to show that they were capable of a united action, both powerful and effective. Therefore, they adopted the policy of non-intercourse under an agreement known as "The Association." By it they pledged themselves not to import, export or consume. British products were not to be brought in after December 1, 1774. The importation of slaves was to cease. A few months later trade with the West Indies was to be sus-

pended. Exports to Great Britain and Ireland were pro-
hibited. Merchants refusing to adopt these boycott agreements were to feel the boycott of the people. The production and manufacture of wool was to be encouraged. Local
committees were to enforce these proposals by the power
of public opinion. The Association enjoined frugality thus:
"We will . . . discountenance and discourage every species
of extravagance and dissipation, especially all horse-
racing, and all kinds of gaming, cock-fighting, exhibitions
of shows, plays and other expensive diversions and enter-
tainents. . . ."

The non-intercourse agreement was to continue until
Parliament repealed the objectionable laws. This bold
measure was denounced by many in England as treasonable,
but it has often been referred to in this country as the
beginning of the movement for independence. Where appeals and supplications had been disregarded, this could
not fail to secure earnest attention.

In the declarations of the Congress there was no note
of defiance, but their very moderation increased their influence. The vigor of their argument and the logic of their
legal position were relied upon to defend their cause. While
there was a growing feeling that conflict impended, the
Congress carefully avoided anything that could be distorted into provocation for a resort to arms. Here was
the great strength of their position. Because of their restraint they secured the confidence of the most influential
forces at home and abroad. They promoted union among
the Colonies while promoting dissension in England. They
compelled the sympathy of the great Whig leaders, who
could not support liberty in England while denying it in
the Colonies.

It would be difficult to find a better illustration of the
superiority of moderation and candor over violence and
deceit in seeking a solution of difficult public questions.

It is easy to draw broad indictments or indulge in sweeping promises. It is no trouble to indulge in invective. But denunciation does not provide a remedy. In moderation and restraint is much more likely to be found a way to agreement upon constructive measures. Appeals to violence and hatred in the first Continental Congress might have produced a rebellion, but they could not have accomplished revolution. They might have led to war, but they could not have secured victory.

Almost all our history as an independent and united nation can be traced back to the assembling of the first Continental Congress, which we are met to celebrate. Our achievements have been wrought by adherence to its policies of reason and restraint, accompanied by firmness and determination. We are not likely to desert that course of action now.

The case which the Congress stated was unanswerable. One side or the other must either give way or maintain its position by force of arms. That conflict for which the Congress had laid the logical foundation was not long in beginning. Liberty never won a more substantial and far-reaching victory than that which resulted from our Revolutionary War. It established the American Nation, with all that it has since meant in the accomplishments of the world and all that it holds of future promise. A form of government was organized in harmony with what Franklin had proposed at Albany in 1754. But the Constitution was not adopted until various experiments with unworkable systems showed some such action necessary. Whatever may be the reputation of that great instrument at home, modified and adapted to local needs, it has been adopted as the fundamental law for republics in every quarter of the world. The influence of that great document, framed in Philadelphia in 1787, can be traced in every constitution on earth, from China to Peru, from the Australian commonwealth to the German republic. They all bear the same testimony.

The idea of a republic was not new, but the practical working out of such a form of government under separate and independent, and yet well-balanced departments, was a very new thing in the world. The governments of the past could fairly be characterized as devices for maintaining in perpetuity the place and position of certain privileged classes, without any ultimate protection for the rights of the people. The Government of the United States is a device for maintaining in perpetuity the rights of the people, with the ultimate extinction of all privileged classes. It is a Constitution which is the product of human experience with all its toil and suffering, its bloodshed and devastation, its oppression and tyranny, but likewise with all its wisdom, its love of liberty and its determination to follow the truth. The first Continental Congress met to redress grievances which were the result of government action. The Revolution was fought to resist those same grievances. And finally, the Constitution was adopted to prevent similar impositions from ever again being inflicted upon the people.

They are all in that precious document, these priceless guarantees. The people do not propose again to entrust their government to others, but to retain it under their own control. No one can tax them or even propose a tax upon them, save themselves and their own representatives. Instead of encroaching upon local Assemblies, it guarantees each state a republican form of government. It regulates suspension of the writ of habeas corpus. It protects the home from the uninvited intrusion of the military force of the Government. It guards the right of jury trial and undertakes to make judicial officers independent, impartial and free from every motive to follow any influence save that of the evidence, the law and the truth. These are representative of the great body of our liberties, of which the Constitution is the sole source and guarantee.

Ours, as you know, is a government of limited powers. The Constitution confers the authority for certain actions upon the President and the Congress, and explicitly prohibits them from taking other actions. This is done to protect the rights and liberties of the people. The Government is limited, only the people are absolute. Whenever the legislative or executive power undertakes to overstep the bounds of its limitations, any person who is injured may resort to the courts for protection and remedy. We do not submit the precious rights of the people to the hazard of a prejudiced and irresponsible political determination, but preserve and protect them by an independent and impartial judicial determination. We do not expose the rights of the weak to the danger of being overcome in the public forum by popular uproar, but protect them in the sanctity of the courtroom, where the still, small voice will not fail to be heard. Any attempt to change this method of procedure is an attempt to put the people again in jeopardy of the impositions and the tyrannies from which the first Continental Congress sought to deliver them. The only position that Americans can take is that they are against all despotism whether it emanate from a monarch, from a parliament, or from a mob.

A significant circumstance of the first Congress, one which ought never to be overlooked, lies in the fact that it resulted from the voluntary effort on the part of the people to redress their own grievances and remedy their own wrongs. We pay too little attention to the reserve power of the people to take care of themselves. We are too solicitous for government intervention, on the theory, first, that the people themselves are helpless, and second, that the Government has superior capacity for action. Often times both of these conclusions are wrong.

Everyone knows that our economic problems are very far from being solved. But we are making constant progress, both in the field of production and distribution. When certain abuses arose, we adopted a policy of government regulation and control. I have no doubt that some action of that kind was necessary, and of course such a policy would be continued. But it has not been, nor can it be hoped that it will be, always wisely administered. While it provides some defence against wrongdoing, its restrictions often hamper development and progress, retard enterprise, and when they fail to produce the perfection promised tend to bring the Government into discredit. The real fact is that in a republic like ours the people are the government, and if they cannot secure perfection in their own economic life it is altogether improbable that the Government can secure it for them. The same human nature which presides over private enterprise must be employed for public action.

It is very difficult to reconcile the American ideal of a sovereign people capable of owning and managing their own government with an inability to own and manage their own business. No doubt there are certain municipalities where some public utilities have been managed through public ownership with a creditable success. But this is very different from a proposal that the National Government should take over railroads and other public utilities. What a strain this would be to our economic system will be realized when it is remembered that public commissions set the value of such utilities at about $35,000,000,000, and that they have about 2,750,000 employees. Such an undertaking would mean about $1,750,000,000 annually in bond interest, and an operating budget estimated at about $9,000,000,000. These utilities are no longer in the hands of a few, directly or indirectly. They are owned by scores of millions of our inhabitants. It would mean a loss in public revenue estimated at $600,000,000 a year, and while in industrial states it might not increase the tax on the farmer more than 3% or 4%, in many agricultural counties it would run as high as 40%. When we recall the appalling loss and the difficulty in the management of $3,500,000,000 worth of ships, we should undoubtedly hesitate about taking on ten times that value in public utilities. But this is no occasion to discuss the details of public ownership.

I have mentioned the desirability for the people to keep control of their own Government and their own property, because I believe that is one of the American ideals of public welfare in harmony with the efforts of the first Continental Congress. They objected to small infractions, which would destroy great principles of liberty. Unless we can maintain the integrity of the courts, where the individual can secure his rights, any kind of tyranny may follow. If the people lose control of the arteries of trade and the natural sources of mechanical power, the nationalization of all industry could soon be expected. Our forefathers were alert to resist all encroachments upon their rights. If we wish to maintain our rights, we can do no less. Through the breaking down of the power of the courts lies an easy way to the confiscation of the property and the destruction of the liberty of the individual. With railways and electrical utilities under political control, the domination of a group would be so firmly intrenched in the whole direction of our Government, that the privilege of citizenship for the rest of the people would consist largely in the payment of taxes. The Fathers sought to escape from any such condition, through the guarantees of our Constitution. They put their faith in a free republic. If we wish to maintain what they established, we shall do well to leave the people in the ownership of their property, in control of their Government, and under the protection of their courts. By a resolute determination to resist all these encroachments we can best show our reverence and appreciation for the men and the work of the first Continental Congress.

XIV

There is a place both present and future in America for true, clean sport. We do not rank it above business, the occupations of our lives, and we do not look with approval upon those who, not being concerned in its performance, spend all their thought, energy and time upon its observance. We recognize, however, that there is something more in life than the grinding routine of daily toil, that we can develop a better manhood and womanhood, a more attractive youth, and a wiser maturity, by rounding out our existence with a wholesome interest in sport.

GOOD SPORTSMANSHIP

As the head of an enterprise which transacts some business and maintains a considerable staff in this town, I have a double satisfaction in welcoming home the victorious Washington Baseball Team. First, you bring the laurels from one of the hardest fought contests in all the history of the national game. Second, I feel hopeful that with this happy result now assured it will be possible for the people of Washington gradually to resume interest in the ordinary concerns of life. So long as we could be satisfied with a prompt report of the score by innings, a reasonable attention to business was still possible. But when the entire population reached the point of requiring the game to be described play by play, I began to doubt whether the highest efficiency was being promoted. I contemplated action of a vigorously disciplinary character, but the outcome makes it impossible. As a result we are a somewhat demoralized community—but exceedingly happy over it.

It may be that at some time in the past a baseball pennant has gone to as widely popular a winner as your team is today. If so, it was in some year when I was not watching the score by innings. Tuesday morning, when I had finished reading details of the decisive battle of Boston and turned to the affairs of government, I found on top of everything else on my desk a telegram which I shall read to you. Whether or not I shall be able to act on its advice, many will agree that it presents a correct, constructive and statesmanlike program for dealing with the present

At the Zero Milestone, Washington, D. C., in welcoming home the Baseball Team, October 1, 1924.

emergency. I have received worse suggestions on more important affairs. It is from a true and thoughtful friend of the people, Congressman John F. Miller, of Seattle. He wires:

"Respectfully suggest it is your patriotic duty to call special session of Congress beginning Saturday, October 4th, so the members of Congress may have an opportunity to sneak out and see Walter Johnson make baseball history. Cannot speak for New York delegation, but hereby pledge all others to root for Washington, and serve without pay or traveling expenses."

Mr. Miller has such judgment and his sense of public psychology is so accurate that I do not need to say what party he represents.

The Washington team won because it deserved to win. It had fought gamely, year after year, for a place at the front; never discouraged, always sure that better things were ahead. Now it appears to have annexed the whole country, with the enthusiastic approval of nearly all concerned. Aside from two or three groups of earnest young men who were willing to accept the championship, the whole country seems agreed that precisely the right thing has happened. That is a real compliment to the fine spirit, the clean play, the good sportsmanship that brought your victory. These have always been characteristics of the work of the Washington team. They have earned for it the affection of the "home town" constituency and the regard of baseball followers throughout the country. Clean sport crowned with victory is a most wholesome sight. I trust it will always be representative of America.

You have come home to receive the plaudits of your city, and to prepare for the greater competition of the World Series. We are all agreed, at least in theory, to the sentiment, "May the best team win." But I want to add that your fellow townsmen of Washington do not need to be told which they regard as the best team. They hold firm convictions about it. And in that full confidence in which the President is privileged to speak when only the public is listening, I may say that I have my opinion about it. I hope the results of the World Series will show we all are right. I know it will show a continuation of clean sport.

Manager Harris, I am directed by a group of your Washington fellow citizens to present to you for the Club this loving cup. It is a symbol of deep and genuine sentiment. It is committed to you and your team-mates in testimony of the feelings that all Washington has for you. With it go the heartiest congratulations on victory already won, and every wish for your success in the contest which is still ahead of you.

There is a place both present and future in America for true, clean sport. We do not rank it above business, the occupations of our lives, and we do not look with approval upon those who, not being concerned in its performance, spend all their thought, energy and time upon its observance. We recognize, however, that there is something more in life than the grinding routine of daily toil, that we can develop a better manhood and womanhood, a more attractive youth, and a wiser maturity, by rounding out our existence with a wholesome interest in sport.

To those who devote themselves to this enterprise in a professional way and by throwing their whole being into it raise it to the level of an art, the country owes a debt of gratitude. They furnish us with amusement, with an outside interest, oftentimes in the open air, that quickens the step, refreshes the mind, rejuvenates and restores us. We pitch with the pitchers, we go to bat with the batters, and make a home run with the hard hitters. The training, the energy, the intelligence which these men lavish upon their profession ought to be an inspiration for a like effort in every walk of life. They are a great band, these armored knights of the bat and ball. They are held up to a high standard of honor on the field, which they have seldom betrayed. While baseball remains our national game our national tastes will be on a higher level and our national ideals on a firmer foundation. By bringing the baseball pennant to Washington, you have made the National Capital more truly the center of worthy and honorable national aspirations.

XV

The great truth cannot be too often repeated that this nation is exactly what the people make it.

PATRIOTISM IN TIME OF PEACE

WE meet to dedicate a monument to the memory of the men of the First Division of the American Expeditionary Forces, who gave their lives in battle for their country. Their surviving comrades bestow this gift upon the Nation. It bears mute but enduring testimony of an affectionate regard for those who made the great sacrifice. This beautiful and stately shaft represents no spirit of self-glorification. It is a tribute of reverence and sorrow to nearly 5,000 of our immortal dead from those who knew and loved them. The figure of winged victory rises above the scrolls of imperishable bronze on which are inscribed alone the ennobled names of those who fell and through their deathless valor left us free. Other soldiers, generals and privates, officers and men, rank on rank, of illustrious fame are unrecorded here. They live. The dead reign here alone.

This memorial stands as a testimony of how the members of the First Division looked upon the War. They did not regard it as a national or personal opportunity for gain or fame or glory, but as a call to sacrifice for the support of humane principles and spiritual ideals. This monument commemorates no man who won anything by the war. It ministers to no aspiration for place or power. But it challenges attention to the cost, suffering and sacrifice that may be demanded of any generation, so long as nations permit a resort to war to settle their disputes. It is a symbol of awful tragedy, of unending sorrow, and of stern warning. Relieved of all attendant considerations, the final lesson

At Washington, October 4, 1924, dedicating the monument to the First Division, A. E. F.

135

which it imparts is the blessing of peace, the supreme blessing of peace with honor.

The First Division has the notable record of being the first to enter France and the last to leave Germany. Hurriedly assembled, largely from Regular Army units, its first four regiments landed at Saint-Nazaire at the end of June, 1917, the advance guard which in a little more than a year was to be swelled to the incredible force of two millions. It had two battalions in the Grand Parade of July 4th in Paris, when tradition claims that a great American Commander laid our wreath at the tomb of the great Frenchman with a salutation which was short but all-embracing in its eloquence: "Lafayette, we are here." Other units, mostly from those who served in Mexico, made the Division so cosmopolitan that it represented every state and all the possessions of the Union. It was comprehensively and truly American.

After short and intensive preparation the Division was ordered from the Gondrecourt training area to the Sommerville sector, where on October 23rd the first American shot was fired. On October 25th the first American officer was wounded, and two days later the first prisoner was taken. On the night of November 2nd Corporal James B. Gresham and Privates Thomas F. Enright and Merle D. Hay, killed when their trenches were raided, were the first Americans lost in the war. In January, 1918, the Division was removed to the Toul sector, where for the first time Americans were given charge of a section of trenches. From here it was sent to Cantigny sector to resist the March drive against Amiens. To this place General Pershing came on a personal visit, warning the officers of the desperate character of the fighting which was soon encountered. The trenches here were imperfect and the troops were constantly exposed to shellfire. The first offensive of an American unit was the attack on Cantigny.

Repeated and desperate efforts were made to recapture the town from the Americans in order that they should not be permitted to record a success, but the town was held and victory remained with the First Division. In July the Division was placed in the Soisson sector to take part in the attack on the German salient. In five days of heavy fighting it advanced 11 kilometers and captured 3500 officers and men, with large quantities of materials. Its own losses were 78 officers and 1458 men killed, 214 officers and 6130 men wounded, 5 prisoners and 390 missing; a heavy price to pay, but the victory at Soisson has been called the turning point of the war.

Following a fortnight for rest and replacements a short service in the Vosges preceded the attack on St. Mihiel. The offensive against this position, which has been held for four years, was the first operation of an American army under an American commander. Under the direction of General Pershing nine American and some French divisions won complete victory, the Americans capturing 16,000 prisoners, 443 guns, and 240 miles of territory. The Division was then sent to the Meuse.

In the great final offensive about a million American troops were engaged in the Argonne sector. After being held in reserve five days after operations opened, the First Division went into action October 4th to open the way on the east for a flank attack upon the forest. From then until the Armistice fighting and marching were continuous. The early successes of the American forces in the Argonne attack started a general German retirement about November 2nd. From then until Armistice Day the advance continued. On the night of November 5th the First Division reached the Meuse. It was ordered to attack Sedan. Between 4:30 in the afternoon of November 5th and midnight November 7th, the Division advanced and fought constantly. The 16th, 18th and 28th Infantry Regiments covered 35 miles each, while the 26th Infantry, under the command of Colonel Theodore Roosevelt, traversed no less than 45 miles. Then came the Armistice. Immediately after the Division was ordered into Germany and stationed at the bridgeheads east of the line, from which it was withdrawn about a year later, the last units reaching New York on September 6, 1919.

Such in barest outline is the war record of the First Division. In little more than a year it lost by death 5,516, of which 4,964 were killed in battle. Over 17,000 were wounded, 170 were reported missing, and 124 were taken prisoners. These numbers nearly equal the original strength of the Division. In General Order No. 201, of November 10, 1918, his only General Order issued referring exclusively to the work of a single Division, after describing your difficult accomplishments, General Pershing concluded thus:

"The Commander-in-Chief has noted in this Division a special pride of service and a high state of morale, never broken by hardship nor battle."

Five different Generals commanded the Division, all of whom won high distinction and commendation. They were William L. Sibert, Robert L. Bullard, Charles P. Summerall, Frank Parker, and Edward F. McGlachlin.

The little that I can say in commendation of the service of your Division is but a slight suggestion of what is deserved. Every unit of the American Army, whether at home or abroad, richly merits its own full measure of recognition. They shrank from no toil, no danger and no hardship, that the liberties of our country might adequately be defended and preserved.

We raise monuments to testify to the honor in which we hold men for the work they have done, and to be a constant reminder to ourselves and future generations of the lessons their actions have taught us. A tradition reminds us of

the ingratitude of republics. That supposition must have
arisen before America was very far advanced. It is true
that we do not pay much attention to those who serve us
in civil life. The honor bestowed during the term of the
office may well be thought adequate recognition. When
our country was young and struggling, poor and unorganized, it found difficulty in even paying those who fought
in the Revolutionary War. It is well known that Washington was not even a dollar a year man, but donated his
great talents to his country. But after our Constitution
was adopted and the national finances were restored to
order, and as the resources of the country grew, the nation
did not fail in its duty toward those that won our independence. The unsurpassing honor in which the nation has
always held its defenders has since that time been reflected
in a policy too familiar to need mention. The great contest which Lincoln directed ended less than sixty years
ago. Those who fought in it and their dependents have
been paid about 6,000 million dollars, averaging $100,000,-
000 a year, and payments are now going on at the rate of
about a quarter of a billion dollars each year. The participants in the Spanish War are being provided for along the
same direction. For that which might be broadly characterized as relief work for the veterans and their dependents
of the World War, the Government has already appropri-
ated well towards 3,000 million dollars. But this is not
the measure, it is only an indication of the high regard and
the abiding honor which America bestows upon its loyal
defenders. It cannot be measured in money. How poor
and cheap and unworthy would be that attitude which
could say: "You have offered your life. Here is your dollar. That discharges the debt. Take it and go." The nation recognizes towards them all a debt which it can never
repay, but which it will never repudiate. Standing to their
credit will forever be an inexhaustible balance of gratitude,

of honor and of praise. In song and story, in monument and memorial, in tradition and history, they will live in the heart of the people forever more.

For the aid and relief of all veterans suffering disability by reason of service, and of their dependents, with the unanimous support of the country the Government is committed to a most broad and liberal policy. Its administration has been difficult from its very magnitude. It had no opportunity to grow and learn by experience. While a military force of about 4,600,000, of which more than 2,000,000 were brought from abroad, had to be demobilized and returned to their homes, and a civil force calculated at about 7,000,000, discharged from war industries, had to be relocated in peacetime occupations, an organization complete in all its functions had to be devised to meet this great emergency of relief. Nevertheless, these 12,000,000 people were restored to a life of peace with little economic loss.

To unify the relation of the Government to this whole problem the Veterans Bureau was established. The Bureau is now functioning in the interest of those it is intended to serve. The scattered mass of laws dealing with relief have been coördinated in the Veterans Act of 1924. Government hospital facilities have been made available to all veterans of all wars, whether the disability was or was not due to military service. The needy are even furnished traveling expenses to reach the hospital. Since 1921 a broad policy of caring for the sick has been established. Over $40,000,000 has been appropriated, 25 new hospitals have been completed with over 10,000 beds, and 7 more with about 1700 beds will soon be ready for occupancy. The 25,000 to 30,000 patients will soon be entirely housed in Government hospitals with several thousand spare beds.

In order that the government might be brought to the Veteran, district organizations provide local relief agencies. Uncertainties are resolved in favor of the service men, and the particular kind of assistance required is supplied. Exceptional benefits accrue to the mentally ill and their dependents. Organization is nationwide to provide employment. In cases of excessive relief, if no fraud is involved the loss falls on the Government. The pension laws for widows and mothers have been liberalized. While there are still 40,000 taking rehabilitation training, over 80,000 have completed these courses and substantially all have been placed in profitable employment.

The caring for those who are the disabled and the dependents by reason of service in time of war is the very first duty of the National Government. I have referred to a few of the representative efforts which our country has made to discharge that duty with an unstinted expenditure which has averaged about half a billion dollars each year. For the relief of stricken veterans and their dependents, America has been proud to establish a new standard.

While this is the first duty, it is by no means the only one. Many others have resulted from the Great War, which must be discharged by the Government and the people. I am well aware that it is impossible to maintain in time of peace the same exalted spirit of patriotism that exists in time of war, and yet, although it may be in a less degree, the country has need of devotion to the same ideals. In our land the people rule. The great truth cannot be too often repeated that this nation is exactly what the people make it. It is necessary to realize that our duties are personal. For each of us our country will be about what we make it. The obligation of citizenship is upon each one of us. We must discharge it in the actions of our daily life. If we are employed, we must be true to that employment. If we are in business, we must be true to that business. What is always of the utmost importance, if we have the privilege to vote we must inform ourselves of the questions at issue and going to the ballot box on election day there vote, as we claim the sacred right of Americans to live, according to the dictates of our own conscience. You who have offered your blood that these supreme rights and privileges might be maintained as a standard of human conduct on this earth must continue to be their chief exponents by what you say and by what you do. The coming generations will reverence your example.

In this presence I am well aware there is no need to urge any support of the American Constitution, but I cannot let this occasion pass without expressing my most strong and emphatic commendation for the reverence which your words and actions constantly express for the liberty-giving provisions of the fundamental law of our land. You have supported the Constitution and the Flag which is its symbol, not only because it represents to you the home-land, but because you know it is the sole source of American freedom. You want your rights protected by the impartial judicial decisions of the courts where you will have a right to be heard and not be exposed to the irresponsible determination of partisan political action. You want to have your earnings and your property secure. You want a free and fair opportunity to conduct your own business and make your way in the world without danger of being overcome by a Government monopoly. When the Government goes into business it lays a tax on everybody else in that business, and uses the money that it collects from its competitors to establish a monopoly and drive them out of business. No one can compete. When the Government really starts into a line of business that door of opportunity is closed to the people. It has always been an American ideal that the door of opportunity should remain open.

But while naturally we think of our own domestic affairs first, we have to remember not only that we are affected by what happens abroad, but that we are one among other nations. If there is anything which is dear to Americans, which they are bound to preserve at all hazards, it is their independence. I mean by that the privilege of reserving to themselves the choice of their own course and the decision of their own actions. We do not propose to entrust to any other power, or combination of powers, any authority to make up our own mind for us. But we recognize that what others do has an effect upon us. Had it not been so, it would not have been necessary for you to go overseas. We recognize too that we are a part of the great brotherhood of mankind, that there are mutual duties and obligations between nations as there are between individuals. America has every wish to discharge its obligations. This is a condition which is not imposed upon us by artificial covenants, but which results from the natural relationship among nations. We wish to recognize these requirements for the promotion of peace. War and destruction are unnatural; peace and progress are natural. It is in that direction that the people of the earth must move. I am in favor of treaties and covenants conforming to the American policy of independence to prevent aggressive war and promote permanent peace. But they have little value unless the sentiment of peace is cherished in the hearts of the people. Peace is the result of mutual understanding and mutual confidence exemplified in honorable action. Your adversaries found that when you made war, you made it with all your might. The nation nourished the war spirit. But now we have made peace. If it is to be real peace, if it is to result in the benefits that ought to accrue from it, it will be because we nourish with equal sincerity the peace spirit, because we seek to establish mutual good will, because we are moved by the sentiment of magnanimity.

No other basis exists for the progress of civilization on earth. We had many motives for entering the war. I shall not attempt to catalogue them. What we need now is to cherish the motives for which we made peace. We want to see the Allies paid, we want to see Germany restored to a condition of productivity and progress, under which she will be able to take up the burden of civilization. Our country has been working toward that end. Our Government suggested a plan, the essence of which was that it should be carried out by private citizens unhampered by political consideration. That was done. The American government was the architect, the experts unconnected with any government built the structure known as the Dawes Plan. The Allies and Germany have adopted it. It remains for private enterprise in this country and Europe to help finance it.

When this is done I believe Europe will begin to revive, and that we shall receive the benefit of a larger market for the products of our farms and our factories. Above that we shall have the satisfaction of knowing that we have done what we could to dispel the hatreds of war, restore the destruction it has wrought, and lay a firmer foundation for industrial prosperity and a more secure peace. To promote these ends, reserving complete jurisdiction over its own internal affairs and complete independence to direct its own actions, America should always stand ready. I have already indicated many times my wish for an International Court and further disarmament.

We cannot claim that under our institutions we have reached perfection, but we are justified in saying that our institutions are the best for the promotion of human welfare that the ingenuity of man has ever been able to devise. We cannot claim that our Government is perfect, but we have the right to believe that it is the best that there is. We do not claim we have been able to discharge our full duty towards the other nations of the earth. But we have a right to believe that we have been the most effectual agency in helping to restore Europe. If anyone doubts the depth and sincerity of the attachment of the American people to their institutions and Government, if anyone doubts the sacrifices which they have been willing to make in behalf of those institutions and for what they believe to be the welfare of other nations, let them gaze upon this monument and other like memorials that have been reared in every quarter of our broad land.   Let them look upon the representative gatherings of our veterans, and let them remember that America has dedicated itself to the service of God and man.

XVI

Our government rests upon religion. It is from that source that we derive our reverence for truth and justice, for equality and liberty, and for the rights of mankind. Unless the people believe in these principles they cannot believe in our government.

RELIGION AND THE REPUBLIC

THIS occasion cannot but recall to our minds in a most impressive way the sacrifice and devotion that has gone into the making of our country. It is impossible to interpret it as the working out of a plan devised by man. The wisest and most far-sighted of them had little conception of the greatness of the structure which was to arise on the foundation which they were making. As we review their accomplishments they constantly admonish us not only that "all things work together for good to them that love God," but that in the direction of the affairs of our country there has been an influence that had a broader vision, a greater wisdom and a wider purpose, than that of mortal man, which we can only ascribe to a Divine Providence. A wide variety of motives has gone into the building of our republic. We can never understand what self-government is or what is necessary to maintain it unless we keep these fundamentals in mind. To one of them, Francis Asbury, the first American Bishop of the Methodist Episcopal Church, and his associates, made a tremendous contribution.

Our government rests upon religion. It is from that source that we derive our reverence for truth and justice, for equality and liberty, and for the rights of mankind. Unless the people believe in these principles they cannot believe in our government. There are only two main theories of government in the world. One rests on righteousness, the other rests on force. One appeals to reason, the other appeals to the sword. One is exemplified in a re-

At the unveiling of the Equestrian Statue of Bishop Francis Asbury, Washington, D. C., October 15, 1924.

public, the other is represented by a despotism. The history of government on this earth has been almost entirely a history of the rule of force held in the hands of a few. Under our constitution America committed itself to the practical application of the rule of reason, with the power held in the hands of the people.

This result was by no means accomplished at once. It came about only by reason of long and difficult preparation, oftentimes accompanied with discouraging failure. The ability for self-government is arrived at only through an extensive training and education. In our own case it required many generations, and we cannot yet say that it is wholly perfected. It is of a great deal of significance that the generation which fought the American Revolution had seen a very extensive religious revival. They had heard the preaching of Jonathan Edwards. They had seen the great revival meetings that were inspired also by the preaching of Whitefield. The religious experiences of those days made a profound impression upon the great body of the people. They made new thoughts and created new interests. They freed the public mind, through a deeper knowledge and more serious contemplation of the truth. By calling the people to righteousness they were a direct preparation for self-government. It was for a continuation of this work that Francis Asbury was raised up.

The religious movement which he represented was distinctly a movement to reach the great body of the people. Just as our Declaration of Independence asserts that all men are created free, so it seems to me the founders of this movement were inspired by the thought that all men were worthy to hear the Word, worthy to be sought out and brought to salvation. It was this motive that took their preachers among the poor and neglected, even to criminals in the jails. As our ideal has been to bring all men to freedom, so their ideal was to bring all men to salvation. It was preëminently a movement in behalf of all the people. It was not a new theory. The American Constitution was not a new theory. But, like it, it was the practical application of an old theory which was very new.

Just as the time was approaching when our country was about to begin the work of establishing a government which was to represent the rule of the people, where not a few but the many were to control public affairs, where the vote of the humblest was to count for as much as the vote of the most exalted, Francis Asbury came to America to preach religion. He had no idea that he was preparing men the better to take part in a great liberal movement, the better to take advantage of free institutions, and the better to perform the functions of self-government. He did not come for political motives. Undoubtedly they were farthest from his mind. Others could look after public affairs. He was a loyal and peaceful subject of the Realm. He came to bring the gospel to the people, to bear witness to the truth and to follow it wheresoever it might lead. Wherever men dwelt, whatever their condition, no matter how remote, no matter how destitute they might be, to him they were souls to be saved.

For this work, the bearing of the testimony of the truth to those who were about to be, and to those who in his later years were, sovereign American citizens, he had a peculiar training and aptitude. He was the son of a father who earned his livelihood by manual labor, of a mother who bore a reputation for piety. By constant effort they provided the ordinary comforts of life and an opportunity for intellectual and religious instruction. It was thus that he came out of a home of the people. Very early, at the age of seventeen, he began his preaching. In 1771, when he was twenty-six years old, responding to a call for volunteers, he was sent by Wesley to America. Landing in Philadelphia, he began that ministry which in the next forty-five years was to take him virtually all through the colonies and their western confines and into Canada, from Maine on the north, almost to the Gulf of Mexico on the south.

He came to America five years after the formation of the first Methodist Society in the city of New York, which had been contemporaneous with his own joining of the British Conference as an itinerant preacher and a gospel missionary. At that time it is reported that there were 316 members of his denomination in this country. The prodigious character of his labors is revealed when we remember that he traveled some 6,000 miles each year, or in all about 270,000 miles, preaching about 15,500 sermons and ordaining more than 4,000 clergymen, besides presiding at no less than 224 Annual Conferences. The highest salary that he received was $80 each year for this kind of service, which meant exposure to summer heat and winter cold, traveling alone through the frontier forests, sharing the rough fare of the pioneer's cabin, until his worn-out frame was laid at last to rest. But he left behind him as one evidence of his labors 695 preachers and 214,235 members of his denomination. The vitality of the cause which he served is further revealed by recalling that the 316 with which he began has now grown to more than 8,000,000.

His problem during the Revolutionary War was that of continuing to perform his duties without undertaking to interfere in civil or military affairs. He had taken for the text of his first sermon in America these very significant words: "For I determined not to know anything among you save Jesus Christ and him crucified." When several of his associates left for England in 1775, he decided to stay. "I can by no means agree to leave such a field for gathering souls to Christ as we have in America," he writes, "therefore I am determined by the grace of God not to leave them, let the consequence be what it may." But he had no lack of loyalty to the early form of American government.

When the inauguration of Washington took place April 30, 1789, the Conference being in session, Bishop Asbury moved the presentation of a congratulatory address to the new President. His suggestion was adopted, and the Bishop being one of those designated for the purpose, presenting the address in person, read it to Washington. How well he fitted into the scheme of things, this circuit rider who spent his life making stronger the foundation on which our government rests and seeking to implant in the hearts of all men, however poor and unworthy they may have seemed, an increased ability to discharge the high duties of their citizenship. His outposts marched with the pioneers, his missionaries visited the hovels of the poor so that all men might be brought to a knowledge of the truth.

A great lesson has been taught us by this holy life. It was because of what Bishop Asbury and his associates preached and what other religious organizations, through their ministry, preached, that our country has developed so much freedom and contributed so much to the civilization of the world. It is well to remember this when we are seeking for social reforms. If we can keep in mind their sources, we shall better understand their limitations.

The government of a country never gets ahead of the religion of a country. There is no way by which we can substitute the authority of law for the virtue of man. Of course we can help to restrain the vicious and furnish a fair degree of security and protection by legislation and police control, but the real reforms which society in these days is seeking will come as a result of our religious convictions, or they will not come at all. Peace, justice, humanity, charity—these cannot be legislated into being. They are the result of a Divine Grace. I have never seen the necessity for reliance upon religion rather than upon law better expressed than in a great truth uttered by Mr. Tiffany Blake, of Chicago, when he said: "Christ spent no time in

the antechamber of Cæsar." An act of Congress may indicate that a reform is being or has been accomplished, but it
does not of itself bring about a reform.

Perhaps, too, there is a lesson in contentment in the life
of this devout man. He never had any of the luxuries of
this life. Even its conveniences did not reach him, and of
its absolute necessaries he had a scanty share. Without
ever having the enjoyment of a real home, constantly on
the move, poorly clad, often wretchedly sheltered, much of
the time insufficiently nourished, yet his great spirit pressed
on to the end, always toward the mark of his high calling.
His recompense was not in the things of the earth. Yet
who can doubt that as he beheld his handiwork, as he saw
his accomplishments grow, there came to him a glorious
satisfaction and a divine peace? No doubt he valued the
material things of this life, and certainly they ought to be
valued and valued greatly, but he regarded it as his work
to put a greater emphasis on the things of the spirit. He
sought to prepare men for the sure maintenance and the
proper enjoyment of liberty, and for the more certain production and the better use of wealth, by inspiring them with
a reverence for the moral values of life.

What a wonderful experience he must have had, this
prophet of the wilderness! Who shall say where his influence, written upon the immortal souls of men, shall end?
How many homes he must have hallowed! What a multitude of frontier mothers must have brought their children
to him to receive his blessing! It is more than probable
that Nancy Hanks, the mother of Lincoln, had heard him
in her youth. Adams and Jefferson must have known him,
and Jackson must have seen in him a flaming spirit as unconquerable as his own. How many temples of worship
dot our landscape; how many institutions of learning, some
of them rejoicing in the name of Wesleyan, all trace the
inspiration of their existence to the sacrifice and service of

this lone circuit rider! He is entitled to rank as one of the builders of our nation.

On the foundation of a religious civilization which he sought to build, our country has enjoyed greater blessing of liberty and prosperity than was ever before the lot of man. These cannot continue if we neglect the work which he did. We cannot depend on the government to do the work of religion. We cannot escape a personal responsibility for our own conduct. We cannot regard those as wise or safe counselors in public affairs who deny these principles and seek to support the theory that society can succeed when the individual fails.

I do not see how any one could recount the story of this early Bishop without feeling a renewed faith in our own country. He met a multitude of storms. Many of them caused him sore trials. But he never wavered. He saw wars and heard rumors of war, but whatever may have been the surface appearance, underneath it all our country manifested then and has continued to manifest a high courage, a remarkable strength of spirit and an unusual ability, in a crisis, to choose the right course. Something has continued to guide the people. No tumult has been loud enough to prevent their hearing the still small voice. No storm has been violent enough to divert inspired men from constantly carrying the word of truth. The contests of the day have but been preparations for victories on the morrow. Through it all our country has acquired an underlying power of judgment and stability of action which has never failed it. It furnishes its own answer to those who would defame it. It can afford to be oblivious to those who would detract from it. America continues its own way unchallenged and unafraid. Above all attacks and all vicissitudes it has arisen calm and triumphant; not perfect, but marching on guided in its great decisions by the same spirit which guided Francis Asbury.

XVII

It is our earnest wish to coöperate and to help in every possible way in restoring the unfortunate countries of the Old World. We want to help them to rid themselves of the bad traditions, the ancient animosities, the long established hostilities. We want our America to continue an example and a demonstration that peace, harmony, coöperation and a truly national patriotic sentiment may be established and perpetuated on an American scale. We believe our first great service to the Old World will be in proving this. And in proving it, we shall be doing the things that will best equip us, spiritually and materially, to give the most effective help toward relieving the suffering nations of the Old World.

THE GENIUS OF AMERICA

THE members of this delegation, whom I have much pleasure in receiving, are all American citizens who chance to have been born in other countries than our own. You have called upon me to testify for yourselves and the millions of others who, though not natives to our soil, are in every other respect thorough-going, loyal and devoted Americans. I am glad to welcome you, not only to this place, but to the full privileges and opportunities, and especially to the full responsibilities and duties, of American citizens. It is not very long, as history views matters, since all of us were alien to this soil. I suppose that if Methuselah were at this time an American in his period of middle life, and should drop in on our little party, he would regard us all as upstarts. Fortunately, American ideas of hospitality have been greatly modified since the times when some of my early American forbears argued the matter with the Indian known as King Philip. He and his Indian supporters regarded themselves as the real Americans, and maintained their case all too effectively.

It is a truism, of course, but it is none the less a fact which we must never forget, that this continent and this American community have been blessed with an unparalleled capacity for assimilating peoples of varying races and nations. The continuing migration which in three centuries has established here this nation of more than a hundred million, has been the greatest that history records as taking place in any such brief period. Viewing it historically, we

To a delegation of foreign-born citizens at the White House, Thursday morning, October 16, 1924 find that the migration to America was little more than a westward projection of the series of great movements of peoples, by which Europe was given its present population. But there is a striking difference between the migrations into Europe, and the later movements of the same racial elements to the New World.

It was the fate of Europe to be always a battleground. Differences in race, in religion, in political genius and social ideals, seemed always, in the atmosphere of our mother continent, to be invitations to contest by battle. From the dawn of history, and we can only conjecture how much longer, the conflicts of races and civilizations, of traditions and usages, have gone on. It is one of the anomalies of the human story that these peoples, who could not be assimilated and unified under the skies of Europe, should on coming to America discover an amazing genius for coöperation, for fusion, and for harmonious effort. Yet they were the same people when they came here that they had been on the other side of the Atlantic. Quite apparently, they found something in our institutions, something in the American system of Government and society which they themselves helped to construct, that furnished to all of them a political and cultural common denominator.

Is it possible for us to make an analysis which will disclose this element that has wrought such a strangely different result here in our country? It must be an element that was present among the peoples of Europe while they were still in Europe. It could not have been brought here except by them. There has been nobody else to bring it. The original human materials were the same in both cases.

It has seemed to me that our search for this mysterious factor of difference must lead to the conclusion that it was not a single factor but the united workings of at least three forces, that brought about the wide difference. Among these I should place, first, the broadly tolerant attitude that has been a characteristic of this country. I use the word in its most inclusive sense, to cover tolerance of religious opinion, tolerance in politics, tolerance in social relationships; in general, the liberal attitude of every citizen toward his fellows. It is this factor which has preserved to all of us that equality of opportunity which enables every American to become the architect of whatever fortune he deserves.

Along with this element of universal tolerance, I should couple our Republican system of Government, which gives to every man a share and a responsibility in the direction of public affairs. And third, I should place our system of universal free education.

I shall not quarrel with anybody who chooses to give these three factors a different order of importance. That is a matter for individual judgment. But I do believe that these three factors largely represent the advantages which our people have enjoyed, and which have made it possible for them to build here a great, harmonious, liberal, community of free people. Starting anew in a land of almost unlimited natural opportunity, the early settlers found that the success of their nation-building experiments must depend upon their working harmoniously together, sinking non-essential differences, coöperating frankly and sincerely in the general interest, and, above all else, forgetting the ancient antagonisms. It has been our good fortune that we have been able to shake off the old traditions, to strike hands with our neighbor in the common effort to preserve our new-found liberties. And along with this, through our system of universal education, we have been able to guard against the revival of old, or the creation of new regional or group hostilities.

You who represent the more recent accretions to our population, know how generously you have been received. You know how free and unquestioned has been your access to the opportunities of this land. You have been expected to do your honest share of the day's work in a community which ranked productive toil as a distinction rather than a degradation. We have all taken our chance on that condition. Because we have been willing to do so, we have been prospered in material things and, what is ever more worth while, in the things of the spirit. Generation after generation, from the beginnings of permanent settlement here, the country has been able to receive and absorb a great number of newcomers from the older countries. That was possible so long as there was cheap land for settlement, and the assurance that industry could put value into it.

But with the passing of the day of lands so cheap as to be well-nigh free, we are coming to confront a new set of conditions. It has been found necessary to inquire whether under these new conditions we can be sure of finding employment for the diverse elements and enormous numbers of new immigrants that are offered to us. We are all agreed, whether we be Americans of the first or of the seventh generation on this soil, that it is not desirable to receive more immigrants than can reasonably be assured of bettering their condition by coming here. For the sake both of those who would come and more especially of those already here, it has been thought wise to avoid the danger of increasing our numbers too fast. It is not a reflection on any race or creed. We might not be able to support them if their numbers were too great. In such event, the first sufferers would be the most recent immigrants, unaccustomed to our life and language and industrial methods. We want to keep wages and living conditions good for everyone who is now here or who may come here.

As a Nation, our first duty must be to those who are already our inhabitants, whether native or immigrants. To them we owe an especial and a weighty obligation. They came to us with stout hearts and high hopes of bettering their estate. They have contributed much to making our country what it is. They magnificently proved their loyalty by contributing their full part when the war made demand for sacrifices by all Americans.

It must be the hope of every American citizen to maintain here as a permanent establishment, and as a perpetual inheritance for Americans of the future, the full measure of benefits and advantages which our people have been privileged to enjoy. It is our earnest wish to coöperate and to help in every possible way in restoring the unfortunate countries of the Old World. We want to help them to rid themselves of the bad traditions, the ancient animosities, the long established hostilities. We want our America to continue an example and a demonstration that peace, harmoney, coöperation and a truly national patriotic sentiment may be established and perpetuated on an American scale. We believe our first great service to the Old World will be in proving this. And in proving it, we shall be doing the things that will best equip us, spiritually and materially, to give the most effective help toward relieving the suffering nations of the Old World.

You have demonstrated again and again that it is useless to appeal to you on any thing but patriotic motives. You are for America, you are for our Constitution, you will not be tempted to take any action that will imperil our society or our Government.

It is the natural and correct attitude of mind for each of us to have regard for our own race and the place of our own origin. There is abundant room here for the preservation and development of the many divergent virtues that are characteristic of the different races which have made America their home. They ought to cling to all these virtues and cultivate them tenaciously. It is my own belief that in this land of freedom new arrivals should especially keep up their devotion to religion. Disregarding the need of the individual for a religious life, I feel that there is a more urgent necessity, based on the requirements of good citizenship and the maintenance of our institutions, for devotion to religion in America than anywhere else in the world. One of the greatest dangers that beset those coming to this country, especially those of the younger generation, is that they will fall away from the religion of their fathers, and never become attached to any other faith.

But in cherishing all that is best in the land of your origin, and in desiring the highest welfare of the people of the old home, the question arises as to how that result can best be secured. I know that there is no better American spirit than that which is exhibited by many of those who have recently come to our shores. It is my belief that those who live here and really want to help some other country, can best accomplish that result by making themselves truly and wholly American. I mean by that, giving their first allegiance to this country and always directing their actions in a course which will be first of all for the best interests of this country. They cannot help other nations by bringing old world race prejudices and race hatreds into action here. In fact, they can best help other countries by scrupulously avoiding any such motives. It can be taken for granted that we all wish to help Europe. We cannot secure that result by proposing or taking any action that would injure America. Nor can we secure it by proposing or taking any action that would seriously injure some European country. The spirit of America is to help everybody and injure nobody. We can be in a position to help only by unifying the American nation, building it up, making it strong, keeping it independent, using its inclination to help and its disclination to injure. Those who cast in their lot with this country can be true to the land of their origin only by first being true to America. When the public sees and realizes that racial groups here are first of all devoted to the interests of this country, there will be little difficulty in securing here the present needed help and assistance for the countries of the old world.

This is the main thought which your presence here brings to my mind. Let us maintain all the high ideals which have been characteristic of our different races at home. Let us keep our desire to help other lands as a great and broad principle, not to help in one place and do harm in another, but to render assistance everywhere. Let us remember also that the best method of promoting this action is by giving undivided allegiance to America, maintaining its institutions, supporting its Government, and, by leaving it internally harmonious, making it eternally powerful in promoting a reign of justice and mercy throughout the earth.

XVIII

I regard a good budget as among the noblest monuments of virtue.

DISCRIMINATING BENEVOLENCE

WHEN the Committee representing your Federation brought me the invitation to address you this evening, I did not receive them with any very profound enthusiasm. To be confidential for a moment, I may confess that an invitation to make a speech is not the rarest experience that comes into a President's life. But I listened with, I hope, proper politeness, down to the point where your spokesman started explaining that you were to devote an evening to the consideration of a budget. Then I began to take real interest, for the budget idea, I may admit, is a sort of obsession with me. I believe in budgets. I want other people to believe in them. I have had a small one to run my own home; and besides that, I am the head of the organization that makes the greatest of all budgets—that of the United States Government. Do you wonder, then, that at times I dream of balance sheets and sinking funds, and deficits, and tax rates, and all the rest?

Yes, I regard a good budget as among the noblest monuments of virtue. It is deserving of all emulation; but there are other topics that afford more obvious inspiration to popular oratory. So when I found that you actually wanted a budget speech, I felt a warming sense of gratitude. Anybody who would deliberately ask for a budget speech ought to be accommodated. I accepted the invitation, and now I want to begin by extending my hearty compliments to my audience. Your practical interest in the budget plan, your adoption of it as the basis of your great charity sys-

Address delivered over the telephone from the White House to the Federation of Jewish Philanthropic Societies of New York City, assembled at the Hotel Pennsylvania, October 26, 1924.

tem, is a fine accomplishment. Wherever the same plan has been adopted, in the financing of benevolences, philanthropies and charities through the "Community Chest" method, it has been productive of the best results. It has eliminated the waste of indiscriminate charity; but that is not by any means its most commendable accomplishment. Far more useful, I think, is the service it has done in organizing these works of human helpfulness so that we may be sure they will not do more harm than good. Nothing is finer than the open hand and the generous heart that prompt free and unselfish giving. But modern social science knows, also, that ill-directed charity is often directly responsible for encouragement of pauperism and mendicancy. The best service we can do for the needy and the unfortunate is to help them in such manner that their self-respect, their ability to help themselves, shall not be injured but augmented Nobody is necessarily *out* merely because he is *down*. But, being down, nobody gets up' again without honest effort of his own. The best help that benevolence and philanthropy can give is that which induces everybody to help himself.

Your Federation for the Support of Jewish Philanthropic Societies in New York is the central financial agency, I am told, for no less than ninety-one various philanthropies, which receive annual support aggregating $7,000,000. Among them are hospitals, orphanages, a great relief society, a loaning organization, a home for Aged and Infirm. The Young Men's Hebrew Association and the Young Women's Hebrew Association do social and educational work of the greatest value. Especial attention is devoted indeed to educational effort for which technical schools are maintained. That is, of course, precisely what we should expect from a great Jewish organization; for the Jews are always among the first to appreciate and to utilize educational opportunities.

Into this entire system of communal services, reaching to every possible department of social relations, the Federation brings order and a proper inter-relationship. Duplication of services, which always means multiplication of expense and division of results, is avoided. The man or woman who gives through this agency, knows that the most good will be done, at the least expense. All administrative costs of the organization have averaged less than four cents on the dollar. Other "Community Chest" activities, which in recent years are getting spread all about the country, make like showings of efficiency and economical management. They have been able, just as your Federation has been able, to enlist the best abilities, the most skilled direction, the widest experience, in systematizing operations that ordinarily are haphazard and wasteful.

But, with all of my regard for the strictly business aspect of this splendid modern program, I must emphasize once more that to me the greatest good of these communal organizations of benevolence lies in their immeasurably greater capacity for real good. There is an impressive array of testimony that the average dollar of indiscriminate, well-meaning, ignorant donation to charity is mostly wasted. Many such dollars are far worse than wasted. You seek no cold and heartless elimination of sentiment from your charitable works. You have, however, sought to substitute sense for sentimentality; and that is altogether to be desired.

The Jewish people have always and everywhere been particularly devoted to the ideal of taking care of their own. This Federation is one of the monuments to their independence and self-reliance. They have sought to protect and preserve that wonderful inheritance of tradition, culture, literature and religion, which has placed the world under so many obligations to them. In their efforts to serve their own highest ideals, they will always be helpful to the wider community of which they are a part. In the work of this Federation they are rendering a service not only to their own people, but to the entire community. Along with that precious service, they are setting up an example of successful practical, helpful business administration which deserves all commendation. It may well be an inspiration to every charitable agency in the land.

I want you to know that I feel you are making good citizens, that you are strengthening the Government, that you are demonstrating the supremacy of the spiritual life and helping establish the Kingdom of God on earth.

XIX

The people of our country are sovereign. If they do not vote they abdicate that sovereignty, and they may be entirely sure that if they relinquish it other forces will seize it, and if they fail to govern themselves some other power will rise up to govern them. The choice is always before them—whether they will be slaves or whether they will be free.

THE DUTIES OF CITIZENSHIP

THE institutions of our country rest upon faith in the people. No decision that the people have made in any great crisis has ever shown that faith in them has been misplaced. It is impossible to divorce that faith which we have in others from the faith which we have in ourselves. The right action of all of us is made up of the right action of each one of us. Unless each of us is determined to meet the duty that comes to us, we can have no right to expect that others will meet the duties that come to them. Certainly we cannot expect them so to act as to save us from the consequences of having failed to act. The immediate and pressing obligation for tomorrow is that each one of us who is qualified shall vote. That is a function which cannot be delegated, which cannot be postponed. The opportunity will never arise again. If the individual fails to discharge that obligation, the whole nation will suffer a loss from that neglect.

America, more thoroughly than any other country, has adopted a system of self-government. Sometimes we refer to it as the rule of the people. Certainly it is a system under which there is every opportunity for self-government and every encouragement for the people to rule. Ours has been described as a government of public opinion. Of course, public opinion functions all the time. It no doubt has its influence on the actions of the executive and legislative branches of our Government, and even though it be imperceptible on any given occasion it is probably, as time passes, reflected in the courts. But all the influence of pub-

Address by radio from the White House, November 3, 1924.

lic opinion, all the opportunity for self-government through the rule of the people, depends upon one single factor. That is the ballot box. If the time comes when our citizens fail to respond to their right and duty, individually and collectively, intelligently and effectively at the ballot box on election day, I do not know what form of government will be substituted for that which we at present have the opportunity to enjoy, but I do know it will no longer be a rule of the people, it will no longer be self-government. The people of our country are sovereign. If they do not vote they abdicate that sovereignty, and they may be entirely sure that if they relinquish it other forces will seize it, and if they fail to govern themselves some other power will rise up to govern them. The choice is always before them—whether they will be slaves or whether they will be free. The only way to be free is to exercise actively and energetically the privileges, and discharge faithfully the duties which make freedom. It is not to be secured by passive resistance. It is the result of energy and action.

To live up to the full measure of citizenship in this nation requires not only action, but it requires intelligent action. It is necessary to secure information and to acquire education. The background of our citizenship is the meeting house and the school house, the place of religious worship and the place of intellectual training. But we cannot abandon our education at the school house door. We have to keep it up through life. A political campaign can be justified only on the grounds that it enables the citizens to become informed as to what policies are best for themselves and for their country, in order that they may vote to elect those who from their past record and present professions they know will put such policies into effect. The purpose of a campaign is to send an intelligent and informed voter to the ballot box. All the speeches, all the literature, all the organization, all the effort, all the time and all the money, which are not finally registered on election day, are wasted.

We are always confronted with the question of whether we wish to be ruled by all the people or a part of the people, by the minority or the majority; whether we wish our elections to be dominated by those who have been misled, through the presentation of half truths, into the formation of hasty, illogical and unsound conclusions; or whether we wish those to determine the course of our Government who have through due deliberation and careful consideration of all the factors involved reached a sound and mature conclusion. We shall always have with us an element of discontent, an element inspired with more zeal than knowledge. They will always be active and energetic, and they seldom fail to vote on election day. But the people at large in this country are not represented by them. They are greatly in the minority. But their number is large enough to be a decisive factor in many elections, unless it is offset by the sober second thought of the people who have something at stake, whether it be earnings from investment or from employment, who are considering not only their own welfare, but the welfare of their children and of coming generations. Our institutions never contemplated that the conduct of this country, the direction of its affairs, the adoption of its policies, the maintenance of its principles, should be decided by a minority moved in part by self-interest and prejudice. They were framed on the theory that decisions would be made by the great body of voters inspired by patriotic motives. Faith in the people does not mean faith in a part of the people. It means faith in all the people. Our country is always safe when decisions are made by a majority of those who are entitled to vote. It is always in peril when decisions are made by a minority.

Lately we have added to our voting population the womanhood of the nation. I do not suppose that George

Washington could be counted as one who would have favored placing upon the women of his time the duty and responsibility of taking part in elections. Nevertheless he had seen a deep realization of the importance of their influence upon public affairs at the time when we were adopting our Federal Constitution, that he wrote to one of them as follows:

"A spirit of accommodation was happily infused into the leading characters of the continent and the minds of men were gradually prepared, by disappointment, for the reception of a good government. Nor could I rob the fairer sex of their share in the glory of a revolution so honorable to human nature, for, indeed, I think you ladies are in the number of the best patriots America can boast."

The praise of Washington was none too high. Without doubt the intuition of the women of his day was quick to reveal what a high promise the patriotic efforts of Washington and his associates held out for the homes and for the children of our new and unfolding republic. What was then done by indirect influence is now possible through direct action. The continuing welfare of the home, the continuing hope of the children, are no longer represented by an expectation. Experience has made them the great reality of America. If the women of that day were willing to support what was only a vision, a promise, surely in this day they will be willing to go to the ballot box to support what has become an actual and permanent realization of their desires.

But the right to vote is conferred upon our citizens not only that they may exercise it for their own benefit, but in order that they may exercise it also for the benefit of others. Persons who have the right to vote are trustees for the benefit of their country and their countrymen. They have no right to say they do not care. They must care. They have no right to say that whatever the result of the election they can get along. They must remember that their country and their countrymen cannot get along, cannot remain sound, cannot preserve its institutions, cannot protect its citizens, cannot maintain its place in the world, unless those who have the right to vote do sustain and do guide the course of public affairs by the thoughtful exercise of that right on election day. They do not hold a mere privilege to be exercised or not, as passing fancy may move them. They are charged with a great trust, one of the most important and most solemn which can be given into the keeping of an American citizen. It should be discharged thoughtfully and seriously, in accordance with its vast importance.

I therefore urge upon all the voters of our country, without reference to party, that they assemble tomorrow at their respective voting places in the exercise of the high office of American citizenship, that they approach the ballot box in the spirit that they would approach a sacrament, and there, disregarding all appeals to passion and prejudice, dedicating themselves truly and wholly to the welfare of their country, they make their choice of public officers solely in the light of their own conscience. When an election is so held, when a choice is so made, it results in the real rule of the people, it warrants and sustains the belief that the voice of the people is the voice of God.

XX

It is all the more necessary under a system of free government that the people should be enlightened, that they should be correctly informed, than it is under an absolute government that they should be ignorant.

THE PRESS UNDER A FREE GOVERNMENT

THE relationship between governments and the press has always been recognized as a matter of large importance. Wherever despotism abounds, the sources of public information are the first to be brought under its control. Wherever the cause of liberty is making its way, one of its highest accomplishments is the guarantee of the freedom of the press. It has always been realized, sometimes instinctively, oftentimes expressly, that truth and freedom are inseparable. An absolutism could never rest upon anything save a perverted and distorted view of human relationships and upon false standards set up and maintained by force. It has always found it necessary to attempt to dominate the entire field of education and instruction. It has thrived on ignorance. While it has sought to train the minds of a few, it has been largely with the purpose of attempting to give them a superior facility for misleading the many. Men have been educated under absolutism, not that they might bear witness to the truth, but that they might be the more ingenious advocates and defenders of false standards and hollow pretenses. This has always been the method of privilege, the method of class and caste, the method of master and slave.

When a community has sufficiently advanced so that its government begins to take on that of the nature of a republic, the processes of education become even more important, but the method is necessarily reversed. It is all the more necessary under a system of free government that

Address before the American Society of Newspaper Editors in Washington, January 17, 1925.

the people should be enlightened, that they should be correctly informed, than it is under an absolute government that they should be ignorant. Under a republic the institutions of learning, while bound by the constitution and laws, are in no way subservient to the government. The principles which they enunciate do not depend for their authority upon whether they square with the wish of the ruling dynasty, but whether they square with the everlasting truth. Under these conditions the press, which had before been made an instrument for concealing or perverting the facts, must be made an instrument for their true representation and their sound and logical interpretation. From the position of a mere organ, constantly bound to servitude, public prints rise to a dignity, not only of independence, but of a great educational and enlightening factor. They attain new powers, which it is almost impossible to measure, and become charged with commensurate responsibilities.

The public press under an autocracy is necessarily a true agency of propaganda. Under a free government it must be the very reverse. Propaganda seeks to present a part of the facts, to distort their relations, and to force conclusions which could not be drawn from a complete and candid survey of all the facts. It has been observed that propaganda seeks to close the mind, while education seeks to open it. This has become one of the dangers of the present day.

The great difficulty in combating unfair propaganda, or even in recognizing it, arises from the fact that at the present time we confront so many new and technical problems that it is an enormous task to keep ourselves accurately informed concerning them. In this respect, you gentlemen of the press face the same perplexities that are encountered by legislators and government administrators. Whoever deals with current public questions is compelled to rely greatly upon the information and judgments of experts and specialists. Unfortunately, not all experts are to be trusted as entirely disinterested. Not all specialists are completely without guile. In our increasing dependence on specialized authority, we tend to become easier victims for the propagandists, and need to cultivate sedulously the habit of the open mind. No doubt every generation feels that its problems are the most intricate and baffling that have ever been presented for solution. But with all recognition of the disposition to exaggerate in this respect, I think we can fairly say that our times in all their social and economic aspects are more complex than any past period. We need to keep our minds free from prejudice and bias. Of education, and of real information we cannot get too much. But of propaganda, which is tainted or perverted information, we cannot have too little.

Newspaper men, therefore, endlessly discuss the question of what is news. I judge that they will go on discussing it as long as there are newspapers. It has seemed to me that quite obviously the news-giving function of a newspaper cannot possibly require that it give a photographic presentation of everything that happens in the community. That is an obvious impossibility. It seems fair to say that the proper presentation of the news bears about the same relation to the whole field of happenings that a painting does to a photograph. The photograph might give the more accurate presentation of details, but in doing so it might sacrifice the opportunity the more clearly to delineate character. My college professor was wont to tell us a good many years ago that if a painting of a tree was only the exact representation of the original, so that it looked just like the tree, there would be no reason for making it; we might as well look at the tree itself. But the painting, if it is of the right sort, gives something that neither a photograph nor a view of the tree conveys. It emphasizes something of character, quality, individuality. We are not lost in looking at thorns and defects; we catch a vision of the grandeur and beauty of a king of the forest.

And so I have conceived that the news, properly presented, should be a sort of cross-section of the character of current human experience. It should delineate character, quality, tendencies and implications. In this way the reporter exercises his genius. Out of the current events he does not make a drab and sordid story, but rather an informing and enlightened epic. His work becomes no longer imitative, but rises to an original art.

Our American newspapers serve a double purpose. They bring knowledge and information to their readers, and at the same time they play a most important part in connection with the business interests of the community, both through their news and advertising departments. Probably there is no rule of your profession to which you gentlemen are more devoted than that which prescribes that the editorial and the business policies of the paper are to be conducted by strictly separate departments. Editorial policy and news policy must not be influenced by business consideration; business policies must not be affected by editorial programs. Such a dictum strikes the outsider as involving a good deal of difficulty in the practical adjustments of every-day management. Yet, in fact, I doubt if those adjustments are any more difficult than have to be made in every other department of human effort. Life is a long succession of compromises and adjustments, and it may be doubted whether the press is compelled to make them more frequently than others do.

When I have contemplated these adjustments of business and editorial policy, it has always seemed to me that American newspapers are peculiarly representative of the practical idealism of our country. Quite recently the construction of a revenue statute resulted in giving publicity to some highly interesting facts about incomes. It must have been observed that nearly all the newspapers published these interesting facts in their news columns, while very many of them protested in their editorial columns that such publicity was a bad policy. Yet this was not inconsistent. I am referring to the incident by way of illustrating what I just said about the newspapers representing the practical idealism of America. As practical newsmen they printed the facts. As editorial idealists they protested that there ought to be no such facts available.

Some people feel concerned about the commercialism of the press. They note that great newspapers are great business enterprises earning large profits and controlled by men of wealth. So they fear that in such control the press may tend to support the private interests of those who own the papers, rather than the general interest of the whole people. It seems to me, however, that the real test is not whether the newspapers are controlled by men of wealth, but whether they are sincerely trying to serve the public interests. There will be little occasion for worry about who owns a newspaper, so long as its attitudes on public questions are such as to promote the general welfare. A press which is actuated by the purpose of genuine usefulness to the public interest can never be too strong financially, so long as its strength is used for the support of popular government.

There does not seem to be cause for alarm in the dual relationship of the press to the public, whereby it is on one side a purveyor of information and opinion and on the other side a purely business enterprise. Rather, it is probable that a press which maintains an intimate touch with the business currents of the nation, is likely to be more reliable than it would be if it were a stranger to these influences. After all, the chief business of the American people is business. They are profoundly concerned with producing, buying, selling, investing and prospering in the world. I am strongly of opinion that the great majority of people will always find these are moving impulses of our life. The opposite view was oracularly and poetically set forth in those lines of Goldsmith which everybody repeats, but few really believe:

> Ill fares the land, to hastening ills a prey,
> Where wealth accumulates, and men decay.

Excellent poetry, but not a good working philosophy. Goldsmith would have been right, if, in fact, the accumulation of wealth meant the decay of men. It is rare indeed that the men who are accumulating wealth decay. It is only when they cease production, when accumulation stops, that an irreparable decay begins. Wealth is the product of industry, ambition, character and untiring effort. In all experience, the accumulation of wealth means the multiplication of schools, the increase of knowledge, the dissemination of intelligence, the encouragement of science, the broadening of outlook, the expansion of liberties, the widening of culture. Of course, the accumulation of wealth cannot be justified as the chief end of existence. But we are compelled to recognize it as a means to well-nigh every desirable achievement. So long as wealth is made the means and not the end, we need not greatly fear it. And there never was a time when wealth was so generally regarded as a means, or so little regarded as an end, as today.

Just a little time ago we read in your newspapers that two leaders of American business, whose efforts at accumulation had been most astonishingly successful, had given fifty or sixty million dollars as endowments to educational works. That was real news. It was characteristic of our American experience with men of large resources. They use their power to serve, not themselves and their own families, but the public. I feel sure that the coming generations, which will benefit by those endowments, will not be easily convinced that they have suffered greatly because of these particular accumulations of wealth.

So there is little cause for the fear that our journalism, merely because it is prosperous, is likely to betray us. But it calls for additional effort to avoid even the appearance of the evil of selfishness. In every worthy profession, of course, there will always be a minority who will appeal to the baser instinct. There always have been, and probably always will be some who will feel that their own temporary interest may be furthered by betraying the interest of others. But these are becoming constantly a less numerous and less potential element in the community. Their influence, whatever it may seem at a particular moment, is always ephemeral. They will not long interfere with the progress of the race which is determined to go its own forward and upward way. They may at times somewhat retard and delay its progress, but in the end their opposition will be overcome. They have no permanent effect. They accomplish no permanent result. The race is not traveling in that direction. The power of the spirit always prevails over the power of the flesh. These furnish us no justification for interfering with the freedom of the press, because all freedom, though it may sometime tend toward excesses, bears within it those remedies which will finally effect a cure for its own disorders.

American newspapers have seemed to me to be particularly representative of this practical idealism of our people. Therefore, I feel secure in saying that they are the best newspapers in the world. I believe that they print more real news and more reliable and characteristic news than any other newspaper. I believe their editorial opinions are less colored in influence by mere partisanship or selfish interest, than are those of any other country. Moreover, I believe that our American press is more independent, more reliable and less partisan today than at any other time in its history. I believe this of our press, precisely as I believe it of those who manage our public affairs. Both are cleaner, finer, less influenced by improper considerations, than ever before. Whoever disagrees with this judgment must take the chance of marking himself as ignorant of conditions which notoriously affected our public life, thoughts and methods, even within the memory of many men who are still among us.

It can safely be assumed that self-interest will always place sufficient emphasis on the business side of newspapers, so that they do not need any outside encouragement for that part of their activities. Important, however, as this factor is, it is not the main element which appeals to the American people. It is only those who do not understand our people, who believe that our national life is entirely absorbed by material motives. We make no concealment of the fact that we want wealth, but there are many other things that we want very much more. We want peace and honor, and that charity which is so strong an element of all civilization. The chief ideal of the American people is idealism. I cannot repeat too often that America is a nation of idealists. That is the only motive to which they ever give any strong and lasting reaction. No newspaper can be a success which fails to appeal to that element of our national life. It is in this direction that the public press can lend its strongest support to our Government. I could not truly criticize the vast importance of the counting room, but my ultimate faith I would place in the high idealism of the editorial room of the American newspaper.

XXI

We have been, and propose to be, more and more American. We believe that we can best serve our own country and most successfully discharge our obligations to humanity by continuing to be openly and candidly, intensely and scrupulously, American. If we have any heritage, it has been that. If we have any destiny, we have found it in that direction.

INAUGURAL ADDRESS, MARCH 4, 1925.

No ONE can contemplate current conditions without finding much that is satisfying and still more that is encouraging. Our own country is leading the world in the general readjustment to the results of the great conflict. Many of its burdens will bear heavily upon us for years, and secondary and indirect effects we must expect to experience for some time. But we are beginning to comprehend more definitely what course should be pursued, what remedies ought to be applied, what actions should be taken for our deliverance, and are clearly manifesting a determined will faithfully and conscientiously to adopt these methods of relief. Already we have sufficiently rearranged our domestic affairs so that confidence has returned, business has revived, and we appear to be entering an era of prosperity which is gradually reaching into every part of the Nation. Realizing that we can not live unto ourselves alone, we have contributed of our resources and our counsel to the relief of the suffering and the settlement of the disputes among the European nations. Because of what America is and what America has done, a firmer courage, a higher hope, inspires the heart of all humanity.

These results have not occurred by mere chance. They have been secured by a constant and enlightened effort marked by many sacrifices and extending over many generations. We can not continue these brilliant successes in the future, unless we continue to learn from the past. It is necessary to keep the former experiences of our country both at home and abroad continually before us, if we are to have any science of government. If we wish to erect

193

new structures, we must have a definite knowledge of the old foundations. We must realize that human nature is about the most constant thing in the universe and that the essentials of human relationship do not change. We must frequently take our bearings from these fixed stars of our political firmament if we expect to hold a true course. If we examine carefully what we have done, we can determine the more accurately what we can do.

We stand at the opening of the one hundred and fiftieth year since our national consciousness first asserted itself by unmistakable action with an array of force. The old sentiment of detached and dependent colonies disappeared in the new sentiment of a united and independent Nation. Men began to discard the narrow confines of a local charter for the broader opportunities of a national constitution. Under the eternal urge of freedom we became an independent Nation. A little less than fifty years later that freedom and independence were reasserted in the face of all the world, and guarded, supported, and secured by the Monroe Doctrine. The narrow fringe of States along the Atlantic seaboard advanced its frontiers across the hills and plains of an intervening continent until it passed down the golden slope to the Pacific. We made freedom a birthright. We extended our domain over distant islands in order to safeguard our own interests and accepted the consequent obligation to bestow justice and liberty upon less favored peoples. In the defense of our own ideals and in the general cause of liberty we entered the Great War. When victory had been fully secured, we withdrew to our own shores and unrecompensed save in the consciousness of duty done.

Throughout all these experiences we have enlarged our freedom, we have strengthened our independence. We have been, and propose to be, more and more American. We believe that we can best serve our own country and most successfully discharge our obligations to humanity by continuing to be openly and candidly, intensely and scrupulously, American. If we have any heritage, it has been that. If we have any destiny, we have found it in that direction.

But if we wish to continue to be distinctly American, we must continue to make that term comprehensive enough to embrace the legitimate desires of a civilized and enlightened people determined in all their relations to pursue a conscientious and religious life. We can not permit ourselves to be narrowed and dwarfed by slogans and phrases. It is not the adjective, but the substantive, which is of real importance. It is not the name of the action, but the result of the action, which is the chief concern. It will be well not to be too much disturbed by the thought of either isolation or entanglements of pacifists and militarists. The physical configuration of the earth has separated us from all of the Old World, but the common brotherhood of man, the highest law of all our being, has united us by inseparable bonds with all humanity. Our country represents nothing but peaceful intentions toward all the earth, but it ought not to fail to maintain such a military force as comports with the dignity and security of a great people. It ought to be a balanced force, intensely modern, capable of defense by sea and land, beneath the surface and in the air. But it should be so conducted that all the world may see in it, not a menace, but an instrument of security and peace.

This Nation believes thoroughly in an honorable peace under which the rights of its citizens are to be everywhere protected. It has never found that the necessary enjoyment of such a peace could be maintained only by a great and threatening array of arms. In common with other nations, it is now more determined than ever to promote peace through friendliness and good will, through mutual understandings and mutual forbearance. We have never practiced the policy of competitive armaments. We have recently committed ourselves by covenants with the other great nations to a limitation of our sea power. As one result of this, our Navy ranks larger, in comparison, than it ever did before. Removing the burden of expense and jealously, which must always accrue from a keen rivalry, is one of the most effective methods of diminishing that unreasonable hysteria and misunderstanding which are the most potent means of fomenting war. This policy represents a new departure in the world. It is a thought, an ideal, which has led to an entirely new line of action. It will not be easy to maintain. Some never move from their old position, some are constantly slipping back to the old ways of thought and the old action of seizing a musket and relying on force. America has taken the lead in this new direction, and that lead America must continue to hold. If we expect others to rely on our fairness and justice we must show that we rely on their fairness and justice.

If we are to judge by past experience, there is much to be hoped for in international relations from frequent conferences and consultations. We have before us the beneficial results of the Washington conference and the various consultations recently held upon European affairs, some of which were in response to our suggestions and in some of which we were active participants. Even the failures can not but be accounted useful and immeasurable advance over threatened or actual warfare. I am strongly in favor of a continuation of this policy, whenever conditions are such that there is even a promise that practical and favorable results might be secured.

In conformity with the principle that a display of reason rather than a threat of force should be the determining factor in the intercourse among nations, we have long advocated the peaceful settlement of disputes by methods of arbitration and have negotiated many treaties to secure that result. The same considerations should lead to our adherence to the Permanent Court of International Justice. Where great principles are involved, where great movements are under way which promise much for the welfare of humnaity by reason of the very fact that many other nations have given such movements their actual support, we ought not to withhold our own sanction because of any small and inessential difference, but only upon the ground of the most important and compelling fundamental reasons. We can not barter away our independence or our sovereignty, but we ought to engage in no refinements of logic, no sophistries, and no subterfuges, to argue away the undoubted duty of this country by reason of the might of its numbers, the power of its resources, and its position of leadership in the world, actively and comprehensively to signify its approval and to bear its full share of the responsibility of a candid and disinterested attempt at the establishment of a tribunal for the administration of even-handed justice between nation and nation. The weight of our enormous influence must be cast upon the side of a reign not of force but of law and trial, not by battle but by reason.

We have never any wish to interfere in the political conditions of any other countries. Especially are we determined not to become implicated in the political controversies of the Old World. With a great deal of hesitation, we have responded to appeals for help to maintain order, protect life and property, and establish responsible government in some of the small countries of the Western Hemisphere. Our private citizens have advanced large sums of money to assist in the necessary financing and relief of the Old World. We have not failed, nor shall we fail to respond, whenever necessary to mitigate human suffering and assist in the rehabilitation of distressed nations. These, too, are requirements which must be met by reason of our vast powers and the place we hold in the world.

Some of the best thought of mankind has long been seeking for a formula for permanent peace. Undoubtedly the clarification of the principles of international law would be helpful, and the efforts of scholars to prepare such a work for adoption by the various nations should have our sympathy and support. Much may be hoped for from the earnest studies of those who advocate the outlawing of aggressive war. But all these plans and preparations, these treaties and covenants, will not of themselves be adequate. One of the greatest dangers to peace lies in the economic pressure to which people find themselves subjected. One of most practical things to be done in the world is to seek arrangements under which such pressure may be removed, so that opportunity may be renewed and hope may be revived. There must be some assurance that effort and endeavor will be followed by success and prosperity. In the making and financing of such adjustments there is not only an opportunity, but a real duty, for America to respond with her counsel and her resources. Conditions must be provided under which people can make a living and work out of their difficulties. But there is another element, more important than all, without which there can not be the slightest hope of a permanent peace. That element lies in the heart of humanity. Unless the desire for peace be cherished there, unless this fundamental and only natural source of brotherly love be cultivated to its highest degree, all artificial efforts will be in vain. Peace will come when there is realization that only under a reign of law, based on righteousness and supported by the religious conviction of the brotherhood of man, can there be any hope of a complete and satisfying life. Parchment will fail, the sword will fail, it is only the spiritual nature of man that can be triumphant.

It seems altogether probable that we can contribute most to these important objects by maintaining our position of political detachment and independence. We are not identified with any Old World interests. This position should be made more and more clear in our relations with all foreign countries. We are at peace with all of them. Our program is never to oppress, but always to assist. But while we do justice to others, we must require that justice be done to us. With us a treaty of peace means peace, and a treaty of amity means amity. We have made great contributions to the settlement of contentious differences in both Europe and Asia. But there is a very definite point beyond which we can not go. We can only help those who help themselves. Mindful of these limitations, the one great duty that stands out requires us to use our enormous powers to trim the balance of the world.

While we can look with a great deal of pleasure upon what we have done abroad, we must remember that our continued success in that direction depends upon what we do at home. Since its very outset, it has been found necessary to conduct our Government by means of political parties. That system would not have survived from generation to generation if it had not been fundamentally sound and provided the best instrumentalities for the most complete expression of the popular will. It is not necessary to claim that it has always worked perfectly. It is enough to know that nothing better has been devised. No one would deny that there should be full and free expression and an opportunity for independence of action within the party. There is no salvation in a narrow and bigoted partisanship. But if there is to be responsible party government, the party label must be something more than a mere device for securing office. Unless those who are elected under the same party designation are willing to assume sufficient responsibility and exhibit sufficient loyalty and coherence, so that they can cooperate with each other in the support of the broad general principles of the party platform, the election is merely a mockery, no decision is made at the polls, and there is no representation of the popular will. Common honesty and good faith with the people who support a party at the polls require that party, when it enters office, to assume the control of that portion of the Government to which it has been elected. Any other course is bad faith and a violation of the party pledges.

When the country has bestowed its confidence upon a party by making it a majority in the Congress, it has a right to expect such unity of action as will make the party majority an effective instrument of government. This administration has come into power with a very clear and definite mandate from the people. The expression of the popular will in favor of maintaining our constitutional guarantees was overwhelming and decisive. There was a manifestation of such faith in the integrity of the courts that we can consider that issue rejected for some time to come. Likewise, the policy of public ownership of railroads and certain electric utilities met with unmistakable defeat. The people declared that they wanted their rights to have not a political but a judicial determination, and their independence and freedom continued and supported by having the ownership and control of their property, not in the Government, but in their own hands. As they always do when they have a fair chance, the people demonstrated that they are sound and are determined to have a sound government.

When we turn from what was rejected to inquire what was accepted, the policy that stands out with the greatest clearness is that of economy in public expenditure with reduction and reform of taxation. The principle involved in this effort is that of conservation. The resources of this country are almost beyond computation. No mind can

comprehend them. But the cost of our combined governments is likewise almost beyond definition. Not only those
who are now making their tax returns, but those who meet
the enhanced cost of existence in their monthly bills, know
by hard experience what this great burden is and what it
does. No matter what others may want, these people
want a drastic economy. They are opposed to waste. They
know that extravagance lengthens the hours and diminishes
the rewards of their labor. I favor the policy of economy,
not because I wish to save money, but because I wish to
save people. The men and women of this country who
toil are the ones who bear the cost of the Government.
Every dollar that we carelessly waste means that their life
will be so much the more meager. Every dollar that we
prudently save means that their life will be so much the
more abundant. Economy is idealism in its most practical
form.

If extravagance were not reflected in taxation, and
through taxation both directly and indirectly injuriously
affecting the people, it would not be of so much consequence. The wisest and soundest method of solving our
tax problem is through economy. Fortunately, of all the
great nations this country is best in a position to adopt that
simple remedy. We do not any longer need war-time revenues. The collection of any taxes which are not absolutely
required, which do not beyond reasonable doubt contribute
to the public welfare, is only a species of legalized larceny.
Under this Republic the rewards of industry belong to those
who earn them. The only constitutional tax is the tax
which ministers to public necessity. The property of the
country belongs to the people of the country. Their title
is absolute. They do not support any privileged class; they
do not need to maintain great military forces; they ought
not to be burdened with a great array of public employees.
They are not required to make any contribution to Govern-

ment expenditures except that which they voluntarily assess upon themselves through the action of their own representatives. Whenever taxes bcome burdensome a remedy can be applied by the people; but if they do not act for themselves, no one can be very successful in acting for them.

The time is arriving when we can have further tax reduction, when, unless we wish to hamper the people in their right to earn a living, we must have tax reform. The method of raising revenue ought not to impede the transaction of business; it ought to encourage it. I am opposed to extremely high rates, because they produce little or no revenue, because they are bad for the country, and, finally, because they are wrong. We can not finance the country, we can not improve social conditions, through any system of injustice, even if we attempt to inflict it upon the rich. Those who suffer the most harm will be the poor. This country believes in prosperity. It is absurd to suppose that it is envious of those who are already prosperous. The wise and correct course to follow in taxation and all other economic legislation is not to destroy those who have already secured success but to create conditions under which every one will have a better chance to be successful. The verdict of the country has been given on this question. That verdict stands. We shall do well to heed it.

These questions involve moral issues. We need not concern ourselves much about the rights of property if we will faithfully observe the rights of persons. Under our institutions their rights are supreme. It is not property but the right to hold property, both great and small, which our Constitution guarantees. All owners of property are charged with a service. These rights and duties have been revealed, through the conscience of society, to have a divine sanction. The very stability of our society rests upon production and conservation. For individuals or for governments to waste and squander their resources is to deny these rights and disregard these obligations. The result of economic dissipation to a nation is always moral decay.

These policies of better international understandings, greater economy, and lower taxes have contributed largely to peaceful and prosperous industrial relations. Under the helpful influences of restrictive immigration and a protective tariff, employment is plentiful, the rate of pay is high, and wage earners are in a state of contentment seldom before seen. Our transportation systems have been gradually recovering and have been able to meet all the requirements of the service. Agriculture has been very slow in reviving, but the price of cereals at last indicates that the day of its deliverance is at hand.

We are not without our problems, but our most important problem is not to secure new advantages but to maintain those which we already possess. Our system of government made up of three separate and independent departments, our divided sovereignty composed of Nation and State, the matchless wisdom that is enshrined in our Constitution, all these need constant effort and tireless vigilance for their protection and support.

In a republic the first rule for the guidance of the citizen is obedience to law. Under a despotism the law may be imposed upon the subject. He has no voice in its making, no influence in its administration, it does not represent him. Under a free government the citizen makes his own laws, chooses his own administrators, which do represent him. Those who want their rights respected under the Constitution and the law ought to set the example themselves of observing the Constitution and the law. While there may be those of high intelligence who violate the law at times, the barbarian and the defective always violate it. Those who disregard the rules of society are not exhibiting a superior intelligence, are not promoting freedom and independence, are not following the path of civilization, but are displaying the traits of ignorance, of servitude, of savagery, and treading the way that leads back to the jungle.

The essence of a republic is representative government. Our Congress represents the people and the States. In all legislative affairs it is the natural collaborator with the President. In spite of all the criticism which often falls to its lot, I do not hesitate to say that there is no more independent and effective legislative body in the world. It is, and should be, jealous of its prerogative. I welcome its cooperation, and expect to share with it not only the responsibility, but the credit, for our common effort to secure beneficial legislation.

These are some of the principles which America represents. We have not by any means put them fully into practice, but we have strongly signified our belief in them. The encouraging feature of our country is not that it has reached its destination, but that it has overwhelmingly expressed its determination to proceed in the right direction. It is true that we could, with profit, be less sectional and more national in our thought. It would be well if we could replace much that is only a false and ignorant prejudice with a true and enlightened pride of race. But the last election showed that appeals to class and nationality had little effect. We were all found loyal to a common citizenship. The fundamental precept of liberty is toleration. We can not permit any inquisition either within or without the law or apply any religious test to the holding of office. The mind of America must be forever free.

It is in such contemplations, my fellow countrymen, which are not exhaustive but only representative, that I find ample warrant for satisfaction and encouragement. We should not let the much that is to do obscure the much which has been done. The past and present show faith and hope and courage fully justified. Here stands our country, an example of tranquillity at home, a patron of tranquillity abroad. Here stands its Government, aware of its might but obedient to its conscience. Here it will continue to stand, seeking peace and prosperity, solicitous for the welfare of the wage earner, promoting enterprise, developing waterways and natural resources, attentive to the intuitive counsel of womanhood, encouraging education, desiring the advancement of religion, supporting the cause of justice and honor among the nations. America seeks no earthly empire built on blood and force. No ambition, no temptation, lures her to thought of foreign dominions. The legions which she sends forth are armed, not with the sword, but with the cross. The higher state to which she seeks the allegiance of all mankind is not of human, but of divine origin. She cherishes no purpose save to merit the favor of Almighty God.

XXII

It must be our untiring effort, to maintain, to improve, and, so far as may be humanly possible, to perfect those institutions which have proved capable of guaranteeing our unity, and strengthening us in advancing the estate of the common man.

THE SPIRITUAL UNIFICATION OF AMERICA

WE HAVE gathered this afternoon to lay with appropriate ceremony and solemnity the cornerstone of a temple. The splendid structure which is to rise here will be the home of the Jewish Community Center of Washington. It will be at once a monument to the achievements of the past, and a help in the expansion of these achievements into a wider field of usefulness in the future. About this institution will be organized, and from it will be radiated, the influences of those civic works in which the genius of the Jewish people has always found such eloquent expression. Such an establishment, so noble in its physical proportions, so generous in its social purposes, is truly a part of the civic endowment of the nation's capital. Beyond that, its existence here at the seat of the national government makes it in a peculiar way a testimony and an example before the entire country.

This year 1925 is a year of national anniversaries, States, cities, and towns throughout all the older part of the country will be celebrating their varied parts in the historic events which a century and half ago marked the beginning of the American Revolution. It will be a year of dedications and re-dedications. It will recall the heroic events from which emerged a great modern nation consecrated to liberty, equality, and human rights. It will remind us, as a nation, of how a common spiritual inspiration was potent to bring and mold and weld together into a national unity, the many and scattered colonial communities that

At the Laying of the Cornerstone of the Jewish Community Center, Washington, May 3, 1925.

had been planted along the Atlantic seaboard. In a time when the need of that unification, understanding and tolerance, which are necessary to a national spirit, is so great, it will recall the fact that the fathers not only confronted these same problems in forms far more difficult than they are today, but also solved them.

Among the peoples of the thirteen colonies, there were few ties of acquaintance, of commercial or industrial interest. There were great differences in political sentiments, even within the local communities, while there were wide divergences among the several colonies, in origin, in religion, in social outlook.

If we would seek a fairly accurate impression of conditions at the beginning of the Revolution, we must attempt a really continental view of North America as it was in 1775. The group of new-born commonwealths which we commonly refer to as "the original thirteen colonies", and which in our minds represent a considerable measure of nationality already achieved, did not in fact even know that they would be thirteen in number. No man, on the day of Lexington, could be altogether sure that the Revolution was more than a New England affair. It might or it might not draw the middle and southern colonies into its armed array of resistence. On the other hand, the thirteen might have been joined by Canada, which was British in sovereignty, but chiefly French in population, by Florida and Louisiana, which were both mainly Spanish. In short, there might have been fourteen, or fifteen, or sixteen original colonies participating in the North American revolution against Europe, or there might have been less than a half dozen of them.

At that time, France had no territory within continental North America. But this condition had existed for only a short time since the end of the Seven Years war. France had by no means become reconciled to this exclusion from a part in the North American empire; and only a little later, in the year 1800, under a new treaty with Spain, resumed the sovereignty of the Mississippi Valley. Three years after this, benefiting by the fortunes of the Napoleonic wars, President Jefferson confronted, and promptly seized the opportunity to buy Louisiana from Napoleon. Even then, many years were yet to pass before the last claims of Spain should be extinguished from this continent.

I have recounted these scraps of territorial history because unless we keep them in mind we shall not at all comprehend the task of unification, of nation building, that the Revolutionary fathers undertook when they not only dared the power of Great Britain, but set themselves against the tradition of the subordination to Europe of America. As we look back, we realize that even among the colonies of England there were few and doubtful common concerns to bind them together. Their chief commercial interests were not among themselves, but with the mother country across the Atlantic. New England was predominantly Puritan, the southern colonies were basically cavalier. New York was in the main Dutch. Pennsylvania had been founded by the Quakers, while New Jersey needed to go back but a short distance to find its beginnings in a migration from Sweden.

There were well-nigh as many divergencies of religious faith as there were of origin, politics and geography. Yet, in the end, these religious differences proved rather unimportant. While the early dangers in some colonies made a unity in belief and all else a necessity to existence, at the bottom of the colonial character lay a stratum of religious liberalism which had animated most of the early comers. From its beginnings, the new continent had seemed destined to be the home of religious tolerance. Those who claimed the right of individual choice for themselves finally had to grant it to others. Beyond that—and this was one of the factors which I think weighed heaviest on the side of unity—the Bible was the one work of literature that was common to all of them. The scriptures were read and studied everywhere. There are many testimonies that their teachings became the most important intellectual and spiritual force for unification. I remember to have read somewhere, I think in the writings of the historian Lecky, the observation that "Hebraic mortar cemented the foundations of American democracy." Lecky had in mind this very influence of the Bible in drawing together the feelings and sympathies of the widely scattered communities. All the way from New Hampshire to Georgia, they found a common ground of faith and reliance in the scriptural writings.

In those days books were few, and even those of a secular character were largely the product of a scholarship which used the scriptures as the model and standard of social interpretation. It was to this, of course, that Lecky referred. He gauged correctly a force too often underestimated and his observation was profoundly wise. It suggests, in a way which none of us can fail to understand, the debt which the young American nation owed to the sacred writing that the Hebrew people gave to the world.

This biblical influence was strikingly impressive in all the New England colonies, and only less so in the others. In the Connecticut code of 1650, the Mosaic model is adopted. The magistrates were authorized to administer justice "according to the laws here established, and, for want of them, according to the word of God." In the New Haven code of 1655, there were 79 topical statutes for the Government, half of which contained references to the Old Testament. The founders of the New Haven colony, John Davenport and Theophilus Eaton, were expert Hebrew scholars. The extent to which they leaned upon the moral and administrative system, laid down by the Hebrew lawgivers, was responsible for their conviction that the Hebrew language and literature ought to be made as familiar as possible to all the people. So it was that John Davenport arranged that in the first public school in New Haven the Hebrew language should be taught. The preachers of those days, saturated in the religion and literature of the Hebrew prophets, were leaders, teachers, moral mentors and even political philosophers for their flocks. A people raised under such leadership, given to much study and contemplation of the scriptures, inevitably became more familiar with the great figures of Hebrew history, with Joshua, Samuel, Moses, Joseph, David, Solomon, Gideon, Elisha—than they were with the stories of their own ancestors as recorded in the pages of profane history.

The sturdy old divines of those days found the Bible a chief source of illumination for their arguments in support of the patriot cause. They knew the Book. They were profoundly familiar with it, and eminently capable in the exposition of all its justifications for rebellion. To them, the record of the exodus from Egypt was indeed an inspired precedent. They knew what arguments from holy writ would most powerfully influence their people. It required no great stretch of logical processes to demonstrate that the children of Israel, making bricks without straw in Egypt, had their modern counterpart in the people of the colonies, enduring the imposition of taxation without representation!

And the Jews themselves, of whom a considerable number were already scattered throughout the colonies, were true to the teachings of their own prophets. The Jewish faith is predominantly the faith of liberty. From the beginnings of the conflict between the colonies and the mother country, they were overwhelmingly on the side of the rising revolution. You will recognize them when I read the names of some among the merchants who unhesitatingly signed the non-importation resolution of 1765: Isaac Moses, Benjamin Levy, Samson Levy, David Franks, Joseph Jacobs, Hayman Levy, Jr.; Matthias Bush, Michael Gratz, Bernard Gratz, Isaac Franks, Moses Mordecai, Benjamin Jacobs, Samuel Lyon and Manuel Mordecai Noah.

Not only did the colonial Jews join early and enthusiastically in the non-intercourse program, but when the time came for raising and sustaining an army, they were ready to serve wherever they could be most useful. There is a romance in the story of Haym Solomon, Polish Jew financier of the Revolution. Born in Poland, he was made prisoner by the British forces in New York, and when he escaped set up in business in Philadelphia. He negotiated for Robert Morris all the loans raised in France and Holland, pledged his personal faith and fortune for enormous amounts, and personally advanced large sums to such men as James Madison, Thomas Jefferson, Baron Steuben, General St. Clair, and many other patriot leaders who testified that without his aid they could not have carried on in the cause.

A considerable number of Jews became officers in the continental forces. The records show at least four Jews who served as Lieutenant Colonels, three as Majors and certainly six, probably more, as Captains. Major Benjamin Nones has been referred to as the Jewish Lafayette. He came from France in 1777, enlisted in the continentals as a volunteer private, served on the staffs of both Washington and Lafayette, and later was attached to the command of Baron De Kalb, in which were a number of Jews. When De Kalb was fatally wounded in the thickest of the fighting at the Battle of Camden, the three officers who were at hand to bear him from the field were Major Nones, Captain De La Motta, and Captain Jacob De Leon, all of them Jews. It is interesting to know that at the time of the Revolution there was a larger Jewish element in the southern colonies than would have been found there at most later periods; and these Jews of the Carolinas and Georgia were ardent supporters of the Revolution. One corps of infantry raised in Charleston, South Carolina, was composed preponderantly of Jews, and they gave a splendid account of themselves in the fighting in that section.

It is easy to understand why a people with the historic background of the Jews should thus overwhelmingly and unhesitatingly have allied themselves with the cause of freedom. From earliest colonial times, America has been a new land of promise to this long-persecuted race.

The Jewish community of the United States is not only the second most numerous in the world, but in respect of its old world origins it is probably the most cosmopolitan. But whatever their origin as a people, they have always come to us eager to adapt themselves to our institutions, to thrive under the influence of liberty, to take their full part as citizens in building and sustaining the nation, and to bear their part in its defense; in order to make a contribution to the national life, fully worthy of the traditions they had inherited.

The institution for which we are today dedicating this splendid home, is not a charity to minister to the body, but rather to the soul. The 14,000 Jews who live in this Capital City have passed, under the favoring auspices of American institutions, beyond the need for any other benevolence. They are planting here a home for community service; fixing a center from which shall go forth the radiations of united effort for advancement in culture, in education, in social opportunity. Here will be the seat of organized influence for the preservation and dissemination of all that is best and most useful, of all that is leading and enlightening, in the culture and philosophy of this "peculiar people" who have so greatly given to the advancement of humanity.

Our country has done much for the Jews who have come

here to accept its citizenship and assume their share of its responsibilities in the world. But I think the greatest thing it has done for them has been to receive them and treat them precisely as it has received and treated all others who have come to it. If our experiment in free institutions has proved anything, it is that the greatest privilege that can be conferred upon people in the mass is to free them from the demoralizing influence of privilege enjoyed by the few. This is proved by the experience here, not alone of the Jews, but of all the other racial and national elements that have entered into the making of this Nation. We have found that when men and women are left free to find the places for which they are best fitted, some few of them will indeed attain less exalted stations than under a regime of privilege; but the vast multitude will rise to a higher level, to wider horizons, to worthier attainments.

To go forward on the same broadening lines that have marked the national development thus far must be our aim. It is an easy thing to say, but not so simple to do. There is no straight and smooth and posted highway into the vast, dim realm of the tomorrows. There are bogs and morasses, blind roads and bad detours. No philosophy of history has ever succeeded in charting accurately the future. No science of social engineering has been able to build wide and easy roads by which to bring up the van of human progress in sure and easy marches. The race is always pioneering. It always has been and always must be. It dare not tire of unending effort and repeated disappointments. It must not in any moment of weariness or inertia cease from pressing on. Least of all can we indulge the satisfactions of complacency, imagining that the sum of useful progress has been attained. The community or the civilization that ceases to progress, begins that hour to recede.

The work of spiritual unification is not completed.

Factional, sectional, social and political lines of conflict yet persist. Despite all experience, society continues to engender the hatreds and jealousies whereof are born domestic strife and international conflicts. But education and enlightenment are breaking their force. Reason is emerging. Every inheritance of the Jewish people, every teaching of their secular history and religious experience, draws them powerfully to the side of charity, liberty and progress. They have always been arrayed on this side, and we may be sure they will not desert it. Made up of so many diverse elements, our country must cling to those fundamentals that have been tried and proved as buttresses of national solidarity.

It must be our untiring effort to maintain, to improve, and, so far as may be humanly possible, to perfect those institutions which have proved capable of guaranteeing our unity, and strengthening us in advancing the estate of the common man. This edifice which you are rearing here is a fine example for other communities. It speaks a purpose to uphold an ancient and noble philosophy of life and living, and yet to assure that such philosophy shall always be adapted to the requirements of changing times, increasing knowledge and developing institutions. It is a guarantee that you will keep step with liberty.

This capacity for adaptation in detail, without sacrifice of essentials, has been one of the special lessons which the marvelous history of the Jewish people has taught. It is a lesson which our country, and every country based on the principle of popular government, must learn and apply, generation by generation, year by year, yes, even day by day. You are raising here a testimonial to the capacity of the Jewish people to do this. In the advancing years, as those who come and go shall gaze upon this civic and social landmark, may it be a constant reminder of the inspiring service that has been rendered to civilization by men and women of the Jewish faith. May they recall the long array of those who have been eminent in statecraft, in science, in literature, in art, in the professions, in business, in finance, in philanthropy and in the spiritual life of the world. May they pause long enough to contemplate that the patriots who laid the foundation of this Republic drew their faith from the Bible. May they give due credit to the people among whom the Holy Scriptures came into being. And as they ponder the assertion that "Hebraic mortar cemented the foundations of American democracy," they cannot escape the conclusion that if American democracy is to remain the greatest hope of humanity, it must continue abundantly in the faith of the Bible.

XXIII

Our country was conceived in the theory of local self-government. It has been dedicated by long practice to that wise and beneficent policy. It is the foundation principle of our system of liberty. It makes the largest promise to the freedom and development of the individual. Its preservation is worth all the effort and all the sacrifice that it may cost.

THE REIGN OF LAW

For those who are the inheritors of a noble estate and a high place in the world, it is a good thing to pause at intervals and consider by what favor of fortune and of ancestry their lines have fallen in such pleasant places. Thus to meditate upon that course of events, which has given them what they have and made them what they are, will tend to remind them how great is their debt and how little is their share of merit.

This is the day on which the American people each year acknowledged that they have such a debt. It has been set aside that a grateful Nation may do fitting honor to the memory of those who have made the greatest and most voluntary contribution to it. Here about us, in this place of beauty and reverence, lies the mortal dust of a noble host, to whom we have come to pay our tribute, as thousands of other like gatherings will do throughout our land. In their youth and strength, their love and loyalty, those who rest here gave to their country all that mortality can give. For what they sacrificed we must give back the pledge of faith to all that they held dear, constantly renewed, constantly justified. Doing less would betray them and dishonor us.

To such a memorial as exists here we can only come in a spirit of humility and of gratitude. We can not hope to repay those whom we are assembled to honor. They were moved by a noble conception of human possibilities and human destiny. But we can undertake to find what was

At the Memorial Exercises, Arlington National Cemetery, Washington, D. C., May 30, 1925.

their inspiration and seek to make it our guide. By that they will be recompensed.

These who are represented here were men in whom courage had reached a high moral quality. They had been brave enough not to shrink from looking at facts and institutions. They had been honest enough to admit that they saw there much that was not good. They glossed over no wrongs, they hid away no skeletons. They did not pretend that wrong was right or ever could be right. They had put much thought to the lessons of hard experience, and had frankly acknowledged that they must deal with a crisis in the Nation's life. They were sure that union was a blessing, that slavery was a wrong, and that domestic war was the supreme human tragedy. This settled, they saw that one of three courses must be taken. They could have had peace with disunion, or they could have had peace and union, with slavery. Freedom with union, they saw at last, meant war. We know how they decided. We know at what fearful cost they supported their decision.

We live far enough away from those times of test and trial to know that sincerity and honesty did not all lie on either side. We know the conflicts of loyalties, traditions, ancestry, and interest which drew men to one side and the other. I doubt if there ever was another so great and elemental a conflict from which men emerged with so much of mutual respect, with so little of bitterness and lingering hostility. The struggle brought the whole Nation at last to see that its only assurance was in unity. United, it could go its way in all security; divided, both sections becoming the prey of jealousy and intrigue, would have dissipated all the power they now have for good in the world.

Our generation has recently lived through times still so vivid as to seem but as yesterday, which have taught us deeply to appreciate the value of union in purpose and effort. We have come to see as through a crystal that in the national variety of talents and resources, of cultures and capacities, of climates and of soils, of occupations and of interests, lies the guaranty of both our power and our authority. More than that, they have taught us how heavy and important is our responsibility in the world.

Conscious of a strength which removes us from either fear or truculence, satisfied with dominions and resources which free us from lust of territory or empire, we see that our highest interest will be promoted by the prosperity and progress of our neighbors. We recognize that what has been accomplished here has largely been due to the capacity of our people for efficient cooperation. We shall continue prosperous at home and helpful abroad, about as we shall maintain and continually adapt to changing conditions the system under which we have come thus far. I mean our Federal system, distributing powers and responsibilities between the States and the National Government. For that is the greatest American contribution to the organization of government over great populations and wide areas. It is the essence of practical administration for a nation placed as ours is. It has become so commonplace to us, and a pattern by so many other peoples, that we do not always realize how great an innovation it was when first formulated, or how great the practical problems which its operation involves. Because of my conviction that some of these problems are at this time in need of deeper consideration, I shall take this occasion to try to turn the public mind in that direction.

When dealing with the distribution of powers between the General Government and the States, Chief Justice Marshall declared:

"When the American people created a national legislature, with certain enumerated powers, it was neither necessary nor proper to define the powers retained by the States. Those powers proceed, not from the people of America, but from the people of the several States, and remain after the adoption of the Constitution what they were before, except in so far as they may be abridged by that instrument."

Our constitutional history started with the States retaining all powers of sovereignty unimpaired, save those conferred upon the National Government. The evolution of the constitutional system has consisted largely in determining the line of demarcation between State and national authority. The cases involved are many and complicated, but there is a fairly good popular understanding of this continuing struggle between these contending sovereignties. Because of better communication and transportation, the constant tendency has been to more and more social and economic unification. The present continent-wide union of forty-eight States is much closer than was the original group of thirteen States.

This increasing unification has well-nigh obliterated State lines so far as concerns many relations of life. Yet, in a country of such enormous expanse, there must always be certain regional differences in social outlook and economic thought. The most familiar illustration of this is found in the history of slavery. The Constitution did not interfere with slavery, except to fix a time when the foreign slave trade should be abolished. Yet within a generation the country was confronting a sharp sectional division on this issue. Changing economic conditions made slavery profitable in the South, but left it unprofitable in the North. The resulting war might have been avoided if the South had adopted a policy of ultimate abolition. But as this method was not pursued the differences grew sharper until they brought on the great conflict.

Though the war ended forever the possibility of disunion, there still remain problems between State and Federal authority. There are divisions of interest, perhaps more apparent than real, among geographical sections or social groups. The seaboard thinks it has interests in maritime transportation and overseas commerce which differ greatly from those of the interior, which is peculiarly dependent upon railroads. Difference in climate and physical conditions throughout so great a territory tend to varied social habits and modes of living which react upon the economic and political attitudes. The industrial development of some sections contrasts with the agricultural character of others. Obviously, these differences give rise to many problems in government, which must always be recognized. But it is hardly conceivable that a really menacing contest between the sovereignty of the States and of the Union could ever again arise.

Our country, having devised this dual system of government, and lived under it longer than any other, is deeply concerned to perfect and adapt it to the changing conditions of organized society. A community comprising half a continent and more than a hundred million people could not possibly be administered under a single government organization. We must maintain a proper measure of local self-government while constantly making adjustments to an increasing interdependence among the political parts.

Our national history has presented various phases of this problem. Slavery showed one; the complexities of interstate commerce have kept others constantly in mind. On the day the Constitution was finished, probably more people would have seen seeds of conflict and dangers to the Union in future commercial relations than in slavery. But commerce became a source of strength, while slavery became a cause of division. It brought the Union into danger; and in the end was destroyed itself. Where there was sincere acceptance of the dual sovereignty theory, where the States sought to do their full part, and accepted the determinations of the National Government as to the rest, the plan worked. Where the States sought more from the

Federal authority than it could give, and resisted national demands—then came dissension and, at length, war.

It would be folly to deny that we still have problems of interstate relations to handle. We boast that this is a land of equal opportunity for all. We insist that there is one law for all the people. But that equality suffers often because of the divergencies between the laws of different States. So long as some can go to a distant State for divorces which others are denied at home, there is not equality in this regard. When some States grant valuable exemptions from taxation which other States impose, one person may enjoy while another is denied these benefits.

A few years ago a majority of the States had adopted prohibition or rigid restrictions on the traffic in intoxicating liquor. But other States did not cooperate in advancing this policy, and ultimately by national action it was extended to all the Union. By failing to meet the requirements of a national demand the States became deprived of the power to act. If questions which the States will not fairly settle on their own account shall have to be settled for them by the Federal authority, it will only be because some States will have refused to discharge obvious duties.

There is another responsibility of the States. It is quite aside from this one of jurisdiction. It is the subject of law enforcement. We are not a lawless people, but we are too frequently a careless one. The multiplicity of laws, the varied possibilities of appeals, the disposition to technicality in procedure, the delays and consequent expense of litigation which inevitably inure to the advantage of wealth and specialized ability—all these have many times been recounted as reproaches to us. It is strange that such laxities should persist in a time like the present, which is marked by a determined upward movement in behalf of the social welfare. But they do exist. They demonstrate a need for better, prompter, less irksome, and expensive administration of the laws. They point the necessity for simplification and codification of laws; for uniformity of procedure; for more accurate delimitation of State and Federal authority.

All these problems constantly come in the work of political and social development. But they stand for a vast progression toward better conditions, a better society, a better economic system. In approaching them, we need to have in mind the Federalist's analysis of our constitutional system:—The powers delegated to the Federal Government are few and defined; those to remain in the hands of the State government are numerous and indefinite.

That statement can not be too much emphasized. The country's growth has compelled the Federal establishment to exceed by far the Government plants of even the greatest States. With this growth in physical extent, in revenue, in personnel, there has inevitably been the suggestion that the Federal Government was overshadowing the States. Yet the State governments deal with far more various and more intimate concerns of the people than does the National Government. All the operations of the minor civil divisions, parishes, wards, school districts, towns, cities, counties, and the like, are dependencies of the State. The maintenance of order through police, the general business of enforcing law, is left to the States. So is education. Property is held and transferred on terms fixed by the States. In short, the structure of social and business relationship is built chiefly about the laws of the States. It depends upon the exercise by the States of that vastly greater share of Government power which resides in them, to the exclusion cf the Federal Government. In ordinary times nearly the entire burden of taxation represents State and local demands. Even now, despite the enormous increase of Federal taxes from pre-war years, State and local taxes far exceed the Federal requirements. Moreover, the national burden is being continually reduced, while that of the local units is growing and likely to continue to grow.

Such is the real distribution of duties, responsibilities, and expenses. Yet people are given to thinking and speaking of the National Government as "the Government." They demand more from it than it was ever intended to provide; and yet in the same breath they complain that Federal authority is stretching itself over areas which do not concern it. On one side, there are demands for more amendments to the Constitution. On the other, there is too much opposition to those that already exist.

Without doubt, the reason for increasing demands on the Federal Government is that the States have not discharged their full duties. Some have done better and some worse, but as a whole they have not done all they should. So demand has grown up for a greater concentration of powers in the Federal Government. If we will fairly consider it, we must conclude that the remedy would be worse than the disease. What we need is not more Federal government but better local government. Yet many people who would agree to this have large responsibility for the lapses of local authority.

From every position of consistency with our system, more centralization ought to be avoided. The States would protest, promptly enough, anything savoring of Federal usurpation. Their protection will lie in discharging the full obligations that have been imposed on them. Once the evasion of local responsibilities becomes a habit, there is no knowing how far the consequences may reach. Every step in such a progression will be unfortunate alike for States and Nation. The country needs, in grappling with the manifold problems of these times, all the courage, intelligence, training, and skill that can be enlisted in both State and national administrations.

One insidious practice which sugar-coats the dose of Federal intrusion is the division of expense for public improvements or services between State and National treasuries. The ardent States-rights advocate sees in this practice a vicious weakening of the State system. The extreme federalist is apt to look upon it in cynical fashion as bribing the States into subordination. The average American, believing in our dual-sovereignty system, must feel that the policy of national doles to the States is bad and may become disastrous. We may go on yet for a time with the easy assumption that "if the States *will not,* the Nation *must.*" But that way lies trouble. When the National Treasury contributes half, there is temptation to extravagance by the State. We have seen some examples in connection with the Federal contributions to road building. Yet there are constant demands for more Federal contributions. Whenever by that plan we take something from one group of States and give it to another group, there is grave danger that we do an economic injustice on one side and a political injury on the other. We impose unfairly on the strength of the strong, and we encourage the weak to indulge their weakness.

When the local government unit evades its responsibility in one direction, it is started in the vicious way of disregard of law and laxity of living. The police force which is administered on the assumption that the violation of some laws may be ignored has started toward demoralization. The community which approves such administration is making dangerous concessions. There is no use disguising the fact that as a nation our attitude toward the prevention and punishment of crime needs more serious attention. I read the other day a survey which showed that in proportion to population we have eight times as many murders as Great Britain, and five times as many as France. Murder rarely goes unpunished in Britain or France; here the reverse is true. The same survey reports many times as many burglaries in parts of America as in all England; and, whereas a very high per cent of burglars in England are caught and punished, in parts of our country only a very low per cent are finally punished. The comparison can not fail to be disturbing. The conclusion is inescapable that laxity of administration reacts upon public opinion, causing cynicism and loss of confidence in both law and its enforcement and therefore in its observance. The failure of local government has a demoralizing effect in every direction.

These are vital issues, in which the Nation greatly needs a revival of interest and concern. It is senseless to boast of our liberty when we find that to so shocking an extent it is merely the liberty to go ill-governed. It is time to take warning that neither the liberties we prize nor the system under which we claim them are safe while such conditions exist.

We shall not correct admitted and grave defects if we hesitate to recognize them. We must be frank with ourselves. We ought to be our own harshest critics. We can afford to be, for in spite of everything we still have a balance of prosperity, of general welfare, of secure freedom, and of righteous purpose, that gives us assurance of leadership among the nations.

What America needs is to hold to its ancient and well-charted course.

Our country was conceived in the theory of local self-government. It has been dedicated by long practice to that wise and beneficent policy. It is the foundation principle of our system of liberty. It makes the largest promise to the freedom and development of the individual. Its preservation is worth all the effort and all the sacrifice that it may cost.

It can not be denied that the present tendency is not in

harmony with this spirit. The individual, instead of working out his own salvation and securing his own freedom by establishing his own economic and moral independence by his own industry and his own self-mastery, tends to throw himself on some vague influence which he denominates society and to hold that in some way responsible for the sufficiency of his support and the morality of his actions. The local political units likewise look to the States, the States look to the Nation, and nations are beginning to look to some vague organization, some nebulous concourse of humanity, to pay their bills and tell them what to do. This is not local self-government. It is not American. It is not the method which has made this country what it is. We can not maintain the western standard of civilization on that theory. If it is supported at all, it will have to be supported on the principle of individual responsibility. If that principle be maintained, the result which I believe America wishes to see produced inevitably will follow.

There is no other foundation on which freedom has ever found a permanent abiding place. We shall have to make our decision whether we wish to maintain our present institutions, or whether we wish to exchange them for something else. If we permit some one to come to support us, we can not prevent some one coming to govern us. If we are too weak to take charge of our own mortality, we shall not be strong enough to take charge of our own liberty. If we can not govern ourselves, if we can not observe the law, nothing remains but to have some one else govern us, to have the law enforced against us, and to step down from the honorable abiding place of freedom to the ignominious abode of servitude.

If these principles are sound, two conclusions follow. The individual and the local, state, and national political units ought to be permitted to assume their own responsi-

bilities. Any other course in the end will be subversive both
of character and liberty. But it is equally clear that they
in their turn must meet their obligations. If there is to be
a continuation of individual and local self-government and
of State sovereignty, the individual and locality must govern themselves and the State must assert its sovereignty.
Otherwise these rights and privileges will be confiscated
under the all-compelling pressure of public necessity for a
better maintenance of order and morality. The whole world
has reached a stage in which, if we do not set ourselves
right, we may be perfectly sure that an authority will be
asserted by others for the purpose of setting us right.

But before we attempt to set ourselves up as exponents
of universal reform, it would be wise to remember that
progress is of slow growth, and also to remember that moderation, patience, forbearance, and charity are virtues in
their own right. The only action which can be effective in
the long run is that which helps others to help themselves.
Before we assume too great responsibilities in the governing of others, it would be the part of wisdom very completely
to discharge our responsibilities for governing ourselves. A
large amount of work has to be done at home before we
can start in on the neighbors, and very considerable duties
have to be performed in America before we undertake the
direction of the rest of the world. But we must at all times
do the best we can for ourselves without forgetting others,
and the best we can for our own country without forgetting
other nations.

Ours is a new land. It has had an almost unbelievable
task to perform, and has performed it well. We have been
called to fit the institutions of ancient civilization to the
conditions of a new country. In that task the leaders of
the Nation have been supported by a deep devotion to the
essentials of freedom. At the bottom of the national character has been a strain of religious earnestness and moral

determination which has never failed to give color and quality to our institutions. Because our history shows us these things, we dare make honest appraisal of our shortcomings. We have not failed. We have succeeded. Because we have been privileged to rely upon generations of men and women ready to serve and to sacrifice, we have magnificently succeeded.

Our gathering here to-day is in testimony of supreme obligation to those who have given most to make and preserve the Nation. They established it upon the dual system of State government and Federal Government, each supreme in its own sphere. But they left to the States the main powers and functions of determining the form and course of society. We have demonstrated in the time of war that under the Constitution we possess an indestructible Union. We must not fail to demonstrate in the time of peace that we are likewise determined to possess and maintain indestructible States. This policy can be greatly advanced by individual observance of the law. It can be strongly supplemented by a vigorous enforcement of the law. The war which established Memorial Day had for its main purpose the enforcement of the Constitution. The peace which followed that war rests upon the universal observance of the Constitution. This Union can only be preserved, the States can only be maintained, under a reign of national, local, and moral law, under the Constitution established by Washington, under the peace provided by Lincoln.

XXIV

We should not forget that, in the world over, the general attitude and one of the strongest attributes of all peoples is a desire to do right. Unless we lay our course in accordance with this principle, the great power for good in the world with which we have been intrusted by a Divine Providence will be turned to a power for evil.

THE NAVY AS AN INSTRUMENT OF PEACE

THE poet reminds us that "Knowledge comes, but wisdom lingers." It may not be difficult to store up in the mind a vast quantity of facts within a comparatively short time, but the ability to form correct judgments requires the severe discipline of hard work and the tempering heat of experience and maturity. By your previous preparation and by your four years' course at this institution, your diploma will testify that you are possessed of knowledge. Your future life will reveal your attainments in wisdom. I have come here to express the faith that your country holds in your abiding worth and in your ability to succeed.

You have chosen a profession which represents one of the great military arms of our Government. You will be a constant testimony throughout your lives that America believes in military preparation for national defense, for the protection of the rights, the security, and peace of her citizens. You will be called to places of responsibility and command. You will be given the power of life and death over fellow countrymen. You will represent the power, the glory, and the honor of this Nation among foreign peoples, with all the prominence that arises from wearing the uniform and carrying the flag. What you are the American sailor will be, and what you represent the American Navy will represent in the ports of our own country and in those of foreign peoples where little will be known of the nature of authority under liberty, save what is learned from you. You have been chosen for this high calling.

Before the Graduating Class, U. S. Naval Academy, Annapolis, Md., June 3, 1925.

But while you will serve the Nation in this special field of endeavor, you will not forget that the real profession of every American is citizenship. Under our institutions each individual is born to sovereignty. Whatever he may adopt as a means of livelihood, his real business is serving his country. He can not hold himself above his fellow men. The greatest place of command is really the place of obedience, and the greatest place of honor is really the place of service. It is your duty in the part you propose to take to make the largest contribution you can to the general citizenship of your country.

Not long ago I heard a Navy chaplain refer to the sage advice of the Apostle to put first things first. It was my understanding that this meant putting proper emphasis on what is essential in life and disregarding so far as possible that which is accidental. The great body of American people will, I hope, always be devoted to civilian life. Their main purpose has been and will be the maintenance of an honorable peace. It may not have occurred to some of you, but I feel warranted in asserting it to be true that your success lies in giving a very large support to the civilian life of the Nation and to the promotion of the public peace. If I were not convinced that this is true, I should question the usefulness of the National Navy.

If we are to heed the admonition to put first things first, a very little deliberation would reveal to us that one of the main essentials which lies at the very beginnings of civilization is that of security. It is only when people can feel that their lives and the property which their industry has produced to-day will continue to be safe on the morrow that there can be that stability of value and that economic progress on which human development has always rested. We do not know of any people in history where this has not been first provided through some form of monarchy supported by a sufficient military force. This condition of security has long been proverbially characterized among English-speaking people as "The King's peace." All violations of that security were crimes against the Crown, as in our Republic they are crimes against the State or the Nation.

It is only when such peace and security have been achieved under well-established customs and the orderly process of the law that there is any opportunity for the advancement of liberty. When a people have begun to respect the rights of each other and maintain common standards of action, they have advanced to a position where they do not constantly require the all-protecting power of force and can begin to take over the making of their own laws and the determination of their own government. Finding that they are secure in the posession of life and property, they can begin the establishment of their liberty. Gradually this policy develops until the last vestige of monarchy disappears and the people become entirely free and self-governing.

There is no need for me to enlarge in this presence upon the privileges which come to the individual in the development of a free people. They are the common experiences of our daily life and the precious heritage of all Americans. Freedom in religion and in expression, popular education, increasing production and more equitable distribution, a larger independence of the mind and of the body, the works of charity and humanity, a broader culture, all mark a material and spiritual advance which follows in the progress of this development. In all this progress and all this advance it has never been possible to maintain that first essential of security without a background of military force. It is that background, that support, that service which your profession helps to provide, that is your contribution, one of the first things, one of the essentials to the civilian life of our country. You may not be actually employed in production, but you are helping to increase the value of production and maintain the public peace without which there could be no production.

It is my firm conviction that the duty of national defense, like the general duty of citizenship, should be broadly extended and borne by all our people. We do not believe in or wish to bear the expense of maintaining large standing military forces. The very genius of a republic would be threatened by that policy. Freedom, independence, self-government are all opposed to anything that assembles a mercenary force. But while military science has advanced to such a degree that it is necessary constantly to maintain a considerable body of trained experts in that profession, the true spirit of American institutions requires that each citizen should be potentially a soldier, ready to take his place in the ranks in time of peril, either in the field or in the necessary productive activity. Not all of our people can pursue a long course of study so as to become trained military experts any more than they can give up the time to become trained physicians, jurists, diplomats, or statesmen. Our military forces on land and sea represent the necessary accomplishment in that profession the same as other professions are represented in civilian life. It is exactly because we wish to keep our standing forces small that the average citizen must give some attention to military affairs, precisely as he gives some attention to other Government affairs, in order that he may express a deliberate and informed judgment at the ballot box.

These are some of the principles that your Government had in mind in giving you a training in the science of naval warfare and reposing in you the public duty of maintaining the learning of that profession for the purposes of national defense. It is for this object that our country remains armed. Though ultimately I believe peace will prevail, I have too much knowledge of the history of mankind and too much experience with the traits of human nature to dare to assert that we shall never again be engaged in war. It is known of all the world that we have no present or traditional enmities, that we covet no territory, harbor no imperialistic designs, and are not arming ourselves with the expectation of attacking or being attacked. The power of our arms is not only consistent with, but ought to be regarded as an additional guaranty of, the peace of the world. And so far as we can look into the future, so far as we can gauge the power and temper of other peoples, there never was a time when it was less likely that any other nation or combination of nations would or could make any attack on us. Both by necessity and by choice the whole world is against war. It has given incomparable hostages to peace. Our own country is disarmed, has adopted the policy of limitation of naval armaments, has voluntarily imposed restrictions upon the traffic in arms, and is taking part in negotiations to secure an agreement to extend such restriction among other nations. The policy of peace through reason rather than peace through force is one in which America has taken and ought always to continue to take a leading part.

As I have already tried to make clear, I regard our Navy as a great instrument of peace. As such it can not fail to secure adequate support from the Public Treasury and command the confidence and admiration of the American people. Whatever aid can be given by voluntary associations in advancing the welfare of the Navy and keeping the public informed of its true aims and purposes and its necessary needs is entirely welcome and thoroughly to be commended. The officers of the Navy are given the fullest latitude in expressing their views before their fellow citizens, subject, of course, to the requirements of not betraying those confidential affairs which would be detrimental to the service. It seems to me perfectly proper for anyone upon any suitable occasion to advocate the maintenance of a Navy in keeping with the greatness and dignity of our country. But as one who is responsible not only for our national defense, but likewise our friendly relations with other peoples and our title to the good opinion of the world, I feel that the occasion will very seldom arise, and I know it does not now exist, when those connected with our Navy are justified, either directly or by inference, in asserting that other specified powers are arming against us, and by arousing national suspicion and hatred attempting to cause us to arm against them.

The suggestion that any other people are harboring a hostile intent toward us is a very serious charge to make. We would not relish having our honorable motives and peaceful intentions questioned; others can not relish having any of us question theirs. We should not forget that in the world over the general attitude and one of the strongest attributes of all peoples is a desire to do right. Unless we lay our course in accordance with this principle, the great power for good in the world with which we have been intrusted by a Divine Providence will be turned to a power for evil. We shall make no progress and be of no benefit to ourselves or to anyone else.

In a recent address made by Ambassador Houghton, who represents us at the Court of St. James, he gave utterance to a great truth most admirably expressed when he said that "Peace is an adventure in faith." That was a thought most appropriate to these times. The chief reliance of the world is faith. We can not maintain any of our necessary relations without it. It is one of those first things which must be put first. It is one of the main elements of the Navy. How far could you proceed in organization or discipline, or what would be the result in battle, if the officers and men did not cherish an almost absolute faith in each other? Such a sentiment of course will be justified only by the knowl-

edge that there exists in each of us qualities which are
worthy of our trust and confidence. I want the Navy when
it attempts to deal with our own people, or with the other
peoples of the earth, to remember that the dominant traits
of mankind are truth and justice and righteousness, and
that the appeal to reason must ultimately prevail. I am
not arguing that there is no evil in the world. We are
painfully aware that it is altogether too prevalent. But
we shall make no progress unless we do more than undertake to recompense evil with evil. We must make our
appeal to the greater realities. We must put the emphasis
not upon the false, but upon the true, not upon corrup-
tion and treachery, but upon purity and honor. Local and
national faith must be extended to international faith.

It is in accordance with these principles which are so
clearly sound that we base our belief in the ability of nations to compose their differences by negotiation, by arbitration and by the judgments of duly constituted courts.
It is under this conception that we try to disarm and
mutually agree to place limits on the extent of military
preparation. Man is a reasonable being and finally reason
must assert itself. We must make our choice between holding to this theory or holding that our only reliance must
be placed on armed force. Carried to its logical conclusion,
that means more and more armaments, more and more
hatreds and suspicions, a return to the old plan of direct
competition in military preparation with the certainty that
as soon as the world can arm and prepare itself after one
war it will be plunged into another.

I am not unfamiliar with the claim that if only we had a
sufficient Military Establishment no one would ever molest
us. I know of no nation in history that has ever been able
to attain that position. I see no reason to expect that we
could be the exception. Although I believe thoroughly in
adequate military preparations, what I am trying to argue

is that they are not sufficient unto themselves. I do not believe the American Navy can succeed if it represents mere naked force. I want to see it represent much more than that. We must place it on a much higher plane. We must make it an instrument of righteousness. If we are to promote peace on earth, we must have a great deal more than the power of the sword. We must call into action the spiritual and moral forces of mankind.

The world moves forward under a reign of law. Our own great Admiral Dewey, the hero of Manila Bay, being approached one time with the suggestion that he become a candidate for office, was asked what platform he would adopt. He replied, "The Constitution and the flag." By that he meant law and loyalty. You will stand peculiarily as the guardians of that great instrument, as supporters of that great symbol. You will always remember the provision of the sixth article, which declares that "This Constitution and the laws of the United States which shall be made in pursuance thereof; and all treaties made, or which shall be made, under the authority of the United States, shall be the supreme law of the land." Acting in accordance with this supreme law of the land, through their duly constituted Government, your fellow citizens are committing into your keeping the solemn and sacred duty of guarding and preserving the integrity of the law of the land and of defending and increasing the honor and glory of the national colors. When the commendations of your fellow countrymen shall come to you, when you shall have won world-wide fame by the faithful discharge of your duty in the service of your country, when in your declining years you shall seek for the last best refuge of human freedom, may your life experience inevitably and unhesitatingly turn your thoughts to the Constitution and the flag.

XXV

If one were seeking proof of a basic brotherhood among all races of men, if one were to challenge the riddle of Babel in support of aspirations for a unity capable of assuring peace to the nations, in such an inquiry I suppose no better testimony could be talen than the experience of this country. Out of the confusion of tongues, the conflict of traditions, the variations of historical setting, the vast differences in talents and tastes there has been evolved a spiritual union accompanied by a range of capacity and genius which marks this Nation for a preeminent destiny.

CONTRIBUTION OF THE NORSEMEN TO AMERICA

How often in the affairs of this world a small and apparently insignificant occurrence turns out to be an event of great importance, carrying in its train a mighty influence for good or evil. Such importance always flows from the character of those concerned. The generations of the earth treasure the rude hut that sheltered the infancy of Abraham Lincoln, seek out the birthplace of Shakespeare, and give to the uninviting soil of Palestine the title of the Holy Land, all because certain obscure happenings in those places produced those who left a broad mark upon the future course of humanity. The character of the participants brought future fame. It is such an event that we meet to commemorate to-day. One hundred years ago a little bark sailed from Norway to America. It was almost unnoticed at the time, save for the daring and hardihood of its navigators; but it brought with it the representatives of a stalwart race, men and women of fixed determination, enduring courage and high character, who were to draw in their retinue a long line of their fellow countrymen destined to change the face of an area broad as an empire, direct the historic course of sovereign States, and contribute to the salvation of a great nation. These mighty works have been wrought because those Norwegian immigrants were well worthy to follow in the wake of the Pilgrim and Cavalier.

This celebration is most happily identified with the present year, which is an anniversary of notable events in the

Before the Norwegian Centennial Celebration, at Minnesota State Fair Grounds, June 8, 1925.

history of our country. We are rounding out a century and a half from the beginning of the American Revolution. It was a half a century from the days of Concord and Lexington to the beginning of that stream of immigration from Norway which was to help guarantee that the spirit of freedom which had been so triumphant in the Colonies should not be lost to the States.

When we consider the astonishing number of immigrants which the Scandinavian countries have contributed in proportion to their own population to making the body of American citizenship, we will appreciate the significance of this anniversary. It well deserves the consideration it is receiving here in this State which has so richly profited by a larger proportion of this north-of-Europe immigration than any other Commonwealth. Minnesota would not be Minnesota, the group of imperial northwestern States would not be what they are, but for the contribution that has been made to them by the Scandinavian countries.

Because of a profound appreciation of that contribution and of its truly national value I have found it an especial pleasure to come here and join in this commemoration. In the midst of loyalties that are all beyond possibility of question, it may be difficult to choose among the many national and racial groups that have sought out America for their home and their country. We are thankful for all of them, and yet more thankful that the experiment of their common citizenship has been so magnificently justified in its results. If one were seeking proof of a basic brotherhood among all races of men, if one were to challenge the riddle of Babel in support of aspirations for a unity capable of assuring peace to the nations, in such an inquiry I suppose no better testimony could be taken than the experience of this country. Out of the confusion of tongues, the conflict of traditions, the variations of historical setting, the vast differences in talents and tastes there has been evolved a spiritual union accompanied by a range of capacity and genius which marks this Nation for a preeminent destiny. The American people have commanded the respect of the world.

It is a good thing that anniversaries such as this are so widely commemorated. The next few years will be filled with a continuing succession of similar occasions. I wish that every one of them might be so impressively celebrated that all Americans would be moved to study the history which each one represents. I can think of no effort that would produce so much inspiration to high and intelligent patriotism. Occasions of this nature bring to our attention whole regions of the past that would otherwise remain unexplored, tend to be forgotten even by scholars, and pass entirely from the public mind. These incentives to special examination of particular historical phases teach us better to understand our country and our countrymen. Anyone who will study the institutions and people of America will come more and more to admire them.

One reason that moved me to accept the cordial invitations to come here to-day was the hope of directing some measure of national attention to the absorbingly interesting subject of the social backgrounds of our country. The making of such a country is not to be told in any mere category of dates, battles, political evolutions, and partisan controversies. Back of all these, which are too often the chief material of history, lies the human story of the unsung millions of plain people whose names are strangers to public place and fame. Their lives have been replete with quiet, unpretentious, modest but none the less heroic virtues. From these has been composed the sum of that magnificent and wondrous adventure, the making of our own America. Somewhere in the epic of struggle to subjugate a continent there will be found a philosophy of human relations that the world will greatly prize. If we could seize and fix it, if we could turn it over, examine and understand it, we would have taken a long step toward solving some of the hardest problems of mankind.

It is not so many years since visitors from other quarters of the world were wont to contemplate our concourse of races, origins, and interests, and shake their heads ominously. They feared that from such a melting pot of diverse elements we could never draw the tested, tempered metal that is the only substance for national character. Even among ourselves were many who listened with serious concern to such forebodings. They were not quite sure whether we had created a nation with the soul of a nation. They wondered if perhaps we had merely brought together a large number of people in a large place. Had these misgivings been justified when the hour of trial came, it would have meant disaster to us and to the world. But instead of crumbling into a chaos of discordant elements, America proved its truly national unity. It demonstrated conclusively that there is a spiritual quality shared by all races and conditions of men which is their universal heritage and common nature. Powerful enough to hold this people to a high ideal in time of supreme trial, why may we not hope that the same influence will at length reach men and women wherever they are found on earth? If fraternity and cooperation are possible on the scale of this continent among people so widely diverse, why not on the scale of a world? It is not a new thought, but it is a profoundly engaging one. I firmly believe it is more than a chimera. I feel it is possible of realization. I am convinced that our national story might somewhat help to guide mankind toward such a goal. Therefore, I urge the deeply thoughtful study and teaching of our history.

No country has a history which starts with its discovery or at its boundaries. For the real beginnings of any people we must go back to the beginnings of all peoples. From the tombs of Egypt and the sands of Mesopotamia men are now unearthing the records of civilizations so ancient that by comparison we think of the recovered wonders of Carthage as almost modern. But all that we shall learn from the glyphs of Ur, the tombs of the Pharaohs, and the monuments of Crete and Carthage is part of our own history, illumination for our to-days, guideposts on the way to our to-morrows. All the past lives in the present. All the works and thoughts of those who have gone before have left their mark on what we think and do.

These Norsemen whose beginnings in the United States we here celebrate have exercised a great influence upon our modern history and western civilization which it is difficult to match among any other like number of people. In many ways their influence upon northern and western Europe may be compared to that of the Greek states upon the civilization of the Mediterranean. They were the first deep-sea navigators. They pioneered the migrations which boldly struck across the western waters. They were at once the terrors of the Western Roman Empire and the guardians of the Eastern. The medieval Mediterranean was a happy hunting ground for them. They branded their name upon French Normandy, and from it descended upon Britain in the Norman conquest from which there was the beginning of modern English history.

But even before William of Normandy had conquered at Hastings, Lief the son of Erik, nearly 500 years before Columbus, appears to have found the New World. Indeed, there seems little doubt that several centuries before Columbus saw the light of day there was born upon American soil, of Norse parents, a boy who afterward became so great a mathematician and astronomer that his studies may have contributed much to the fund of knowledge which helped Columbus formulate his vision of the world as we know it. Among the fascinating chapters in the history of the dark ages is the story of Iceland. As a little Norse Republic it maintained itself for several centuries as one of the real repositories of ancient culture in a world whose lamp of learning seemed near to flickering out. We have long known of the noble Icelandic literature which was produced during those generations of the intellectual twilight; but we know too little of the part which Iceland performed as an outpost of the sturdy northern culture in bridging over the gulf of darkness between the ancient and modern eras of history.

These sons of Thor and Odin and the great free North shape themselves in the mind's eye as very princes of high and hardy adventure. From Norway to Iceland, from Iceland to Greenland, from Greenland to the mainland, step by step they worked their way across the north Atlantic. They found the western ocean, and it was a Norseman who first traversed Bering Strait and demonstrated that there was no land connection between Asia and North America. One wonders whither these Northmen would turn for adventure if the earth should ever be so completely charted that exploration offered no more challenges. Within a very few years one of them first traversed the northwest passage from Atlantic to Pacific; and the same one, Amundsen, carried the flag of Norway to the South Pole; and now, within a few days past, he has been the first to make large explorations in the region of the North Pole in an airplane, tempting a fate which, as I write, is unknown.

One likes to linger over these tales of adventure and exploration. One of them has a special significance in connection with this celebration which entitles it to more particular reference. This, of course, is the voyage of the little sloop *Restaurationen*, which in 1825 brought the first organized party of Norwegian immigrants to this country. One reared on the New England tradition of the *Mayflower* will find all the materials for a new legend of pioneering in the voyage of the *Restaurationen.* She was a sloop of 45 tons, whereas the *Mayflower* was rated as 180 tons. The *Restaurationen* sailed from Stavanger, Norway, on July 4, 1825, with a desperately heavy cargo of iron and a party of fifty-two people. She came safely into the port of New York after a voyage of fourteen weeks, which compares with nine weeks required for the historic passage of the *Mayflower.*

The arrival of the *Restaurationen* created a sensation among those inured to the sea. It was claimed that she was the smallest vessel that had ever made the trans-Atlantic crossing. The New York authorities threatened to deny her the privileges of the port on the ground that she carried too many passengers and too much cargo. She was ultimately released, apparently through the influence of the Society of Friends. Most of her passengers seemed to have been members of a Norwegian religious community intimately related to the Quakers, and it appears that one of their reasons for coming to this country was that they had not enjoyed entire liberty of religious opinion at home. Thus the parallel between the voyages of the *Mayflower* and of the *Restaurationen,* despite that they were separated by more than 200 years, is impressive in several ways.

Almost without money or supplies, the little company of immigrants were taken in charge by the New York Quakers who raised funds to send them to Kendall, Orleans County, N. Y. There they secured lands and established the first Norwegian settlement in this country. It is a curious circumstance that although the Norwegians are among the greatest seafaring peoples, this party was composed almost entirely of farmers, so that their first interest was to get land. And ever since, the greater share of Norwegians have come in search of homes on the land. These first immigrants having practically no money, bought a tract on the shore of Lake Ontario for $5 per acre to be paid for in ten

annual instalments. It is hard to realize that western
New York so late as 1825 was so far on the frontier. Their
land was heavily timbered, and they were compelled not
only to clear it but to build their own shelter. The first
house is said to have been a log cabin twelve feet square,
with a garret. In this twenty-one of them lived for a time,
the men seeking such scanty employment as was to be found
in the neighborhood to support them through the winter.
The only one in the party who could speak English was
Capt. Lars Olson and he had remained in New York.

Despite poverty and hardships, the colony thrived, and
its members were shortly writing letters back to Norway
describing the opportunities of America and urging friends
to come. From this beginning the stream of Norwegian
immigration set in, but most of the later comers went much
farther west. A few years after the settlement at Kendall
another party went to La Salle County, Ill. Already the
west was fascinating them and many of the original Kendall
colony sold out and went on to Illinois. Thence the migration spread to other States of the middle west and northwest. Even before it was formed into a Territory, Iowa had
received its first Norwegians, and from about 1835 they
spread rapidly into Wisconsin, Minnesota, the Dakotas,
and other States.

It is not possible, as it is certainly not needful on this
occasion, even to summarize the story of Norwegian immigration. But it should be explained that while the settlement of 1825 in Orleans County, N. Y., was the first
Norwegian settlement and represented the first organized
immigration, these pioneers of the *Restaurationen* were not
the first Norwegians to come here. Considerable numbers
had come even before the Revolutionary War and some as
far back as the earliest colonial years. There were Norwegians in both Army and Navy during the Revolution
and the War of 1812. But the fact remains that the great

movement which established Norwegian communities all over the northwest and contributed so greatly to the building of that part of the country began with the voyage of the *Restaurationen*. It is said that Norwegians and their descendants in this country are now just about as numerous as the population of Norway itself. Norway is credited with furnishing a larger number of settlers to the United States in proportion to its population than any other European country except one.

It is frequently noted regarding immigration that the newcomers from Europe commonly sought climatic conditions here like those in which they had been raised. So the Scandinavians are found chiefly in the northern parts of this country. About eighty per cent of the population of Norway is agricultural, the remainder maritime and industrial. These proportions are closely carried out in the occupational distribution here. A great majority sought the land, but considerable numbers have always followed the sea. Some of the coincidences in connection with this migration are oddly interesting. Thus we have noted that the little sloop *Restaurationen* brought a cargo of iron; to-day Minnesota has more Norwegians and produces more iron ore than any other State. Again, Norway is a land of wonderful fresh-water lakes, and it is closely matched by Minnesota.

There is one phase in the story of immigration which seems always to characterize it. Once the tide had set in from a particular European country, the movement thereafter has invariably been encouraged by the early comers. Not only did they urge relatives and friends in the old home to come, but they devoted their new-found prosperity to help them. On this subject there is an opportunity for some useful historical research. In the pre-Revolutionary days immigration to America seems to have been encouraged from the other side, partly from political and partly from business motives. The colonizing countries of Europe competed to control the best parts of the New World by occupying it with their colonies. Immigration was encouraged both by the Governments and by companies of merchant adventurers. At that stage of the movement, of course, the colonies possessed no wealth to help their friends to come. But after the Revolution the situation greatly changed. New political conditions made this country more attractive than ever before, and developing wealth and opportunity emphasized its invitation. So we find the people of our Republic deliberately and consciously encouraging the movement in this direction. There is opportunity for a much more detailed examination of these factors in the European migration than has yet been undertaken. It would be a profoundly interesting contribution to the story of this greatest of all migrations that humanity has ever accomplished if we could know more of the precise motives which have animated it.

The contribution of this country to financing immigration of the last century and a third has certainly run into hundreds of millions of dollars, perhaps into billions. It has had a profound social influence, both here and in Europe. Its economic consequences could hardly be overestimated. A detailed inquiry into these facts should include a close consideration of all the great migrations which have marked the distribution of men throughout the world. Man seems to have been from his beginnings the most migratory of animals. His earlier movements appear to have had their chief motive in adventure and the desire to find the regions where existence was most comfortable. There could hardly have been a very serious pressure of population, for it is only in recent historic times that this factor has existed. Some very early migrations were doubtless due to climatic or other physical conditions. Later on political, social, religious, and economic reasons caused the movements. Some went forth to make conquests, others were driven out by conquest. The children of Israel migrated into Egypt to escape from famine. They left Egypt to escape from bondage and to recover their religious liberty. The old Romans and Phœnicians were great colonizers, the Romans from imperialistic motives and the Phœnicians from desire to extend their trade. The European migration to the American Continent represented in its various phases all the causes that have operated through the ages to bring about such shifts of population. In the beginning there was chiefly the motive of exploration and adventure. Later came the desire to be freed from onerous clerical or political restrictions. Then, with the realization of America's enormous resources, there was the wish to share in its developing riches. Only in the later stages of the movement did the people of this country reach their hand of welcome to the friends across the Atlantic, both urging and assisting them to come.

Though I make no pretense to deep studies in the subject, yet I have been impressed that in this last regard the shift of Old-World peoples to this side of the Atlantic was perhaps unique. From the time when their fast-developing institutions of popular government, religious freedom, and intellectual liberality had begun to take definite and attractive forms, the people of the Colonies took a new interest in inducing their European relatives to follow them thither. They engaged in an inverted crusade, a conquest without invasion and without force. The new country offered not only material opportunities, but possibilities of a spiritual and intellectual emancipation which they ardently wished their friends on the other side to share. Citizenship in the New World meant something that it had not meant in the Old. It was seen that the New World offered something new. There was increasing realization that many burdensome traditions and institutions had somehow been shed. Here at last the individual was lord of himself, master of his own destiny, keeper of his own sovereignty. Here he was free.

With the eighteenth century's epoch of intellectual liberalism there came yet more sharp realization that the new country was not bound to ancient manners and prejudices, and that therefore it offered to the common man a better chance. Here he might realize that ideal of equality which by this time was so generally finding a lodgment in European minds. This spiritual evolution moved rather slowly during the first two-thirds of the eighteenth century. The Seven Years' War, or as we commonly call it, the French and Indian War, was for the Colonies a period of rapid awakening and realization. They began to find themselves, to formulate more definite aspirations for their future. But it does not appear that this new conception of American destiny began in any important way to be shared in Europe until the Revolution, independence and the establishment of the Federal Government forced it upon the old countries. Then a new idea began to fix itself in the European mind. The new country was seen as an essentially, vitally, basically different conception of human relationships. It appeared not merely as a new country, but as a different kind of country. It was considered not only different from Europe, but different from any earlier social creations. The European peoples had been greatly stirred by the intellectual awakening of the eighteenth century, and the liberals among them had been deeply disappointed at the seeming meager results which accrued from it. We may well wonder what would have been the fate of Europe after 1815, if the liberalism of both England and the Continent had settled down to disappointment and cynicism. We can not doubt that during this period, say from 1815 to 1848, the beacon which they saw had been lighted over the western Atlantic was a lamp to the feet and a hope to the hearts of liberals throughout Europe.

Within this period immigration from the north and west of Europe was not only rapidly building this country into numbers, wealth, and authority in the world, but it was having a tremendous reflex upon Europe itself. But for American example and influence the democratic movements of 1832 and 1848 in Europe might have been long postponed. The broadly democratic evolution which swayed Europe so greatly in the latter half of the nineteenth century might have failed entirely.

In the period we have been discussing nearly all the immigration to the United States was from northern and western Europe. Through its reactions upon Europe it gave constant encouragement there to liberal thought and action. In this country, by gradually giving the North a great preponderance in numbers, it hastened the downfall of slavery and helped rid our institutions of that great and threatening anomaly.

These Northmen, one of whose anniversaries we are celebrating to-day, have from their first appearance on the margin of history been the children of freedom. Native to a rigorous climate and a none too productive soil, they had learned the necessity for hard work and careful management. They were moved by that aspiration for a free holding in the land which has always marked peoples in whom the democratic ideal was pressing for recognition. Eager for both political and economic independence, they realized the necessity for popular education, and so have always been among the most devoted supporters of public schools. Thousands of them volunteered in the service of the country during the Civil and Spanish Wars, and tens of thousands in the World War. The institutions and the manners of democracy came naturally to them. Their glory is all about you, their living and their mighty dead. They have given great soldiers, statesmen, scientists, educators and men of business to the upbuilding of their adopted country. They have been rapidly amalgamated into the body of citizenship, contributing to it many of its best and most characteristic elements. To their adaptability the Nation owes much for its success in the enormous process of assimilation and spiritual unification that has made our Nation what it is and our people what they are.

Although this movement of people originated in Norway, in its essence and its meaning it is peculiarly American. It has nothing about it of class or caste. It has no tinge of aristocracy. It was not produced through the leadership of some great figure. It is represented almost entirely by that stalwart strain who make the final decisions in this world, which we designate the common people. It has about it the strength of the home and the fireside; the family ties of the father and the mother, the children and the kindred. It has all been carried on very close to the soil, it has all been extremely human. When I consider the marvelous results it has accomplished I can not but believe that it was inspired by a Higher Power. Here is something vital, firm, and abiding, which I can only describe as a great reality.

An enormous power has come to you, but you are charged with equally enormous responsibilities. Those responsibilities you have never failed to meet, that power you have never failed to sanctify. Therein lies the sole title to all the glory you have achieved in the past and therein will lie the sole title to all the glory that you will achieve in the future. Believing that there resides in an enlightened people an all-compelling force for righteousness, I have every faith that through the vigorous performance of your duties you will add new luster to your glory in the days to come.

Our America with all that it represents of hope in the world is now and will be what you make it. Its institutions of religious liberty, of educational and economic opportunity, of constitutional rights, of the integrity of the law, are the most precious possessions of the human race. These do not emanate from the Government. Their abiding place is with the people. They come from the consecration of the father, the love of the mother, and the devotion of the children. They are the product of that honest, earnest, and tireless effort that goes into the rearing of the family altar and the making of the home of our country. They can have no stronger supporters, no more loyal defenders, than that great body of our citizenship which you represent. When I look upon you and realize what you are and what you have done, I know that in your hands our country is secure. You have laid up your treasure in what America represents, and there will your heart be also. You have given your pledge to the Land of the Free. The pledge of the Norwegian people has never yet gone unredeemed.

XXVI

The world has tried war with force and has utterly failed. The only hope of success lies in peace with justice. No other principle conforms to the teaching of Washington; no other standard is worthy of the spirit of America; no other course makes so much promise for the regeneration of the world.

WASHINGTON

After 150 anniversaries repeatedly observed, followed during the last three months by intensive celebration, in this neighborhood where it had its beginnings, the American Revolution should be fairly well understood. If it needs any justification, if it needs any praise, it is enough to say that its product is America. It ought to be unnecessary on this occasion to dwell very much on that event and its yet more remarkable results. But no great movement in the progress of mankind has ever been accomplished without the guidance of an inspired leadership. Of this accepted truth, there is no more preeminent example than that which was revealed by the war which made this country independent. Wherever men love liberty, wherever they believe in patriotism, wherever they exalt high character, by universal consent they turn to the name of George Washington. No occasion could be conceived more worthy, more truly and comprehensively American, than that which is chosen to commemorate this divinely appointed captain. The contemplation of his life and work will forever strengthen our faith in our country and in our country's God.

Those men who have taken great parts in the world are commonly ranked by posterity according to their accomplishments while living, and the permanent worth of the monuments representing their achievements which remain after they are gone. By this standard I think we may regard George Washington as the first lay citizen of the

Address delivered at the celebration of the 150th anniversary of George Washington taking command of the Continental Army, Cambridge, Mass., July 3, 1925, at 4. p.m.

world of all time. He was one in whom the elements of greatness were so evenly blended, so accurately proportioned, that his character has well-nigh defied analysis. Others have created wider commotion and deeper impression in the hour of their eminence. But we shall hardly find one who in his own day achieved so much as Washington and left his work so firmly established that posterity, generation after generation, can only increase its tributes to his ability, his wisdom, his patriotism, and his rounded perfection in the character of a Christian citizen.

No figure in profane history has inspired so many testimonies of admiration. The highest eloquence, the most profound sincerity, have been invoked to picture him as the very sum of public capacities and civic virtues. No pride of race or country has even attempted to set up rivals to him. Envy and malice have stood rebuked in the presence of his towering form. There is no language of literature and culture which does not boast among its adornments noble eulogies of the work and character of Washington. Although, as history reckons its periods, it is but a little time since he passed from the stage of life, he has been claimed, wherever men struggle and aspire, as the possession of all humanity, the first citizen of all the ages.

So he must be a strangely bold and self-confident eulogist who would attempt even on such an occasion as this to add anything to the total of affection, admiration, and reverence which has been reared as the true memorial of Washington. It is impossible for us to add to or take from the estimate which has been fixed by the generations of the world.

But if the preeminent place of Washington is thus established beyond possibility of change at our hands, it is only the more desirable that on this anniversary we should come here to do our reverence and to seek replenishment of the inspiration which is always to be drawn from consideration of his life and works. To the people of the

Republic whose existence is due to his leadership, his life
is the full and finished teaching of citizenship. To others,
who may claim him only by virtue of the right of humanity
to be heir to all the ages, his story is replete with example
and admonition peculiarly applicable to the problems of
the world and its peoples in these times.

We have come here because this day a century and a
half ago, and in this place, Washington formally assumed
command of the armies of the Colonies. His feet trod this
soil. Here was his headquarters. Here was his place of
worship. Our first view therefore is of Washington the
soldier. But he was indeed so much more than the soldier;
his talents were so many and so perfectly proportioned,
that it is impossible to study him in any one of his capacities, to the exclusion of the others. In him, we find also a
marvelous instinct for statecraft, supporting and sustaining
an equal genius for camp and field. We see moreover the
qualities of a great man of business, which he brings to
serve the vast task of organizing and equipping his armies.
We find him on one day writing a noble and eloquent re-
buke to a commander of the King's forces who was bent
on waiving the laws of civilized warfare; and on another,
addressing compelling counsels of patriotism, energy, and
executive sense, to the Continental Congress and the provincial legislatures. In everything he was called to be the
leader. In everything, his leadership wrought results which
completely vindicated the confidence reposed in him.

The complaint has been many times uttered that Washington was so nearly a paragon of abilities and virtues that
it is impossible to see through the aura of perfections to
the real, simple, human man. But there is a phase of
Washington's career which, fully studied and understood,
will give us the picture of him as one of the most human
men in history. To inform ourselves of this human side,
we need only to know of the long years of arduous prepara-

tion which preceded the historic event which took place here 150 years ago to-day.

From his earliest manhood, Washington's life had been a part of great affairs. Many of those affairs were vastly greater and more significant than he himself, or indeed anybody else, could possibly have realized at the time. He had come up through a schooling of strangely mingled adversities and successes. He had devoted hard and disappointing years to activities which resulted, aside from the training which he derived, in little more than hopeless futilities. Nobody can know the real Washington, the man Washington, without studying closely his services to the Virginia Colony and the British Crown, during the years immediately preceding and covering the old French War. Here we see him as a young man, in whom the combination of rare and remarkable parts is most easily discerned. We find him, at times, hot-headed and impetuous, always intensely impatient with incompetency in places of authority.

From the beginning we discover a special genius for commanding the respect and attention of older men. When hardly more than a boy he was chosen for a responsible and difficult mission to the French on the western frontier. This mission brought him in contact with an important French officer who reported to his Government that this young man was likely to make more trouble for French interests in America than any fifty other people. That observation was more profound than its maker could have realized. Washington had been sent with a small force, as the emissary of Governor Dinwiddie, of Virginia, to notify the French that their aggressions in the upper Ohio territory were occasion of deep concern to the British colonies, and must cease. It was the wish of Washington and his superiors that the message be delivered without bringing about any clash at arms. But events decreed otherwise, and a skirmish took place in the wilderness in which a number of men were killed and wounded, among them a French officer of some rank and importance. It is deeply suggestive of the destiny which had marked Washington that this backwoods brush at arms should have occasioned the first bloodshed in that long series of wars which was to drench the Western World for near two generations, and did not end until the downfall of Napoleon.

From the day of that clash in the western forests of Pennsylvania, precipitated by the determination of Washington to execute his mission, the Seven Years' War was a foregone conclusion. Washington was denounced in France as a murderer, a man-eating freebooter of the wilds. In England his boldness and determination won him a good deal of reputation. In the Colonies there was much difference of opinion, for the time being, whether his course was justified or had brought the country face to face with the possibility of a disastrous struggle.

At any rate, from that day until the downfall of Napoleon at Waterloo, there was no peace in either Europe or America, save for brief periods which represented little more than temporary truces. Doubtless that long and fearful series of conflicts was inevitable. Whether it was or not, the facts of history show Washington, a youth of twenty-two, as the commander whose order proved the torch to set a world on fire. From that hour, responsible men in both Britain and France realized that there could be no lasting peace until those countries had fought the duel which should determine the supremacy of one or the other in the New World. There was not room for both.

So came the Seven Years' War and the establishment of British domination in North America. A little later came the American Revolution, the French Revolution, and the Napoleonic wars. One can but wonder what might have been the reflections of Washington, if he could have imagined on that July morning of 1754, when he resolved that he must fight, if he could have known the train of events that would follow upon his determination. But such conjecture is of little value. To us there is more of immediate interest in the curious coincidence that the skirmish for possession of Fort Necessity took place on July 3, 1754, exactly twenty-one years before the day when Washington in this place assumed command of the Continental Army.

And those twenty-one years, as Washington lived them, constituted a fitting probation for the career that awaited him. The echoes of the little battle of Fort Necessity reverberated throughout the American Colonies and the European courts as if it had been an engagement of Titans. Its political effects were tremendous. It made Washington a marked man throughout the Colonies and gave him a real European reputation.

His part in the Braddock expedition, though vastly better known, probably had less effect in forming his character or directing his career than this expedition to Fort Necessity. Nevertheless, his reputation was further increased by his conduct in the Braddock campaign. But that heroic episode was followed by a long and disappointing experience as head of the Virginia forces defending the western frontier. He saw little of satisfying service during this period. But he learned the supreme importance of organization and preparation in connection with military operations. In the end it was his privilege to lead his Virginians to the occupation of Fort Pitt, when it was finally surrendered by the French. But the real campaign for control of the Ohio Valley was made from the north by General Wolfe on the Plains of Abraham rather than from Virginia, and Washington found his part in it disappointingly small.

Not only the Braddock campaign of 1755, but his earlier operations, both diplomatic and military, on the upper Ohio, marked him as a man of caution, sagacity, and wisdom in planning and conducting military operations. At the same time, they showed him as the intrepid and fearless fighting soldier in the hours of action.

One thing that Washington learned during the French War must have contributed greatly to form his opinions about relations between Britain and the Colonies. He was brought to realize that the form of colonial government, with which bitter experience made him so familiar, could not long satisfy the people of the larger, wealthier, and fast-growing Colonies. With Washington, the idea of substantial freedom long preceded that of independence. Like most of the colonial youth, he hoped that a more enlightened policy in London and a more sympathetic execution of it by the royal governors might compose the growing differences. During the troublous epoch between the French War and the Revolution he thought deeply of these matters, and his correspondence gives evidence of the growing impression that a contest must come. He followed the development of events in Massachusetts with a close and understanding concern. His writings and occasional public pronouncements during this period show him acutely anxious that the Colonies should present a united front when the test came. One in his position of leadership, authority, and independent fortune, living as a Virginia gentleman, might easily enough have felt that the troubles of the Massachusetts Bay Colony had small concern for him. High Churchman, conformist in most things, enjoying excellent repute in England and with English officials in America, his influence might logically enough have been thrown to the royalists. Yet, as early as the spring of 1769, he wrote declaring, "Our lordly masters in Great Britain will be satisfied with nothing less than the deprivation of American freedom * * *." And, inquiring what could be done to avert such a calamity, he added, "That no man should scruple or hesitate a moment to use arms in defense of so valuable a blessing is clearly my opinion. Yet, arms,

I would beg to add, should be the last resource." A little later, in that same year, Washington, at a public meeting, offered a non-importation resolution and secured its adoption.

In short, it is plain that he was anxious to keep the sentiment of the southern Colonies fully in step and sympathy with the attitude of the New England patriots who at the moment were bearing the brunt of the struggle for colonial rights. Seemingly, the Boston port bill convinced him that the Colonies must prepare for the harshest eventualities. At a meeting of the citizens of his county he helped draft a petition and remonstrance to the King, which concluded with the ominous words, "From our sovereign there can be but one appeal." Such a declaration, coming from one whose repute was high in all the Colonies, and who was beginning to speak with the voice of something like authority for the southern communities, could not fail to strengthen the arm and purpose of the New Englanders.

The selection of Washington to command the Continental Armies has, I think, been too much attributed to his high military repute and too little to the fact that he had long taken the view of a true statesman regarding the impending crisis. The fact is that he had all along seen the struggle as a continental and national one. He realized that Massachusetts could not win alone, nor could New England. In helping to set up the committee of correspondence, in molding the sentiment of Virginia, in his service as member of the Continental Congress, the ideal of a firm and whole-hearted union of all the Colonies was plainly fundamental. Repeatedly, in his writings, even long before the struggle had seriously suggested the possibility of war, he used the phrase, "Our Country," giving it an application vastly broader than the domain or concerns of any single colony. He was among the first to see the vision of an American Nation. No other man so early grasped certain physical and geographic arguments which urged nationality as inevitable.

In this his engineering training, together with his intimate knowledge of the topography of the Ohio and Potomac Valleys, had an important part. As a young surveyor he realized the importance of that break through the Allegheny system which these two valleys mark. Many years later he pointed out its strategic importance in connection with the defense and unity of the Colonies fronting the Atlantic. Before the Ohio was much more than a myth to most people, even in Virginia, Washington saw that the Ohio basin must be controlled by the Colonies if they were to be secure.

Thus it was that a complete and clear vision of all the arguments for national unity was due to the many-sidedness of the Washington mind. He saw it as politician, as statesman, as military man, as engineer. Without such a grasp of all the elements, he could not have taken the statesmanly and essentially national view of the problem before hostilities began. Nor could he have dealt effectively with its military aspects during the war. He possessed one of those rarely endowed minds which not only recognize all the factors, but assign to each its proper weight.

He was in truth a consummate politician. When he went to the sittings of the Continental Congress, wearing his Virginia uniform of buff and blue, some were inclined to ridicule the display of military predilection. They accused him of swashbuckling, and pointed to his uniform as equivalent to announcement of his candidacy for Commander in Chief. In the first, they were utterly wrong; in the second, quite probably right. That uniform, when he presided over the committees on military preparation, could hardly have been construed as meaning anything other than that its wearer realized what was ahead and was willing to force some part of that realization on others.

I suppose if we were to pick any two men out of that

gathering, to be set down as something other than politicians, Washington and sturdy old John Adams would be well toward the top in the polling. Though they approached the matter from utterly different angles, they were both led by the sagacity of great politicians to the same conclusion. To both, the crisis was essentially national. A nation must be created to deal with it. The army before Boston must be taken over by the Congress as a national army. There must be a Commander in Chief, supreme in the military field. All this we look back upon as illumined statesmanship. But statesmanship is nothing more than good, sound politics, tested and proved. That is what it was when John Adams conceived the great strategy of calling a man of the South to the chief command. A more provincial man might have dreamed of Massachusetts, aided by the other colonies, taking and holding the lead and garnering the lion's share of glory. But Adams was planning in terms of a nation, not of provinces; and Washington had for years been writing of "Our Country." So Washington put on his uniform in testimony of his readiness for whatever might happen, and Adams, after some period of misgivings, set about convincing the delegates from New England and the middle Colonies that there must be a nation, and a national army, with a Commander in Chief, and that must be Washington.

It was a stroke of political genius that Adams, soul of Puritanic idealism, should have moved the adoption of the army by Congress and the selection of Washington as Commander in Chief. The selection was made without a dissenting vote, though it is not true to say that Washington was unanimously preferred. Already there were clashing ambitions and divergent community interests. But Adams saw, and made others see, the peculiar reasons that urged Washington. The middle Colonies, dominated by their landed aristocracies, had much in common with the social and economic system of the South. To them Washington meant the enlistment of property, substance, and eminent respectability. In presenting his name to the Congress Adams described him in terms which seem prophetic, and which we can hardly improve: "A gentleman, whose skill and experience as an officer, whose independent fortune, great talents, and excellent universal character would command the approbation of all America and unite the cordial exertions of all the Colonies better than any other person in the Union."

Let it ever be set down to the glory of Massachusetts that John Adams made George Washington Commander in Chief of the Continental Armies and John Marshall Chief Justice of the United States. Destiny could have done no more.

Immediately after his selection, Washington set out from Philadelphia for Boston. On the way he received first tidings of the Battle of Bunker Hill, which had been fought two days after he was named commander. He inquired eagerly about the behavior of the continental troops, and when he learned how splendidly they had fought against the British regulars he quietly declared that the liberties of the country were safe. In that anxious hour the battle of twenty years earlier in the Pennsylvania's woods, wherein his Virginia militia had saved Braddock's regulars from destruction, no doubt was near the top of his mind. To be assured that the raw levies of New England were capable of behaving just as well in 1775 as his Virginians had done in 1755 must have been intensely reassuring.

Knowing the story of the Revolution as we do, we can not doubt that the historic event which took place here 150 years ago to-day marked one of its crises. Even with Washington, the struggle was well-nigh lost at several periods. Of course, the ultimate separation of the Colonies from the mother country was inevitable. Had the Revolution of 1775 failed, as it must have failed without Washington, there would have been harsh and vindictive reprisals. Nobody can read the arrogant pronouncements of Lord North's government or the still more arrogant letters of General Gage to Washington and avoid conviction that the British Government and its American military representatives would have vied with each other in efforts to estrange the Colonies. Such a policy would have established traditions of animosity that would have kept the struggle alive even after a nominal peace. In the end separation would have come. But it might have been delayed through many recurrences of turbulence and struggle. It was vastly to the good of both the mother country and the Colonies that, the conflict being once begun, it was brought to a decisive conclusion.

There is another reason why the final victory of the Colonies was important to the world. It was just as necessary for the maintenance of the British Empire as for the proper development of the American community. I believe this view is now generally accepted by British students as well as Americans. We may be sure that it was in the mind of the great Chatham, who had laid the foundations of the British Empire in the Seven Years' War. If there was a man in all that realm who might well have been given attention when the American crisis was developing, that man was Chatham. He had found Britain weak and had built it into strength. He had well-nigh made the whole North American Continent British. He had reestablished the empire and extended it in many directions. Yet Chatham knew that Lord North's policies would surely cost the loss of the American dominion. Emerging from a long political retirement, defying the doctors he hated and the King he had served, the grand old man hurried down to the House of Lords to pronounce his allegiance to the cause of the Colonies. "When your lordships," said he, "look at the

papers transmitted to us from America; when you consider
their decency, their firmness, their wisdom, you can not but
respect their cause and wish to make it your own." That
decency, firmness, and wisdom were in no small part George
Washington.

Chatham knew what it had been to build an empire; he
would not see it thrown away without having his protest
heard. He spoke the voice of liberalism in England; but
the King and his ministers had no ear for such counsels.
They had fixed their course and could not be swerved.

Washington's assumption of the command gave the colonial cause an effective national character. Had he not possessed the genius and the power to impress others with that
conception, it is hardly conceivable that disaster could long
have been postponed. He found himself in command of an
unorganized, undisciplined, unprovisioned, and unmuni-
tioned body of some 14,000 militia, opposing an army of
11,000 regulars shut up in Boston and supported by a naval
power that completely commanded the seas. Washington
was called first to make an army, then to drive his enemy
out of Boston, and then to meet attack at whatever point
along the coast the enemy might choose. Where many
others, quite as sincere in their patriotism, fondly imagined
that the evacuation of Boston would move the London government to make peace, he was convinced that it would be
little more than the beginning. For the long struggle he
foresaw, he had to prepare, not only by creating an army
but by convincing the civil authority and the people that
he must have the utmost measure of their support and cooperation. So we find him, immediately upon assuming
his command, dividing his time between military tasks and
the writing of endless letters to the leaders of the Congress,
to the provincial assemblies, to men of importance everywhere, designed to impress them with the enormity of the
coming struggle.

This is not the time or place for a review of Washington's military career. Yet there are phases of that career which I am never able to pass over without a word of wonder and admiration because of some of the exploits which it includes.

It is recorded that a few evenings after the surrender of Lord Cornwallis at Yorktown a banquet was given by Washington and his staff to the British commander and his staff. One likes to contemplate the sportsmanship of that function. Amiabilities and good wishes were duly exchanged, and finally Lord Cornwallis rose to present his compliments to Washington. There had been much talk of past campaigning experiences, and Cornwallis, turning to Washington, expressed the judgment that when history's verdict was made up "the brightest garlands for your excellency will be gathered, not from the shores of the Chesapeake, but from the banks of the Delaware." We may fairly assume that Cornwallis, in the fullness of a very personal experience, was qualified to judge. Washington had outgeneralled and defeated him both on the banks of the Delaware and the shores of the Chesapeake. In giving the laurels to the Trenton-Princeton campaign, he expressed not only his own judgment, but the estimate which was afterwards pronounced by Frederick the Great, who declared that the Trenton-Princeton campaign was the most brilliant military performance of the century. For myself, without pretense of military wisdom, the lightning-like stroke of Trenton and Princeton in its supreme audacity and ideal execution has always seemed the most perfectly timed combination of military genius and political wisdom that we find in the records of warfare.

On the other hand, much can be urged to support the claim that Yorktown was the most brilliant campaign of Washington. With an army on the point of disintegration, he was almost utterly unable to get supplies and transport. Yet he managed to withdraw his forces from before New

York and get them well on the way to Virginia before his enemy seriously suspected his design. It was a miracle of military skill, diplomacy, and determination, to effect on the Virginia Peninsula that consolidation of forces from south and north, along with the French army and fleet, at precisely the right moment. The essence of strategy is to divide the forces of the enemy and defeat them in detail; and there are few campaigns which show a commander accomplishing this through operations covering so extended a territory and involving so many difficulties.

In the Yorktown campaign we see all the varied elements of Washington's genius at work. He had to deal at once with an inert Congress that was threatening at this critical moment actually to reduce the Army. He had to find supplies and money or get along without them. In part he did one, in part the other. He had to effect a junction of widely separated forces and to maintain secrecy to the last moment. Everything must be done within a period of time so short that it might well have made success appear utterly impossible, because he could not count on the co-operation of the French for a longer period. All these things he accomplished. Accomplishing them, he won the war, as in the campaign of Trenton and Princeton he had saved the Revolution. No man could have rendered his service to the Revolution who was not both a soldier and statesman. He understood, and he never underestimated, the political bearings of every move.

When he retired to Mount Vernon, Washington entered upon a new phase of his career. He had won the war but he was a man of peace. His experience as Commander in Chief had completely convinced him that the form of government under the confederation could not possibly serve the necessities of the country. It is not possible here to outline the discouragements which threatened the country with all manner of disasters. Washington, as the most in-

280 FOUNDATIONS OF THE REPUBLIC

fluential citizen, was the inevitable leader in preparing for the Constitutional Convention of 1787 and the establishment of a real nation. That task he took up early, and to it he devoted an energy and a wisdom that were alike amazing. It was quite natural that he should be chosen to preside over the Constitutional Convention. When its work was done, his influence was one of the chief forces to bring about ratification. After that, there was none to question that he must be the first President under the new régime.

Perhaps no character in history has been subjected to more close study or sympathetic analysis than that of Washington. The volume of his writings which have been left to us is enormous. Moreover, from earliest manhood his life was lived almost continuously under intense public observation. It is therefore remarkable that biographers and eulogists should be so generally accused of failing to give us a satisfying picture of him. The fault, however, is not his, but theirs. The explanation is that no biographer has possessed, and probably none ever will possess, the full-rounded measure of qualification to appreciate, to understand, to apportion, and to weigh all the elements that made this man. Unfortunately, a vast myth was early built around Washington, difficult to avoid, and not even yet entirely dissipated. Among his biographers and eulogists, some have seen first and most admiringly the great soldier. Some have been most engaged with him as the statesman-politician, dealing with great affairs from day to day as circumstances demanded. Others have devoted themselves particularly to portraying him as the constructive student of government, and builder of institutions. Still others have found their first inspiration in his work as a wise, firm, and discriminating administrator.

Volumes have been written, and they are exceedingly interesting volumes, on Washington as a pioneer of modern scientific agriculture. It is interesting to recall that in their tastes for agriculture Washington and his great antagonist, King George III, stood on a common ground. Whoever cares to familiarize himself with this particular detail in the careers of Washington and the King will find that these two might in other circumstances have been the best of friends. For both were devoted admirers and supporters of Arthur Young, the famous English traveler and agricultural authority. In the last year or two before the beginning of the French Revolution, Young traveled extensively throughout France. He kept a journal of his observations and experiences that has since been invaluable to whoever wished to know conditions in the France of that time. Besides all this Arthur Young was almost the founder of the modern science and technique of advanced agriculture. He wrote and published voluminously on such subjects as rotation of crops, scientific fertilization, farm drainage, the breeding of livestock, the growing of plants, and many other subjects which are now commonplaces. King George became interested in his work and turned over to him some farms of the royal domain to be conducted as the earliest agricultural experiment stations.

Young published an agricultural journal devoted to his theories and experiments, and to it Washington became a subscriber. This led him into a correspondence with Young, which seems to have been quite extended. Convinced that the Young program represented much of value to American agriculture, Washington offered to set aside one of his farms, to be managed by English experts, if Young would enlist them. Apparently nothing finally came of this proposal, but the fact that it was made, and seriously considered, shows how near Washington and King George came to an intimate association for the betterment of agriculture. Indeed, inside of two years after the end of the Revolution, Washington appealed to Young to buy and ship to him an invoice of agricultural implements and seeds with which Washington desired to experiment. On investigation, Young discovered that British law forbade these exports. So he went to the Minister for Home Affairs, Lord Grenville, and pleaded for permission to send them. It was immediately granted, and by the courtesy of the British Government the entire order was filled. The incident is an interesting indication of the liberal disposition manifested, so soon after the war, by leading men of both countries.

It is a pleasant thing to be privileged to recall on an occasion like this such a bit of evidence touching the underlying community of interest between the old Kingdom and the new Republic in matters of common concern and human advancement. Washington was the last person to harbor resentments; and in this and other instances he more than once found his former enemies ready to meet him half way. As we look back now on a century and more of uninterrupted peace between the two nations, we can not but feel that such peace and the long period of international cooperation which it has made possible have been in no small part a testimony to the generous willingness of all men everywhere to recognize as the first citizen of the world him who has been so long acclaimed as the first American.

It had been my expectation to confine my address to General Washington and leave the stately and solemn grandeur of this great figure as the sole subject for the thought of those who might hear me. I shall not enter into the vain speculation of what he might do if he were living to-day. Yet his farewell address shows conclusively that he hoped to be able to lay down certain principles of conduct for his fellow countrymen which would be of advantage to them so long as the Nation into which he had wrought his life might endure. No doubt he knew the whole world would hear him. He had seen the life of the soldier in time of war and after that of the statesman in time of peace. He had an abiding faith in honesty. He believed mightily in his fellow men. The vigor with which he insisted on the prosecution of war was no less than the vigor with which he insisted on the observance of peace. He cherished no resentments, he harbored no hatreds, he forgave his enemies. He felt the same obligation to execute the terms of a treaty made for the benefit of a former foe that he felt to require the observance of those made for the benefit of his own country. He realized that peace could be the result only of mutual forbearance and mutual good faith.

He harmonized the divergent and conflicting interests of different nationalities and different colonial governments by conference and agreement. He demonstrated by his arguments, and our country has demonstrated by experience, that more progress can be made by cooperation than by conflict. To agree quickly with your adversary always pays.

The world has not outgrown, it can never outgrow, the absolute necessity for conformity to these eternal principles. I want to see America assume a leadership among the nations in the reliance upon the good faith of mankind. I do not see how civilization can expect permanent progress on any other theory. If what is saved in the productive peace of to-day is to be lost in the destructive war of to-morrow, the people of this earth can look forward to nothing but everlasting servitude. There is no justification for hope. This was not the conception which Washington had of life.

If the people of the Old World are mutually distrustful of each other let them enter into mutual covenants for their mutual security, and when such covenants have been made let them be solemnly observed no matter what the sacrifice. They have settled the far more difficult problems of reparations, they are in process of funding their debts to us, why can they not agree on permanent terms of peace and fully reestablish international faith and credit? If there be differences which can not be adjusted at the moment, if there be conditions which can not be foreseen, let them be resolved in the future by methods of arbitration and by the forms of judicial determination.

While our own country should refrain from making political commitments where it does not have political interests, such covenants would always have the moral support of our Government and could not fail to have the commendation of the public opinion of the world. Such a course would be sure to endow the participating nations with an abundant material and spiritual reward. On what other basis can there be any encouragement for a disposition to attempt to finance a revival of Europe? The world has tried war with force and has utterly failed. The only hope of success lies in peace with justice. No other principle conforms to the teaching of Washington; no other standard is worthy of the spirit of America; no other course makes so much promise for the regeneration of the world.

XXVII

If we are to have that harmony and tranquillity, that union of spirit which is the foundation of real national genius and national progress, we must all realize that there are true Americans who did not happen to be born in our section of the country, who do not attend our place of religious worship, who are not of our racial stock, or who are not proficient in our language. If we are to create on this continent a free Republic and an enlightened civilization that will be capable of reflecting the true greatness and glory of mankind, it will be necessary to regard these differences as accidental and unessential.. We shall have to look beyond the outward manifestations of race and creed. Divine Providence has not bestowed upon any race a monopoly of patriotism and character.

TOLERATION AND LIBERALISM

IT is a high privilege to sit as a member of this convention. Those who exercise it have been raised to the rank of a true nobility. It is a mark of personal merit which did not come by right of birth but by right of conquest. No one can ever question your title as patriots. No one can ever doubt the place of affection and honor which you hold forevermore in the heart of the Nation. Your right to be here results from what you dared and what you did and the sacrifices which you made for our common country. It is all a glorious story of American enterprise and American valor.

The magnitude of the service which you rendered to your country and to humanity is beyond estimation. Sharp outlines here and there we know, but the whole account of the World War would be on a scale so stupendous that it could never be recorded. In the victory which was finally gained by you and your foreign comrades, you represented on the battle field the united efforts of our whole people. You were there as the result of a great resurgence of the old American spirit, which manifested itself in a thousand ways—by the pouring out of vast sums of money in credits and charities, by the organization and quickening of every hand in our extended industries, by the expansion of agriculture until it met the demands of famishing continents, by the manufacture of an unending stream of munitions and supplies, by the creation of vast fleets of war and transport ships, and, finally, when the tide of battle was turning

Before the American Legion Convention at Omaha, Nebraska, October 6, 1925.

against our associates, by bringing into action a great armed force on sea and land of a character that the world had never seen before, which, when it finally took its place in the line, never ceased to advance, carrying the cause of liberty to a triumphant conclusion. You reaffirmed the position of this Nation in the estimation of mankind. You saved civilization from a gigantic reverse. Nobody says now that Americans can not fight.

Our people were influenced by many motives to undertake to carry on this gigantic conflict, but we went in and came out singularly free from those questionable causes and results which have often characterized other wars. We were not moved by the age-old antagonisms of racial jealousies and hatreds. We were not seeking to gratify the ambitions of any reigning dynasty. We were not inspired by trade and commercial rivalries. We harbored no imperialistic designs. We feared no other country. We coveted no territory. But the time came when we were compelled to defend our own property and protect the rights and lives of our own citizens. We believed, moreover, that those institutions which we cherish with a supreme affection, and which lie at the foundation of our whole scheme of human relationship, the right of freedom, of equality, of self-government, were all in jeopardy. We thought the question was involved of whether the people of the earth were to rule or whether they were to be ruled. We thought that we were helping to determine whether the principle of despotism or the principle of liberty should be the prevailing standard among the nations. Then, too, our country all came under the influence of a great wave of idealism. The crusading spirit was aroused. The cause of civilization, the cause of humanity, made a compelling appeal. No doubt there were other motives, but these appear to me the chief causes which drew America into the World War.

In a conflict which engaged all the major nations of the

earth and lasted for a period exceeding four years, there could be no expectation of material gains. War in its very essence means destruction. Never before were contending peoples so well equipped with every kind of infernal engine calculated to spread desolation on land and over the face of the deep. Our country is only but now righting itself and beginning a moderate but steady recovery from the great economic loss which it sustained. That tremendous debt must be liquidated through the laborious toil of our people. Modern warfare becomes more and more to mean utter loss, destruction, and desolation of the best that there is of any people, its valiant youth and its accumulated treasure. If our country secured any benefit, if it met with any gain, it must have been in moral and spiritual values. It must be not because it made its fortune but because it found its soul. Others may disagree with me, but in spite of some incidental and trifling difficulties it is my firm opinion that America has come out of the war with a stronger determination to live by the rule of righteousness and pursue the course of truth and justice in both our domestic and foreign relations. No one can deny that we have protected the rights of our citizens, laid a firmer foundation for our institutions of liberty, and made our contribution to the cause of civilization and humanity. In doing all this we found that, though of many different nationalities, our people had a spiritual bond. They were all Americans.

When we look over the rest of the world, in spite of all its devastation there is encouragement to believe it is on a firmer moral foundation than it was in 1914. Much of the old despotism has been swept away. While some of it comes creeping back disguised under new names, no one can doubt that the general admission of the right of the people to self-government has made tremendous progress in nearly every quarter of the globe. In spite of the staggering losses and the grievous burden of taxation, there is a new note of hope for the individual to be more secure in his rights, which is unmistakably clearer than ever before. With all the troubles that beset the Old World, the former cloud of fear is evidently not now so appalling. It is impossible to believe that any nation now feels that it could better itself by war, and it is apparent to me that there has been a very distinct advance in the policy of peaceful and honorable adjustment of international differences. War has become less probable; peace has become more secure. The price which has been paid to bring about this new condition is utterly beyond comprehension. We can not see why it should not have come in orderly and peaceful methods without the attendant shock of fire and sword and carnage. We only know that it is here. We believe that on the ruins of the old order a better civilization is being constructed.

We had our domestic problems which resulted from the war. The chief of these was the care and relief of the afflicted veterans and their dependents. This was a tremendous task, on which about $3,000,000,000 has already been expended. No doubt there have been cases where the unworthy have secured aid, while the worthy have gone unrelieved. Some mistakes were inevitable, but our people and our Government have at all times been especially solicitous to discharge most faithfully this prime obligation. What is now being done is related to you in detail by General Hines, of the Veterans' Bureau, a public official of demonstrated merit, so that I shall not dwell upon it. During the past year, under the distinguished and efficient leadership of Commander Drain, the Legion itself has undertaken to provide an endowment fund of $5,000,000 to minister to the charitable requirements of their comrades. The response to this appeal has been most generous and the results appear most promising. The Government can do much, but it can never supply the personal relationship that comes from the ministrations of a private charity of that kind.

The next most pressing problem was the better ordering of the finances of the Nation. Our Government was costing almost more than it was worth. It had more people on the pay roll than were necessary, all of which made expenses too much and taxes too high. This inflated condition contributed to the depression which began in 1920. But the Government expenditures have been almost cut in two, taxes have been twice reduced, and the incoming Congress will provide further reductions. Deflation has run its course and an era of business activity and general prosperity, exceeding anything ever before experienced in this country and fairly well distributed among all our people, is already at hand.

Our country has a larger Army and a more powerful Navy, costing annually almost twice as much as it ever before had in time of peace. I am a thorough believer in a policy of adequate military preparation. We are constantly working to perfect our defenses in every branch, land forces, air forces, surface and submarine forces. That work will continue. Our Military Establishment of the Army and Navy, the National Guard, and the Reserve Corps is far superior to anything we have ever maintained before, except in time of war. In the past six years we have expended about $4,000,000,000 for this purpose. That ought to show results, and those who have correct information know that it does show results. The country can rest assured that if security lies in military force, it was never so secure before in all its history.

We have been attempting to relieve ourselves and the other nations from the old theory of competitive armaments. In spite of all the arguments in favor of great military forces, no nation ever had an army large enough to guarantee it against attack in time of peace or to insure its victory in time of war. No nation ever will. Peace and security are more likely to result from fair and honorable dealings, and mutual agreements for a limitation of armaments among nations, than by any attempt at competition in squadrons and battalions. No doubt this country could, if it wished to spend more money, make a better military force, but that is only part of the problem which confronts our Government. The real question is whether spending more money to make a better military force would really make a better country. I would be the last to disparage the military art. It is an honorable and patriotic calling of the highest rank. But I can see no merit in any unnecessary expenditure of money to hire men to build fleets and carry muskets when international relations and agreements permit the turning of such resources into the making of good roads, the building of better homes, the promotion of education, and all the other arts of peace which minister to the advancement of human welfare. Happily, the position of our country is such among the other nations of the world that we have been and shall be warranted in proceeding in this direction.

While it is true that we are paying out far more money and maintaining a much stronger Military Establishment than ever before, because of the conditions stated, we have been able to pursue a moderate course. Our people have had all the war, all the taxation, and all the military service that they want. They have therefore wished to emphasize their attachment to our ancient policy of peace. They have insisted upon economy. They have supported the principle of limitation of armaments. They have been able to do this because of their position and their strength in numbers and in resources. We have a tremendous natural power which supplements our arms. We are conscious that no other nation harbors any design to put us in jeopardy.

It is our purpose in our intercourse with foreign powers to rely not on the strength of our fleets and our armies but on the justice of our cause. For these reasons our country has not wished to maintain huge military forces. It has been convinced that it could better serve itself and better serve humanity by using its resources for other purposes.

In dealing with our military problems there is one principle that is exceedingly important. Our institutions are founded not on military power but on civil authority. We are irrevocably committed to the theory of a government by the people. We have our constitutions and our laws, our executives, our legislatures, and our courts, but ultimately we are governed by public opinion. Our forefathers had seen so much of militarism, and suffered so much from it, that they desired to banish it forever. They believed and declared in at least one of their State constitutions that the military power should be subordinate to and governed by the civil authority. It is for this reason that any organization of men in the military service bent on inflaming the public mind for the purpose of forcing Government action through the pressure of public opinion is an exceedingly dangerous undertaking and precedent. This is so whatever form it might take, whether it be for the purpose of influencing the Executive, the legislature, or the heads of departments. It is for the civil authority to determine what appropriations shall be granted, what appointments shall be made, and what rules shall be adopted for the conduct of its armed forces. Whenever the military power starts dictating to the civil authority, by whatsoever means adopted, the liberties of the country are beginning to end. National defense should at all times be supported, but any form of militarism should be resisted.

Undoubtedly one of the most important provisions in the preparation for national defense is a proper and sound selective service act. Such a law ought to give authority for a very broad mobilization of all the resources of the country, both persons and materials. I can see some difficulties in the application of the principle, for it is the payment of a higher price that stimulates an increased production, but whenever it can be done without economic dislocation such limits ought to be established in time of war as would prevent so far as possible all kinds of profiteering. There is little defense which can be made of a system which puts some men in the ranks on very small pay and leaves others undisturbed to reap very large profits. Even the income tax, which recaptured for the benefit of the National Treasury alone about 75 per cent of such profits, while local governments took part of the remainder, is not a complete answer. The laying of taxes is, of course, in itself a conscription of whatever is necessary of the wealth of the country for national defense, but taxation does not meet the full requirements of the situation. In the advent of war, power should be lodged somewhere for the stabilization of prices as far as that might be possible in justice to the country and its defenders.

But it will always be impossible to harmonize justice and war. It is always possible to purchase materials with money, but patriotism can not be purchased. Unless the people are willing to defend their country because of their belief in it, because of their affection for it, and because it is representative of their home, their country can not be defended. If we are looking for a more complete reign of justice, a more complete supremacy of law, a more complete social harmony, we must seek it in the paths of peace. Progress in these directions under the present order of the world is not likely to be made except during a state of domestic and international tranquillity. One of the great questions before the nations to-day is how to promote such tranquillity.

The economic problems of society are important. On

the whole, we are meeting them fairly well. They are so personal and so pressing that they never fail to receive constant attention. But they are only a part. We need to put a proper emphasis on the other problems of society. We need to consider what attitude of the public mind it is necessary to cultivate in order that a mixed population like our own may dwell together more harmoniously and the family of nations reach a better state of understanding. You who have been in the service know how absolutely necessary it is in a military organization that the individual subordinate some part of his personality for the general good. That is the one great lesson which results from the training of a soldier. Whoever has been taught that lesson in camp and field is thereafter the better equipped to appreciate that it is equally applicable in other departments of life. It is necessary in the home, in industry and commerce, in scientific and intellectual development. At the foundation of every strong and mature character we find this trait which is best described as being subject to discipline. The essence of it is toleration. It is toleration in the broadest and most inclusive sense, a liberality of mind, which gives to the opinions and judgments of others the same generous consideration that it asks for its own, and which is moved by the spirit of the philosopher who declared that "To know all is to forgive all." It may not be given to infinite beings to attain that ideal, but it is none the less one toward which we should strive.

One of the most natural of reactions during the war was intolerance. But the inevitable disregard for the opinions and feelings of minorities is none the less a disturbing product of war psychology. The slow and difficult advances which tolerance and liberalism have made through long periods of development are dissipated almost in a night when the necessary war-time habits of thought hold the minds of the people. The necessity for a common purpose and a united intellectual front becomes paramount to everything else. But when the need for such a solidarity is past there should be a quick and generous readiness to revert to the old and normal habits of thought. There should be an intellectual demobilization as well as a military demobilization. Progress depends very largely on the encouragement of variety. Whatever tends to standardize the community, to establish fixed and rigid modes of thought, tends to fossilize society. If we all believed the same thing and thought the same thoughts and applied the same valuations to all the occurrences about us, we should reach a state of equilibrium closely akin to an intellectual and spiritual paralysis. It is the ferment of ideas, the clash of disagreeing judgments, the privilege of the individual to develop his own thoughts and shape his own character, that makes progress possible. It is not possible to learn much from those who uniformly agree with us. But many useful things are learned from those who disagree with us; and even when we can gain nothing our differences are likely to do us no harm.

In this period of after-war rigidity, suspicion, and intolerance our own country has not been exempt from unfortunate experiences. Thanks to our comparative isolation, we have known less of the international frictions and rivalries than some other countries less fortunately situated. But among some of the varying racial, religious, and social groups of our people there have been manifestations of an intolerance of opinion, a narrowness to outlook, a fixity of judgment, against which we may well be warned. It is not easy to conceive of anything that would be more unfortunate in a community based upon the ideals of which Americans boast than any considerable development of intolerance as regards religion. To a great extent this country owes its beginnings to the determination of our hardy ancestors to maintain complete freedom in religion. Instead of a state church we have decreed that every citizen shall be free to follow the dictates of his own conscience as to his religious beliefs and affiliations. Under that guaranty we have erected a system which certainly is justified by its fruits. Under no other could we have dared to invite the peoples of all countries and creeds to come here and unite with us in creating the State of which we are all citizens.

But having invited them here, having accepted their great and varied contributions to the building of the Nation, it is for us to maintain in all good faith those liberal institutions and traditions which have been so productive of good. The bringing together of all these different national, racial, religious, and cultural elements has made our country a kind of composite of the rest of the world, and we can render no greater service than by demonstrating the possibility of harmonious cooperation among so many various groups. Every one of them has something characteristic and significant of great value to cast into the common fund of our material, intellectual, and spiritual resources.

The war brought a great test of our experiment in amalgamating these varied factors into a real Nation, with the ideals and aspirations of a united people. None was excepted from the obligation to serve when the hour of danger struck. The event proved that our theory had been sound. On a solid foundation of a national unity there had been erected a superstructure which in its varied parts had offered full opportunity to develop all the range of talents and genius that had gone into its making. Well-nigh all the races, religions, and nationalities of the world were represented in the armed forces of this Nation, as they were in the body of our population. No man's patriotism was impugned or service questioned because of his racial origin. his political opinion, or his religious convictions. Immigrants and sons of immigrants from the central European countries fought side by side with those who descended from the countries which were our allies; with the sons of equa-

torial Africa; and with the Red men of our own aboriginal
population, all of them equally proud of the name Americans.

We must not, in times of peace, permit ourselves to lose
any part from this structure of patriotic unity. I make
no plea for leniency toward those who are criminal or
vicious, are open enemies of society and are not prepared
to accept the true standards of our citizenship. By tolerance I do not mean indifference to evil. I mean respect for
different kinds of good. Whether one traces his American-
isms back three centuries to the *Mayflower,* or three years
to the steerage, is not half so important as whether his
Americanism of to-day is real and genuine. No matter by
what various crafts we came here, we are all now in the
same boat. You men constituted the crew of our "Ship of
State" during her passage through the roughest waters.
You made up the watch and held the danger posts when
the storm was fiercest. You brought her safely and trium-
phantly into port. Out of that experience you have learned
the lessons of discipline, tolerance, respect for authority,
and regard for the basic manhood of your neighbor. You
bore aloft a standard of patriotic conduct and civic integrity, to which all could repair. Such a standard, with a
like common appeal, must be upheld just as firmly and
unitedly now in time of peace. Among citizens honestly
devoted to the maintenance of that standard, there need be
small concern about differences of individual opinion in
other regards. Granting first the essentials of loyalty to
our country and to our fundamental institutions, we may
not only overlook, but we may encourage differences of
opinion as to other things. For differences of this kind will
certainly be elements of strength rather than of weakness.
They will give variety to our tastes and interests. They
will broaden our vision, strengthen our understanding, encourage the true humanities, and enrich our whole mode

and conception of life. I recognize the full and complete necessity of 100 per cent Americanism, but 100 per cent Americanism may be made up of many various elements.

If we are to have that harmony and tranquillity, that union of spirit which is the foundation of real national genius and national progress, we must all realize that there are true Americans who did not happen to be born in our section of the country, who do not attend our place of religious worship, who are not of our racial stock, or who are not proficient in our language. If we are to create on this continent a free Republic and an enlightened civilization that will be capable of reflecting the true greatness and glory of mankind, it will be necessary to regard these differences as accidental and unessential. We shall have to look beyond the outward manifestations of race and creed. Divine Providence has not bestowed upon any race a monopoly of patriotism and character.

The same principle that it is necessary to apply to the attitude of mind among our own people it is also necessary to apply to the attitude of mind among the different nations. During the war we were required not only to put a strong emphasis on everything that appealed to our own national pride but an equally strong emphasis on that which tended to disparage other peoples. There was an intensive cultivation of animosities and hatreds and enmities, together with a blind appeal to force, that took possession of substantially all the peoples of the earth. Of course, these ministered to the war spirit. They supplied the incentive for destruction, the motive for conquest. But in time of peace these sentiments are not helps but hindrances; they are not constructive. The generally expressed desire of "America first" can not be criticized. It is a perfectly correct aspiration for our people to cherish. But the problem which we have to solve is how to make America first. It can not be done by the cultivation of national bigotry, arrogance, or selfishness. Hatreds, jealousies, and suspicions will not be productive of any benefits in this direction. Here again we must apply the rule of toleration. Because there are other peoples whose ways are not our ways, and whose thoughts are not our thoughts, we are not warranted in drawing the conclusion that they are adding nothing to the sum of civilization. We can make little contribution to the welfare of humanity on the theory that we are a superior people and all others are an inferior people. We do not need to be too loud in the assertion of our own righteousness. It is true that we live under most favorable circumstances. But before we come to the final and irrevocable decision that we are better than everybody else we need to consider what we might do if we had their provocations and their difficulties. We are not likely to improve our own condition or help humanity very much until we come to the sympathetic understanding that human nature is about the same everywhere, that it is rather evenly distributed over the surface of the earth, and that we are all united in a common brotherhood. We can only make America first in the true sense which that means by cultivating a spirit of friendship and good will, by the exercise of the virtues of patience and forbearance, by being "plenteous in mercy," and·through progress at home and helpfulness abroad standing as an example of real service to humanity.

It is for these reasons that it seems clear that the results of the war will be lost and we shall only be entering a period of preparation for another conflict unless we can demobilize the racial antagonisms, fears, hatreds, and suspicions, and create an attitude of toleration in the public mind of the peoples of the earth. If our country is to have any position of leadership, I trust it may be in that direction, and I believe that the place where it should begin is at home. Let us cast off our hatreds. Let us candidly accept our treaties and our natural obligations of peace. We know and everyone knows that these old systems, antagonisms, and reliance on force have failed. If the world has made any progress, it has been the result of the development of other ideals. If we are to maintain and perfect our own civilization, if we are to be of any benefit to the rest of mankind, we must turn aside from the thoughts of destruction and cultivate the thoughts of construction. We can not place our main reliance upon material forces. We must reaffirm and reinforce our ancient faith in truth and justice, in charitableness and tolerance. We must make our supreme commitment to the everlasting spiritual forces of life. We must mobilize the conscience of mankind.

Your gatherings are a living testimony of a determination to support these principles. It would be impossible to come into this presence, which is a symbol of more than 300 years of our advancing civilization, which represents to such a degree the hope of our consecrated living and the prayers of our hallowed dead, without a firmer conviction of the deep and abiding purpose of our country to live in accordance with this vision. There have been and will be lapses and discouragements, surface storms and disturbances. The shallows will murmur, but the deep is still. We shall be made aware of the boisterous and turbulent forces of evil about us seeking the things which are temporal. But we shall also be made aware of the still small voice arising from the fireside of every devoted home in the land seeking the things which are eternal. To such a country, to such a cause, the American Legion has dedicated itself. Upon this rock you stand for the service of humanity. Against it no power can prevail.

XXVIII

The history of relationships among the nations of the New World has been a continuing story of effort to substitute the rule of arbitration, of mediation, of adjudication and confidence, for the rule of force and war.

JOSÉ DE SAN MARTIN, LATIN AMERICAN LIBERATOR

GREAT men belong to humanity. They are the incarnation of the truth. Although they are almost always developed by local circumstances, in the end their influence becomes world-wide. It is that which makes appropriate the rearing of monuments within our own land to those who have been instrumental in advancing human welfare in other countries. It is a recognition of a universal standard of action and a common brotherhood among all men. We are all servants of the truth.

As I listened to the eloquent and generous words of the distinguished ambassador from Argentina, speaking on behalf of his Government and people, in presenting this noble monument of civic virtue and patriotic achievement to the people of the United States, I was again reminded how closely parallel have run the lines of experience, how intimate have been the spiritual associations, among the members of the American family of Republics. To the people of the United States it has been a matter of pride and gratification that their ancestors were providentially chosen to initiate the movement for independence in the New World. If that movement had not started where and when it did, we may be sure it would have started at some other place and time, and that at last its results would have been substantially the same. It was not among the human possibilities that the communities of these new-found continents should permanently be maintained as dependencies

At the dedication of a monument to General José de San Martin given by Argentina to the United States, Washington, D. C., October 28, 1925.

of the mother states in Europe. We can see now that their destiny to establish themselves independently was just as certain as that a patriarchal system of government must ultimately be displaced by a more progressive form.

It was not possible that these sturdy communities should merely contribute to the world a distorted reflection from the light of older states and ancient institutions. The discovery of America to the world was providentially fixed in a time of spiritual and intellectual awakening. It was an epoch of new lights and new aspirations, of mighty clashes between the traditions of the old and the spirit of the new time. The New World proved a fruitful field for testing out of new ideas of man's relations both to his Creator and to his fellow men. In the warming sunshine of such an opportunity, in the fertility of such a virgin soil, these experiments found that full and fair scope which made possible their triumphant conclusion.

It may be well to consider for a moment the essential similarities which marked the experiences of all the new American communities during their struggles for independence and later during their trying era of institution building. By doing this we can better realize that the American contribution could not have been made save from the soil of a new country. You can not transplant an ancient and rigid social system to a new country without many and revolutionary modifications. You can not expect that these new institutions will have adequate opportunity for development unless they grow in the light of human independence and spiritual liberty.

This realization came early to the great leaders of thought in all the American countries. So we find that as North American aspirations produced our Washington, Jefferson, Adams, Hamilton, and Franklin—so the countries to the south of us brought forth their Miranda, their Bolivar, their Hidalgo, their Artigas, their O'Higgins, their Sucré, their

Morazan, and finally their San Martin—patriot, statesman, immortal contributor to the founding of three Republics. It is to honor the memory of San Martin, and to acclaim his achievements, that we are gathered to-day.

It was the fortune of our thirteen North American Colonies to be first in attaining the fact and recognition of independence. Deeply appreciating their own high fortune, the people of the new United States were from the beginning profoundly sympathetic with every movement for liberty and independence throughout these continents. And, in this connection, Mr. Ambassador, permit me to thank you for the generous reference you made a few moments ago to the services of Henry Clay in the cause of Pan American freedom. You have reminded us of his persistent and eloquent pleadings in behalf of the struggling peoples in the other American countries. The high tribute of Mr. Clay to the State papers produced during that period by the Latin American leaders was only equaled by that accorded by the great liberal leaders in England to the State papers of our Revolutionary period. In expressing complete agreement with the estimate placed upon them by Mr. Clay, I wish to call attention to a happy coincidence of this occasion. In Mr. Clay's great speech in the House of Representatives on March 24, 1818, championing the cause of the South American Republics, he referred in especially glowing terms to the far-seeing statesmanship of the Argentine patriot who was then director of the United Provinces of La Plata. I am sure your excellency will pardon me an allusion to a relationship which your modesty has forbidden you to mention. For to me it is a happy and auspicious circumstance that you, Argentina's ambassador to our Government, chance to be the grand-nephew of the wise and courageous statesman, Don Juan Martin Pueyrredon, whom Mr. Clay so appropriately eulogized.

On such an occasion as this it is utterly impossible to attempt a recounting of the services, in arms and in counsel, of such a man as José de San Martin. Just as so many of the military figures in the North American struggle for independence had had European training during the Seven Years' War, so San Martin had had a varied and useful experience in the Napoleonic struggles. As George Washington learned military science on the frontiers of Pennsylvania while a youth, so San Martin received his education in the European and African wars of Spain a generation later. And these American soldiers of independence learned their lessons well. As some distinguished military critics have described Washington's campaign of Trenton and Princeton as a military exploit of unparalleled brilliancy, so in the annals of the southern wars of independence others describe San Martin's passage of the Andes with his little patriot army as a more notable achievement than the crossing of the Alps by either Hannibal or Napoleon. I do not pretend to pass on these questions of military organization and direction; but I can not refrain from pointing out the basic similarity between the strategy of the North American and the South American revolutionary epochs. The North American revolutionists chose the great Washington, citizen of a southern colony, to lead a revolutionary movement that had been begun, and in its early stages was chiefly sustained by the people of the north. Likewise, when San Martin was made the supreme military leader of Argentina, he saw that the success of Argentina depended upon strengthening and sustaining the revolution in Chile and Peru.

But it is not my purpose to-day to attempt to analyze the military genius of San Martin. For that I refer you to the writings of men truly capable of giving it an adequate estimate. He was, like our Washington, one of those seemingly inspired military chieftains who are capable of thinking at the same moment of terms of war and of politics, of the battle field and the great human forum. For me the great significance of San Martin and his deeds and times lies less in their brilliancy in the moment of accomplishment and more in the justifying verdict which a later time and a riper experience have pronounced upon them.

This is a subject which I believe worthy of greater development than my time will permit. We who to-day study the lessons of modern history possess advantages unknown to our predecessors of even a few years ago. We see many things which we could not then have recognized. Thus we see your South America suddenly lifted to a place of impressive eminence among the grand divisions of the world. For it stands to-day as the only continent that has escaped from deep and critical involvement in the most widespread and terrific struggle that has been waged for the domination of the destiny of mankind. There is not one among us here to-day who, having passed the meridian of life, can not recall the days when our American experiments were still looked upon throughout a large part of the world as of doubtful value and dubious success. We recall that the sophisticated statesmanship of an older world entertained profound misgivings as to the ultimate fate of these American Republics. These critics wondered whether with their liberal and democratic organization these new countries would prove able to play their full part and emerge secure and sound from one of the vast periodical convulsions to which our race has seemed to be inevitably subjected. Now, I am glad to say, we hear less of such misgivings. The world has had its test. The institutions of men have been through their trial. That trial has quite definitely answered the questionings of pessimism. It has provided us with much specific information by which we may judge for ourselves whether the institutions of a republican New World or of a monarchial Old World were best adapted as conservators of human happiness and human progress. We are content to leave the final verdict to history. The republican peoples of the Americas are prepared to take their chance on that judgment.

It was no mere accident or coincidence that saved the countries of South America from a far more intimate and disastrous connection with the recent world convulsion. Whoever has given even casual consideration to the past century's evolution of international relationships in that continent must recognize that not only its aspirations but its practical working processes for dealing with difficult issues between nations have steadily tended toward the insuring of peace. They have looked to the substitution of reason for force. They have repeatedly recognized, in the most practical fashion and difficult circumstances, that even issues of vital interest to the national welfare may be determined to the advantage of all concerned without resort to hostilities. Such problems as international boundary disputes involving sovereignty over great areas and populations have been settled through arbitrations or adjudications time and again. And these settlements have been followed by demonstrations of good will and mutual confidence, where war, no matter what its verdict, would surely have added to the exasperations of both parties and left a heritage of that mutual distrust which so commonly is responsible for increased armaments and future wars. I do not pretend to controvert the facts of history by denying that South America has had its share of international wars. I am seeking merely to call attention to the fact that there would have been more wars, and more disastrous ones, but for the fact that South American statesmanship has on the whole been dominated by an earnest and increasingly successful purpose to devise and adopt a variety of methods for avoidance of armed conflict. The will to peace has been present, even though the way to it was not always open.

The present occasion naturally brings some reflections

upon the workings of the republican system that for a well-rounded century has prevailed throughout the greater part of the Americas. If we will go back over a century of the New World's history, we will find many evidences that these American institutions have peculiarly lent themselves to the support of those fundamental international efforts which look to the maintenance of peace and the prevention of war. It is almost precisely a century since the first Pan American conference was held at Panama City. Its accomplishments did not seem impressive, but even at that it was well remembered as a fine and hopeful gesture. It was seen as an invitation to understanding, to coöperation, and to sincere effort at maintaining peace on this side of the Atlantic.

From that day to this the history of relationships among the nations of the New World has been a continuing story of effort to substitute the rule of arbitration, of mediation, of adjudicating and confidence, for the rule of force and war. To the scholarly statesmanship of the Latin American nations the world owes a debt which it has been too tardy in acknowledging. The truth is that they have demonstrated a peculiar genius in the realm of international accommodation and accord. The high and humane doctrines of international relationship which were expounded by such men as Calvo, Drago, Alvarez, Bello, Ruy Barbosa, Rio Branco, and a long list of others are now recognized universally. The record of arbitrations, mediations, and adjudications among the Latin American countries constitutes one of the fairest pages in a century's story of mankind's effort to eliminate the causes of war. Among their international treaties we will find models of effective covenants for the limitation of armament and the prevention of strife in arms.

The present is a time when men and nations are all giving heed to the voice which pleads for peace. Everywhere they are yearning as never before for a leadership that will direct them into the inviting paths of progress, prosperity, and genuine fellowship. A clearer vision has shown them not alone the horrors but the terrible futility of war. In such a time as this, they will do well to turn their thoughts in all sincerity to these lessons from the statesmanship, the experience, and the constant aspiration of the South American nations. The continent which of all the world has known less of war and more of peace than any other through this trying period is well entitled to pride in the service it has rendered to its own people and in the example which it has set before the rest of mankind.

So the present occasion has appealed to me not merely as appropriate for the exchange of the ordinary felicitations but as one on which these contributions of Latin America in moral and intellectual leadership might be given something of the recognition they have deserved. It is not possible to do more than suggest the subject. But even so fragmentary an allusion to such an inviting field, I hope may serve a useful purpose. It would be worth the effort of men and women who seek means of preventing wars and reducing armaments to study the experiences of the American Republics. I commend them to the close attention of all who would like to see peace as nearly as possible assured and war as far as possible outlawed from the earth.

Among the leaders whose courage and genius brought realization of the New World's dream of liberty with independence, none was moved by a deeper horror of war than San Martin. None among his colleagues would give more ardent approval than he to the work of later statesmen who had a vision of a continent dedicated to peace and the true welfare of its people. To his sagacity, more than that of any other man, is due the distribution of the South American Continent within its present national lines, because he possessed the foresight of the statesman along with the qualities of the brilliant soldier and the eager patriot.

As has happened too often to the foremost benefactors of their fellowmen, San Martin was denied during his own life those testimonies of gratitude and reverence which other times and all peoples have been proud to shower upon his memory. I have been told that monuments to him have been dedicated in almost all the capitals of South America. To-day the country which gave him to the cause of freedom is presenting to the Government of my own Nation this statue of him. It is a welcome duty which comes to me, in behalf of the Government and people of the United States, to express their pleasure in accepting it. May it stand through the centuries as an inspiration to all who love liberty. May it ever be an added reminder of the fellowship between the great nation which gives and that which is honored to receive it. May it serve to keep in the minds and hearts of all humankind the realization of the noble and honored place which is held by that republican system of the New World, of which he was one of the foremost creators.

XXIX

True business represents the mutual organized effort of society to minister to the economic requirements of civilization. It is an effort by which men provide for the material needs of each other. While it is not an end in itself, it is the important means for the attainment of a supreme end. It rests squarely on the law of service. It has for its main reliance truth and faith and justice. In its larger sense it is one of the greatest contributing forces to the moral and spiritual advancement of the race.

GOVERNMENT AND BUSINESS

THIS time and place naturally suggest some consideration of commerce in its relation to Government and society.
We are finishing a year which can justly be said to surpass
all others in the overwhelming success of general business.
We are met not only in the greatest American metropolis,
but in the greatest center of population and business that
the world has ever known. If any one wishes to gauge the
power which is represented by the genius of the American
spirit, let him contemplate the wonders which have been
wrought in this region in the short space of 200 years. Not
only does it stand unequaled by any other place on earth,
but it is impossible to conceive of any other place where
it could be equaled.

The foundation of this enormous development rests upon
commerce. New York is an imperial city, but it is not a
seat of government. The empire over which it rules is not
political, but commercial. The great cities of the ancient
world were the seats of both government and industrial
power. The Middle Ages furnished a few exceptions. The
great capitals of former times were not only seats of government but they actually governed. In the modern world
government is inclined to be merely a tenant of the city.
Political life and industrial life flow on side by side, but
practically separated from each other. When we contemplate the enormous power, autocratic and uncontrolled,
which would have been created by joining the authority of
government with the influence of business, we can better

Address before the Chamber of Commerce of the State of New York,
New York City, November 19, 1925.

317

appreciate the wisdom of the fathers in their wise dispensation which made Washington the political center of the country and left New York to develop into its business center. They wrought mightily for freedom.

The great advantages of this arrangement seem to me to be obvious. The only disadvantages which appear lie in the possibility that otherwise business and government might have had a better understanding of each other and been less likely to develop mutual misapprehensions and suspicions. If a contest could be held to determine how much those who are really prominent in our government life know about business, and how much those who are really prominent in our business life know about government, it is my firm conviction that the prize would be awarded to those who are in government life. This is as it ought to be, for those who have the greater authority ought to have the greater knowledge. But it is my even firmer conviction that the general welfare of our country could be very much advanced through a better knowledge by both of those parties of the multifold problems with which each has to deal. While our system gives an opportunity for great benefit by encouraging detachment and breadth of vision which ought not to be sacrificed, it does not have the advantages which could be secured if each had a better conception of their mutual requirements.

While I have spoken of what I believed would be the advantages of a more sympathetic understanding, I should put an even stronger emphasis on the desirability of the largest possible independence between government and business. Each ought to be sovereign in its own sphere. When government comes unduly under the influence of business, the tendency is to develop an administration which closes the door of opportunity; becomes narrow and selfish in its outlook, and results in an oligarchy. When government enters the field of business with its great resources, it has a tendency to extravagance and inefficiency, but, having the power to crush all competitors, likewise closes the door of opportunity and results in monopoly. It is always a problem in a republic to maintain on the one side that efficiency which comes only from trained and skillful management without running into fossilization and autocracy, and to maintain on the other that equality of opportunity which is the result of political and economic liberty without running into dissolution and anarchy. The general results in our country, our freedom and prosperity, warrant the assertion that our system of institutions has been advancing in the right direction in the attempt to solve these problems. We have order, opportunity, wealth, and progress.

While there has been in the past and will be in the future a considerable effort in this country of different business interests to attempt to run the Government in such a way as to set up a system of privilege, and while there have been and will be those who are constantly seeking to commit the Government to a policy of infringing upon the domain of private business, both of these efforts have been very largely discredited, and with reasonable vigilance on the part of the people to preserve their freedom do not now appear to be dangerous.

When I have been referring to business, I have used the word in its all-inclusive sense to denote alike the employer and employee, the production of agriculture and industry, the distribution of transportation and commerce, and the service of finance and banking. It is the work of the world. In modern life, with all its intricacies, business has come to hold a very dominant position in the thoughts of all enlightened peoples. Rightly understood, this is not a criticism, but a compliment. In its great economic organization it does not represent, as some have hastily concluded, a mere desire to minister to selfishness. The New York

Chamber of Commerce is not made up of men merely animated with a purpose to get the better of each other. It
is something far more important than a sordid desire for
gain. It could not successively succeed on that basis. It
is dominated by a more worthy impulse; its rests on a
higher law. True business represents the mutual organized effort of society to minister to the economic requirements of civilization. It is an effort by which men provide
for the material needs of each other. While it is not an
end in itself, it is the important means for the attainment
of a supreme end. It rests squarely on the law of service.
It has for its main reliance truth and faith and justice. In
its larger sense it is one of the greatest contributing forces
to the moral and spiritual advancement of the race.

It is the important and righteous position that business
holds in relation to life which gives warrant to the great
interest which the National Government constantly exercises for the promotion of its success. This is not exercised
as has been the autocratic practice abroad of directly supporting and financing different business projects, except in
case of great emergency; but we have rather held to a democratic policy of cherishing the general structure of business while holding its avenues open to the widest competition, in order that its opportunities and its benefits might
be given the broadest possible participation. While it is
true that the Government ought not to be and is not committed to certain methods of acquisition which, while par-
taking of the nature of unfair practices, try to masquerade
under the guise of business, the Government is and ought
to be thoroughly committed to every endeavor of production and distribution which is entitled to be designated as
true business. Those who are so engaged, instead of regarding the Government as their opponent and enemy,
ought to regard it as their vigilant supporter and friend.

It is only in exceptional instances that this means a

change on the part of the national administration so much as it means a change on the part of trade. Except for the requirements of safety, health and taxation, the law enters very little into the work of production. It is mostly when we come to the problems of distribution that we meet the more rigid exactions of legislation. The main reason why certain practices in this direction have been denounced is because they are a species of unfair competition on the one hand or tend to monopoly and restraint of trade on the other. The whole policy of the Government in its system of opposition to monopoly, and its public regulation of transportation and trade, has been animated by a desire to have business remain business. We are politically free people and must be an economically free people.

It is my belief that the whole material development of our country has been enormously stimulated by reason of the general insistence on the part of the public authorities that economic effort ought not to partake of privilege, and that business should be unhampered and free. This could never have been done under a system of freight-rate discriminations or monopolistic trade associations. These might have enriched a few for a limited period, but they never would have enriched the country, while on the firmer foundation of justice we have achieved even more ample individual fortunes and a perfectly unprecedented era of general prosperity. This has resulted in no small part from the general acceptance on the part of those who own and control the wealth of the Nation, that it is to be used not to oppress but to serve. It is that policy, sometimes perhaps imperfectly expressed and clumsily administered, that has animated the National Government. In its observance there is unlimited opportunity for progress and prosperity.

It would be difficult, if not impossible, to estimate the contribution which government makes to business. It is notorious that where the government is bad, business is bad. The mere fundamental precepts of the administration of justice, the providing of order and security, are price-less. The prime element in the value of all property is the knowledge that its peaceful enjoyment will be publicly defended. If disorder should break out in your city, if there should be a conviction extending over any length of time that the rights of persons and property could no longer be protected by law, the value of your tall buildings would shrink to about the price of what are now water fronts of old Carthage or what are now corner lots in ancient Baby-lon. It is really the extension of these fundamental rights that the Government is constantly attempting to apply to modern business. It wants its rightful possessors to rest in security, it wants any wrongs that they may suffer to have a legal remedy, and it is all the time striving through administrative machinery to prevent in advance the in-fliction of injustice.

These undoubtedly represent policies which are wise and sound and necessary. That they have often been mis-applied and many times run into excesses, nobody can deny. Regulation has often become restriction, and in-spection has too frequently been little less than obstruc-tion. This was the natural result of those times in the past when there were practices in business which warranted severe disapprobation. It was only natural that when these abuses were reformed by an aroused public opinion a great deal of prejudice which ought to have been discriminating and directed only at certain evil practices came to include almost the whole domain of business, especially where it had been gathered into large units. After the abuses had been discontinued the prejudice remained to produce a large amount of legislation, which, however well meant in its application to trade, undoubtedly hampered but did not improve. It is this misconception and misapplication, disturbing and wasteful in their results, which the National Government is attempting to avoid. Proper regulation and control are disagreeable and expensive. They represent the suffering that the just must endure because of the unjust. They are a part of the price which must be paid to promote the cause of economic justice.

Undoubtedly if public vigilance were relaxed, the generation to come might suffer a relapse. But the present generation of business almost universally throughout its responsible organization and management has shown every disposition to correct its own abuses with as little intervention of the Government as possible. This position is recognized by the public, and due to the appreciation of the needs which the country has for great units of production in time of war, and to the better understanding of the service which they perform in time of peace, resulting very largely from the discussion of our tax problems, a new attitude of the public mind is distinctly discernible toward great aggregations of capital. Their prosperity goes very far to insure the prosperity of all the country. The contending elements have each learned a most profitable lesson.

This development has left the Government free to advance from the problems of reform and repression to those of economy and construction. A very large progress is being made in these directions. Our country is in a state of unexampled and apparently sound and well distributed prosperity. It did not gain wealth, as some might hastily conclude, as a result of the war. Here and there individuals may have profited greatly, but the country as a whole was a heavy loser. Forty billions of the wealth of the Nation was directly exhausted, while the indirect expenditure and depreciation can not be estimated. The Government appreciated that the only method of regeneration lay in economy and production. It has followed a policy of economy in national expenditures. By an enormous reduction in taxation it has released great amounts of capital for use in productive effort. It has sought to stimulate domestic production by a moderate application of the system of protective tariff duties. The results of these efforts are known to all the world.

Another phase of this progress is not so well understood, but upon its continuance depends our future ability to meet the competition of the lower standards of living in foreign countries. During the past five years the Department of Commerce has unceasingly directed attention to the necessity for the elimination of waste. This effort has been directed toward better cooperation to improve efficiency in the use of labor and materials in all branches of business. This has been sought by the necessary cooperative action among individual concerns within industrial groups, and between producers and consumers. This does not imply any diminution of fair competition or any violation of the laws against restraint of trade. In fact, these proposals have been a protection to the smaller units of business and a most valuable asset alike to the producer, wage earner and consumer.

The result of the realization of these wastes and the large cooperative effort that has been instituted in the community to cure them, whether with the assistance of the Government departments or by independent action of the groups, has been the most profound factor in this recovery made in the past five years. There can be no question that great wastes have been eliminated by these activities in the business community through such actions as the abolition of car shortages; by improved equipment and methods of management of our railways; the cooperation with shippers to save delays; the remarkable advance in electrification of the country with all of its economies in labor and coal; the provision of better economic and statistical information as to production, stocks, and consumption of all commodities in order that producers and consumers may better adjust supply to demand, thereby eliminating speculation and loss; the great progress made in the technology of standardizing quality and dimensions in heavy manufactured products like building materials and commodities generally which do not involve problems of style or individuality; the reduction of seasonal employment in the construction and other industries and of losses through fire and through traffic accidents; advancement of commercial arbitration; development of farmers' cooperatives for the more economical and stable marketing of farm produce; and in general the elimination of waste due to lost motion and material throughout our whole economic fabric.

All this represents a movement as important as that of twenty years ago for the regulation of corporations and conservation of our natural resources. This effort for conservation of use of materials and conservation of energy in which our whole country has engaged during these five years has been in no small part responsible for the rich reward in the increasing comfort and living standards of the people. But in addition to bringing about a condition in which the Government debt is being rapidly liquidated while at the same time taxes are greatly reduced, capital has become abundant and prosperity reigns. The most remarkable results of economy and the elimination of waste are shown in the wage and commodity indexes. In 1920 wages were about 100 per cent above the pre-war rates and the average wholesale price of commodities was about 120 per cent above the pre-war rates. A steady increase in the wage index took place, so that during the last year it was 120 per cent above the pre-war rate. As the cost of our production is so largely a matter of wages, and as tax returns show that for the last year profits were ample, it would naturally have been expected that the prices of commodities would have increased. Yet during this period the average wholesale price level of commodities declined from 120 per cent above the pre-war level that it was in 1920, to only 57 per cent above the pre-war level in 1925. Thus, as a result of greater economy and efficiency, and the elimination of waste in the conduct of the National Government and of the business of the country, prices went down while wages went up. The wage earner receives more, while the dollar of the consumer will purchase more. The significance and importance of this result can not be overestimated.

This is real and solid progress. No one can deny that it represents an increase in national efficiency. It must be maintained. Great as the accomplishments have been, they are yet but partly completed. We need further improvement in transportation facilities by development of inland waterways; we need railroad consolidations; we need further improvement of our railway terminals for more economical distribution of commodities in the great congested centers; we need reorganization of Government departments; we need still larger extension of electrification; in general, we need still further effort against all the various categories of waste which the Department of Commerce has enumerated and so actively attacked, for in this direction lies not only increased economic progress but the maintenance of that progress against foreign competition. There is still plenty of work for business to do.

By these wise policies, pursued with tremendous economic effort, our country has reached its present prosperous condition. The people have been willing to work because they have had something to work for. The per capita production has greatly increased. Out of our surplus savings we have been able to advance great sums for refinancing the Old World and developing the New. While Europe has attracted more public attention, Latin America, Japan, and even Australia, have been very large participators in these loans. If rightly directed, they ought to be of benefit to both lender and borrower. If used to establish industry and support commerce abroad, through adding to the wealth and productive capacity of those countries, they create their own security and increase consuming power to the probable advantage of our trade. But when used in ways that are not productive, like the maintenance of great military establishments or to meet municipal expenditures which should either be eliminated by government economy or supplied by taxation, they do not appear to serve a useful purpose and ought to be discouraged. Our bankers have a great deal of responsibility in relation to the soundness of these loans when they undertake to invest the savings of our country abroad. I should regret very much to see our possession of resources which are available to meet needs in other countries be the cause of any sentiment of envy or unfriendliness toward us. It ought everywhere to be welcomed with rejoicing and considered as a part of the good fortune of the entire world that such an economic reservoir exists here which can be made available in case of need.

Everyone knows that it was our resources that saved Europe from a complete collapse immediately following the armistice. Without the benefit of our credit an appalling famine would have prevailed over great areas. In accordance with the light of all past history, disorder and revolution, with the utter breaking down of all legal restraints and the loosing of all the passions which had been aroused by four years of conflict, would have rapidly followed. Others did what they could, and no doubt made larger proportionate sacrifices, but it was the credits and food which we supplied that saved the situation.

When the work of restoring the fiscal condition of Europe began, it was accomplished again with our assistance. When Austria determined to put her financial house in order, we furnished a part of the capital. When Germany

sought to establish a sound fiscal condition, we again contributed a large proportion of the necessary gold loan.
Without this, the reparations plan would have utterly failed.
Germany could not otherwise have paid. The armies of
occupation would have gone on increasing international
irritation and ill will. It was our large guarantee of credit
that assisted Great Britain to return to a gold basis. What
we have done for France, Italy, Belgium, Czechoslovakia,
Poland, and other countries, is all a piece of the same endeavor. These efforts and accomplishments, whether they
be appreciated at home or received with gratitude abroad,
which have been brought about by the business interests of
our country, constitute an enormous world service. Others
have made plans and adopted agreements for future action
which hold a rank of great importance. But when we
come to the consideration of what has been done, when we
turn aside from what has been promised, to examine what
has been performed, no positive and constructive accomplishment of the past five years compares with the support
which America has contributed to the financial stability of
the world. It clearly marks a new epoch.

This holds a distinctly higher rank than a mere barter
and sale. It reaches above the ordinary business transaction into a broader realm. America has disbanded her
huge armies and reduced her powerful fleet, but in attempting to deal justly through the sharing of our financial
resources we have done more for peace than we could have
done with all our military power. Peace, we know, rests
to a great extent upon justice, but it is very difficult for
the public mind to divorce justice from economic opportunity. The problem for which we have been attempting
a solution is in the first instance to place the people of the
earth back into avenues of profitable employment. It
was necessary to restore hope, to renew courage. A great
contribution to this end has been made with American

money. The work is not all done yet. No doubt it will develop that this has not been accomplished without some mistakes, but the important fact remains that when the world needed to be revived we did respond. As nations see their way to a safer economic existence, they will see their way to a more peaceful existence. Possessed of the means to meet personal and public obligations, people are re-establishing their self-respect. The financial strength of America has contributed to the spiritual restoration of the world. It has risen into the domain of true business.

Accompanying these efforts to assist in rehabilitation have lately come the negotiations for the settlement of our foreign debts. Ten nations have already made settlements for $6,383,411,669 of these debts, exclusive of accrued interest. The principal sums and interest which have been funded and are to be paid to the United States aggregate $15,056,486,000. There remain nine nations, with debts in the principal amount of $3,673,342,362, which have not yet been settled. Of the nine nations, France represents $3,340,000,000, Greece $15,000,000, and Yugoslavia $51,-000,000. Of the remaining six, Rumania is now negotiating a settlement, Nicaragua is paying currently, and a moratorium for twenty years has been granted Austria by act of Congress. Armenia has ceased to exist as a nation, the Government of Russia has not been recognized, and Liberia owes but $26,000.

It has been the belief of the Government that no permanent stabilization of European finances and European currency can be accomplished without a definite adjustment of these obligations. While we realize that it is for our advantage to have these debts paid, it is also realized that it is greatly for the advantage of our debtors to have them finally liquidated. We created these values and sent them abroad in a period of about two years. We are extending the time for their return over a term of sixty-two years.

While settlements already made and ratified by Congress, and those which will be presented for ratification, are very generous, I believe they will be alike beneficial to ourselves and the countries concerned. They maintain the principle of the integrity of international obligations. They help foreign governments to reestablish their fiscal operations and will contribute to the economic recovery of their people. They will assist both in the continuance of friendly relations, which are always jeopardized by unsettled differences, and the mutual improvement of trade opportunities by increasing the prosperity of the countries involved.

The working out of these problems of regulation, Government economy, the elimination of waste in the use of human effort and of materials, conservation and the proper investment of our savings both at home and abroad, is all a part of the mighty task which was imposed upon mankind of subduing the earth. America must either perform her full share in the accomplishment of this great world destiny or fail. For almost three centuries we were intent upon our domestic development. We sought the help of the people and the wealth of other lands by which to increase our numerical strength and augment our national fortune. We have grown exceedingly great in population and in riches. This power and this prosperity we can continue for ourselves if we will but proceed with moderation. If our people will but use those resources which have been intrusted to them, whether of command over large numbers of men or of command over large investments of capital, not selfishly but generously, not to exploit others but to serve others, there will be no doubt of an increasing production and distribution of wealth.

All of these efforts represent the processes of reducing our domestic and foreign relations to a system of law. They consist of a determination of clear and definite rules of action. It is a civilizing and humanizing method adopted by means of conference, discussion, deliberation, and determination. If it is to have any continuing success, or any permanent value, it will be because it has not been brought about by one will compelling another by force, but has resulted from men reasoning together. It has sought to remove compulsion from the business life of the country and from our relationship with other nations. It has sought to bestow a greater freedom upon our own people and upon the people of the world. We have worshiped the ideals of force long enough. We have turned to worship at the true shrine of understanding and reason.

In our domestic affairs we have adopted practical methods for the accomplishment of our ideals. We have translated our aspirations into appropriate actions. We have followed the declaration that we believe in justice, by establishing tribunals that would insure the administration of justice. What we have been able to do in this respect in relation to the different States of our Union, we ought to encourage and support in its proper application in relation to the different nations of the world. With our already enormous and constantly increasing interests abroad, there are constantly accumulating reasons why we should signify our adherence to the Permanent Court of International Justice. Mindful of our determination to avoid all interference in the political affairs, which do not concern us, of other nations, I can think of no more reassuring action than the declaration of America that it will whole-heartedly join with others in the support of the tribunal for the administration of international justice which they have created. I can conceive of nothing that we could do, which involves assuming so few obligations on our part, that would be likely to prove of so much value to the world. Beyond its practical effect, which might be somewhat small, it would have a sentimental effect which would be tremendous. It would be public notice that the enormous influences of our country were to be cast upon the side of the enlightening processes of civilization. It would be the beginning of a new world spirit.

This is the land of George Washington. We can do no less than work toward the realization of his hope. It ought to be our ambition to see the institutions which he founded grow in the blessings which they bestow upon our own citizens and increase in the good which their influence casts upon all the world. He did not hesitate to meet peril or encounter danger or make sacrifices. There is no cause which can be supported by any other methods. We can not listen to the counsels of perfection; we can not pursue a timorous policy; we can not avoid the obligations of a common humanity. We must meet our perils; we must encounter our dangers; we must make our sacrifices; or history will recount that the works of Washington have failed. I do not believe the future is to be dismayed by that record. The truth and faith and justice of the ancient days have not departed from us.

XXX

America is not without a true nobility, but it is not supported by privilege. It rests on worth.

THE FARMER AND THE NATION

No one can travel across the vast area that lies between the Alleghenies and the Rockies without being thoroughly impressed with the enormous expansion of American agriculture. Other sections of our country, acre for acre, are just as important and just as productive, but it is in this region that the cultivation of the land holds its most dominant position. It is to serve the farmers of this great open country that teeming cities have arisen, great stretches of navigation have been opened, a mighty network of railways has been constructed, a fast increasing mileage of highways has been laid out, and modern inventions have stretched their lines of communication among all the various communities and into nearly every home. Agriculture holds a position in this country that it was never before able to secure anywhere else on earth.

It is the development which has taken place within this area, mostly within the last seventy-five years, which has given agriculture a new standing in the world. By bringing the tillage of the soil under a new technique it has given to the people on the farm a new relationship to commerce, industry, and society. The ownership of land has always been a mark of privilege and distinction, but in other times and places the laborious effort of farming, the hard work of cultivating the soil—which was done almost entirely by hand—the comparative isolation of rural existence, was traditionally an unattractive life assigned to the serf and the uncultured peasant. It still partakes of that nature in

Address before the annual convention of the American Farm Bureau Federation, Chicago, Ill., December 7, 1925.

most countries.   But in America the farm has long since ceased to be associated with a mode of life that could be called rustic.   It has become a great industrial enterprise, requiring a broad knowledge in its management, a technical skill in its labor, intricate machinery in its processes, and trained merchandising in its marketings.   Agriculture in America has been raised to the rank of a profession.   It does not draw any artificial support from industry or from the Government.   It rests squarely on a foundation of its own.   It is independent.

The place which agriculture holds to-day in this country, superior to that which it ever held before in time of peace in this or any other land, is by reason of its very eminence one of increasing exactions and difficulties.   It does not require much talent or any great foresight to live on an inferior scale, limited and impoverished, nor does it evoke much eulogy, but to maintain freedom and independence, to rise in the economic scale to the ownership and profitable management of a great property amid all the perils of our competitive life, requires a high degree of industry and ability.   Those who achieve that position in a community will always be entitled to the highest commendation.   Whatever other obstacles the American people have had to meet and overcome, of every station in life, they have never permitted themselves to be hampered by a condition of dependence.   As what they have had was secured not by favor or by bounty, but by their own efforts, no one else has had any power to deprive them of it.   Unencumbered by any special artificial support, they have stood secure on their own foundation.   America is not without a true nobility, but it is not supported by privilege.   It rests on worth.

It is our farm life that is particularly representative of this standard of American citizenship.   It is made up of many different types and races; it includes many different modes of thought and living. Stretching from the North, with its months of frost, to the Gulf, with its perpetual summer, it embraces a wide variety of production. But it is all a partaker of the same high measure of achievement and character. It rises in its importance above the products of the land and puts a stamp of its own upon the quality of our people. It is not merely for a supply of food that we look to the farms, but as a never-failing source, if others become exhausted, from which we can always replenish the manhood and womanhood of the Nation. It is for this reason that our whole country entertains the greatest solicitude for the welfare of the people who make up our agricultural population. The importance of their continued success and progress can not be overestimated. It affects not only the material prosperity but reaches beyond that into the moral and spiritual life of America.

It was the people of this stamp and character who were mainly instrumental in founding American institutions. It was well on into the nineteenth century before the great industrial development of our country began. In the old days there were some professional men and there were the clergy who exercised in a high degree an inspired leadership not only in the religious and educational, but to a marked extent in the political, life of their day. But the people were of the farm. Their living came from the soil. Their sturdy industry, their determination to be free, resulted in no small part from their occupation and mode of life. Wherever there is a farm, there is the greatest opportunity for a true home. It was the loyalty and perseverance bred of the home life of the American farmer that supported Washington through seven years of conflict and provided the necessary self-restraint to translate his victory into the abiding institutions of freedom. It is the spirit of those homes that our country must forever cherish.

But the gratitude of America, and I think of the whole

world, is due not only to "the embattled farmers" who stood at Concord bridge and "fired the shot heard round the world," but to those tillers of the soil of the great prairie States, prophets and pioneers of freedom, who rose to power in time to make it possible for Lincoln to save the Union, and also to the informed, improved, and well-equipped agriculture of our own day, which, while giving generously of their own manhood and womanhood, put forth those stupendous efforts which provided food, cotton, wool, and other materials that turned the tide for the cause of liberty in the Great War. It is the existence of this superb power, both of resources and of people, which has its home in the great open country, that has made possible not only the independence and freedom of our own land and the extension of liberty throughout the world, but has furnished the foundation on which has been built the great expansion in the industrial and commercial life of the Nation. Our statesmanship can be dedicated to no more worthy purpose than the perpetuation of this high standard of American farm life.

All of these results would appear to lead to the inevitable conclusion that to a very large extent the underlying support to the strength and character and greatness of America has been furnished by the strength and character and greatness of its agriculture. Our country has been developed under the influence of a new spirit. In the early beginnings of organized society the main form of wealth which was plentiful consisted of land. It was almost the sole source of production. Always in theory, and usually in practice, all land belonged to the Crown. It was the custom for the ruler to bestow upon his retainers not only landed estates, but to provide in addition the serfs who were attached to the soil, in order that they might supply the necessary labor for its productivity. The workers in the field were held in servitude, while their masters usually lived many miles from the land, sometimes in their castles, sometimes in towns and cities. This was the established condition all over the Old World. The position of the country thus became stationary. It was in the cities and towns, where opportunity came for exchange of ideas and educational advancement, that there started that progress toward freedom and self-government which marked the beginning of the modern age. The importance of the cities and towns became predominant. Even after freedom was granted to the serfs, the tillers of the soil never became a great influence. Their interests were always subordinated to the stronger, more aggressive life of the industrial population and of the ruling classes.

But America never fully came under this blighting influence. It was a different type of individual that formed the great bulk of our early settlers. They gained their livelihood by cultivating the soil, but there was no large and overmastering city or industrial population. The expansion of our country down to almost as late as 1880 was an agricultural expansion. A large majority of our inhabitants were engaged in that occupation. They not only tilled the soil, but they owned it. They not only directed the Government, but they made it. The fertile lands and generous homestead laws under American institutions all worked together to produce an entirely new position of place and power for agriculture. When there was added to this the marvelous inventions of farm machinery which have come into modern life, it made it possible to establish here the first agricultural empire which did not rest upon an oppressed peasantry. This was a stupendous achievement.

Following this came the vast business growth which brought great changes. The town and industrial population for the first time began to exceed that of the farms. From the surplus of food products requiring foreign markets we began to reach something like a balance between domestic production and consumption. Before 1910, so wise a man as James J. Hill expressed the opinion that in the near future we should be importers of wheat.

Under normal conditions Mr. Hill might have been correct, but the World War intervened. The enormous demand from abroad brought the high prices which so stimulated production that it reached a new record in amount and value. Without this service, famine undoubtedly would have prevailed over wide areas. This resulted in a great inflation and in an overproduction, reaching its summit in 1919, which was followed by the inevitable deflation of 1920 and 1921. The best economic authority tells us this was inevitable. Whether it was or not, it came. It afflicted both agriculture and industry. The values of manufacturing plants and their stocks on hand went down, their orders were canceled, their operations ceased, and the buying capacity of their wage earners being greatly reduced, the consumption of food products declined, causing a fall in prices that reached back to the farm. The resulting losses have never been fully recovered either in industry or agriculture, but starting from the low point of 1920 and 1921 both have made progress and from every indication appear to be entering an era of prosperity.

It has seemed to me desirable to consider thus briefly the development of our American agriculture, in order that by a better understanding of the method of its progress and the position it now holds we may better comprehend its needs and better estimate what the future promises for it. Everyone knows that the farmer, who is often least able to bear it, went through the most drastic deflation. Considered as a whole, his position has steadily improved since 1921. I do not mean that land values or prices have reached their former level. That was not to be expected. But I do mean that, generally speaking, the present business of farming as a whole is beginning to be profitable. Of course there are exceptions to be made of localities, individuals, and crops. Some people would grow poor on a mountain of gold, while others would make a good living on a rock. We can not bend our course to meet the exceptions; we must treat agriculture as a whole, and if, as a whole, it can be placed in a prosperous condition the exceptions will tend to eliminate themselves.

There have been discussions which seem to indicate some fear that our agriculture is becoming decadent, that it has already reached its highest point, and that, becoming unprofitable, it is likely to diminish. Nothing in the appearance of the country or of its people as I have traveled over it has seemed to indicate any deterioration, nor do I find anything in the farm census and reports that warrants this conclusion.

It is true that there is an increasing interchange of population between the city and the country. With the coming of the automobile many of the city people are moving out into the country, and with the increasing use of machinery some of those formerly employed on the farm have been released for employment in the industries. For the past fifteen years urban population has been increasing, while farm population and the number of farms have slightly decreased. This has reversed the condition that existed before that period. But this is only a part of the story.

The real question is not the numbers employed but the amount of production. If that should appear to be inadequate to meet our requirements for food and raw materials, if the morale of the farmers should be breaking down, the situation might be serious. Such does not appear to be the fact. In intelligence, in education, in the general standards of living, farm life was never so well equipped as it is today. In the past forty-five years, which roughly marks our great industrial development, the index number of production rose from 100 to 237, while that for population is estimated to be but 226. Production has outrun population, according to the statistics of the Harvard Service. While the number of farms and people engaged in farming was slightly less in 1924 than in 1910, production in 1923 and 1924 was 15 per cent greater than in 1910. Fewer people but more production means each person on the farm will receive more.

It is not only production, however, but price that is important to the farmer. The value of his produce for 1924, excluding crops fed to animals, was about $12,136,000,000. The estimates for the present year are about the same. This compares with $3,549,000,000 in 1900. According to estimates, the number of people on farms in 1924 was about 10 per cent greater than in 1900. The amount of money received was about 350 per cent greater. But as the general price level of all commodities had greatly advanced, measured in purchasing power the amount received was only about 90 per cent greater. This means that 110 per cent of people engaged in agriculture received 190 per cent more in 1924 than they did in 1900. While it is true that there was a great decline in farm prices in 1920 and 1921, and an even greater decline in the purchasing power of farm produce compared with other commodities, yet since that time farm prices have risen more rapidly than other commodities, so that the purchasing power of farm produce has risen also. The tendency appears to be to bring agriculture as a whole back to the same relative economic position that it occupied before the war. While general production, prices, and living conditions on the farm are improving, there is little ground for fear that agriculture is becoming decadent; yet some areas are still depressed; debts and taxes still remain.

Although it is gratifying to know that farm conditions as a whole are encouraging, yet we ought not to cease our efforts for their constant improvement. We can not claim that they have reached perfection anywhere, and in too many instances there is still much distress. Various suggestions of artificial relief have been made. Production has been ample, but prices compared with the war era have been very much reduced, although they are now considerably improved. The proposals made have, therefore, had the purpose of increasing prices.

One of the methods by which this has been sought, though put forward chiefly as an emergency measure as I understand from its proponents, was to have corporations organized through which the Government would directly or indirectly fix prices or engage in buying and selling farm produce. This would be a dangerous undertaking, and as the emergency is not so acute, it seems at present to have lost much of its support. No matter how it is disguised, the moment the Government engages in buying and selling, by that act it is fixing prices. Moreover, it would apparently destroy cooperative associations and all other marketing machinery, for no one can compete with the Government. Ultimately it would end the independence which the farmers of this country enjoy as a result of centuries of struggle and prevent the exercise of their own judgment and control in cultivating their land and marketing their produce.

Government control can not be divorced from political control. The overwhelming interest of the consumer, not the smaller interest of the producer, would be sure to dominate in the end. I am reliably informed that the secretary of agriculture of a great foreign power has recently fixed the wages of farm labor in his country at less than $5 per week. The government price is not always a high price. Unless we fix correspoding prices for other commodities, a high fixed price for agriculture would simply stimulate overproduction that would end in complete collapse. However attractive this proposal was at first thought, careful consideration of it has led to much opposition on the part of the farmers. They realize that even the United States Government is not strong enough, either directly or indirectly, to fix prices which would constantly guarantee success. They are opposed to submitting themselves to the control of a great Government bureaucracy. They prefer the sound policy of maintaining their freedom and their own initiative as individuals, or to limit them only as they voluntarily form group associations. They do not wish to put the Government into the farming business.

Others have thought that the tariff rates were unfavorable to the farmer. If this should be a fact, it ought to be corrected. Let us examine our imports. Last year their gross value was $3,610,000,000, but $2,080,000,000, or 57%10 per cent, came in wholly free of duty. This free list was constructed especially to favor the farmer, and contains more than 50 articles which he purchases, like fertilizer, leather harnesses, farm machinery, coffee, binder twine, barbed wire, and gasoline.

Of the $1,530,000,000 of goods paying imports, $780,000,000 was upon agricultural products, levied solely to protect the farmer, including animal and dairy products, grain, flax, wool, sugar, nuts, citrus fruits, and many others. If any farmer wants to get an accurate and full list of his products which are protected and his purchases which come in free, let him go to his public library and consult Official Document No. 33, comparing the last three tariff acts. Thus 80 per cent of our imports either come in free or pay a duty to protect the farmer. This must be further increased by $250,000,000 more of imported luxuries like diamonds, fine rugs, silks, cut glass, jewelry, and mahogany. These items can not affect the prosperity of the farmer. This brings the total of imports up to 88 per cent which are either free, or luxuries, or protected to help the farmer, and leaves only 12 per cent of our imports upon which the agricultural industry pays any part of the tariff.

But, on the other hand, our industrial and city population pays the tariff on the $780,000,000 worth of agricultural imports and also participates in the $500,000,000 worth of imports outside of luxuries. While the farmer pays part of the duties on 12 per cent of our imports which do not benefit him, industry and commerce pay part of the duty on 36 per cent of the imports which do not benefit them.

But if we take all that the farmer buys for his household and farm operation and subtract from it articles dutiable to protect the farmer, the free list, and luxuries, we should have left less than 10 per cent of his expenditures. This means that less than 10 per cent of farm purchases are at an increased cost which is adverse to the farmer. Admitting that the price of these purchases is increased by the full amount of the duty, this means that the total adverse cost to the farmer on account of the tariff is only between 2 per cent and 3 per cent of his purchases.

Many economists consider that even this calculation as to the contribution of our farmers to the tariff is overestimated. As their expenditures include many items for labor and service on which there is no duty, the proportion of total expenditure on dutiable articles outside the three lists above mentioned is not 10 per cent, but only 3 per cent or 4 per cent of his total expenditures. Thus, even assuming that the farmer pays tariff on this ratio of goods, his expenditures would only be increased by one-third of 3 per cent or 4 per cent, or not over 1⅓ per cent.

On the other side, protection is a great benefit to agriculture as a whole. The $780,000,000 of agricultural produce imported last year had to pay $260,000,000 for the privilege of coming in to compete with our own farm production. If these were admitted free of duty, they would no doubt greatly increase in volume, reduce present farm prices, and result in much lower standards of living on our farms. We are also exporters as well as importers. Protection greatly aids diversification and so eliminates an unprofitable surplus. Under our tariff our flax acreage has increased from 1,641,000 in 1921 to 3,093,000 in 1925. Much of this would otherwise have been devoted to wheat, increasing the surplus and further demoralizing that market. The same principle holds in relation to sugar, wool, and other agricultural products.

It has been thought that protection does not help agricultural products. Any study of dairy products, flax, wool, and the many other commodities, will demonstrate that it does. Even wheat, where we are exporters, shows its effect. If we take Buffalo, to secure a point of common contact, American No. 1 Dark Northern is 25 cents to 35 cents higher than Canadian, No. 2 Dark Hard Winter is 37 cents to 42 cents higher, and No. 2 Red would be 45 cents to 46 cents higher. Contract wheat for future delivery in Chicago has been usually as high as future deliveries in Liverpool, although the difference in freight is about 20 cents a bushel, which means that our wheat is now about that much above world price levels. The question is complicated with different grades and qualities, some of which do not show the same differences.

But the largest benefits accruing to the farmer come from supplying him with home markets. What the farmer raises must either be sold at home or sent abroad. Our per capita consumption of butter, sugar, meats, eggs, milk, and tobacco is far above those of foreign countries. When the depression of 1920 came and 5,000,000 of our wage earners were unemployed, their consumption of the more expensive agricultural supplies, such as animal products, fell 18 per cent below what it had been before and what it became again when employment increased. This was more than the amount of our exports. Prosperity in our industries is of more value to the farmer than the whole export market for foodstuffs. Protection has contributed in our country to making employment plentiful with the highest wages and highest standards of living in the world, which is of inestimable benefit to both our agricultural and industrial population. General economic stability is of the utmost importance to the farmer, and a depression in industry with the attendant unemployment would do the farmer an incalculable injury.

If the price fixing and tariff revision do not seem to be helpful, there are other proposals that do promise improvements. For financing the farmer we are developing the farm loan and intermediate credit banks. These have put out about $1,200,000,000 of loans at moderate rates to about 350,000 farmers. In addition, there is the general banking system, National and State. All of these agencies need to give more informed attention to farm needs. They need more energy in administration. They should be equipped to supply not only credit but sound business advice, and the farmers to a much better extent should learn to use all these facilities.

For a more orderly marketing calculated to secure a better range of prices the cooperative movement promises the greatest success. Already they are handling $2,500,000,000 of farm produce, or nearly one-fifth of the annual production. The disposition of surplus produce has been discussed. If by this is meant the constant raising of a larger supply than is needed, it is difficult to conceive of any remedy except reduced production in any such commodity. But there are, of course, accidental surpluses due to more favorable weather conditions, which are unavoidable and which ought to be managed so that they can be spread over a year or two without depressing prices. The initiative of the farmers themselves, with such assistance as can be given them by the Government without assuming responsibility for business management, through financing and through the cooperative movement, would appear to be a wise method of solving this problem. Of course, I should be willing to approve any plan that can be devised in accordance with sound economic principles.

To have agriculture worth anything, it must rest on an independent business basis. It can not at the same time be part private business and part Government business. I believe the Government ought to give it every assistance, but it ought to leave it as the support, the benefit, and the business of the people. The interest which the National Government takes in agriculture is manifest by an appropriation of about $140,000,000 a year, which is nearly one-fifth of our total expenditure, exclusive of the Post Office, prior to the war. I do not need to recount what is being done for education and good roads, for opening up our waterways, or the enormous activities of the Department of Agriculture which reach to almost every farmer in the land.

The most important development of late years has been the cooperative movement. With the economic information furnished by the department, which was of such great value to the hog and potato industries for the last year or two, with better warehouse and storage facilities and a better credit structure, much can be done to take care of the ordinary surplus. With a production influenced by information from the department, with adequate storage, supplied with necessary credit and the orderly marketing effected through cooperative action, agriculture could be placed on a sound and independent business basis. While the Government ought not to undertake to control or direct, it should supplement and assist all efforts in this direction. The leaders in the cooperative movement, with the advice of the Department of Agriculture, have prepared what is believed to be an adequate bill embodying these principles, which will be presented to the Congress for enactment. I propose actively and energetically to assist the farmers to promote their welfare through cooperative marketing.

Under the working out of the provisions of this bill the farmers would have the active and energetic assistance of the Government in meeting the problem of surplus production. Through consultation and conference the best experts of the country would be employed as the needs require and methods of storage, credit, and marketing would be devised. The agencies created would have at their disposal the active cooperation of the great organizations of the Departments of Agriculture, Commerce, and Federal banking. Their representatives at home and abroad would be engaged in locating and supplying domestic and foreign markets. The fundamental soundness of this proposal rests on the principle that it is helping the farmer to help himself. Already the cooperative effort in raisins and other products has met with marked success by adopting this plan.

It would be a great mistake to underestimate the difficulties under which the farmers labor. They are entitled to all the sympathy and help which the Government can give them. But I feel they are also entitled to consider the encouraging features of their situation. Human nature is on their side. We are all consumers of food. The more prosperous we become, the more we consume of the higher-priced products. In the past, farm prices have always tended to get the better of industrial prices. In the period from 1820 to 1860 there was a general rise of all commodities, but farm prices increased about 50 per cent more than other commodities. After the Civil War, from the seventies to 1896, there was a decline in all commodities, but farm prices declined less, so that their purchasing power actually increased. From 1896 to 1913, according to the Bureau of

Labor Statistics, the index number of farm prices rose 82 per cent while that of other prices rose but 37 per cent. It was this great increase in the price of food products which brought about the complaint and discussion of the high cost of living, which everyone will recall became acute about 1911 and remained a problem of economic adjustment unsolved when the World War began.

With the coming of the great conflict an entire transformation took place. The price of all commodities rose and the price of land rose. There was a great temptation to expand. Farmers bought more land at very high prices. Then came the terrible world depression which left many involved in great debts and everybody with shrunken land values. Farm produce decreased in price faster than other commodities. These debts and shrunken values still remain as a great burden. On top of them are the war taxes which the Nation has greatly reduced, but which the local communities still tend to increase.

It is this burden which is causing distress, but history is again showing signs of repeating itself. In 1921 the price of farm produce reached its low point. According to the Department of Agriculture, however, the end of this four-year period sees the price of farm products substantially increased. Much of the debts and taxes remain, but with the prices now received the present business of farming is very much improved.

I believe that the past history of the relative trend of prices between farm products and other commodities is of tremendous significance. The surplus lands of the country are exhausted. The industrial population is outstripping the farm population. Manufacturing is expanding. These must come to the farmers for their food and their raw materials. While we can produce more, the markets for food are increasing much faster than present farm productivity. The future of agriculture looks to be exceedingly secure.

The real wealth of our country, its productive capacity, its great manufacturing plants, its far-reaching railroad system, its mighty commerce, and its agriculture did not come into being all at once, but is the result of a vast multitude of small increments brought about by long, slow, and laborious toil. Whatever a few individuals may do, the Nation as a whole and its great subdivisions of industry, transportation, commerce, and agriculture can increase by no other method. The percentage of yearly returns upon all the property of this country is low, but in the aggregate it is a stupendous sum. Unless all past experience is to be disregarded, notwithstanding its present embarrassments, agriculture as a whole should lead industry in future prosperity.

In all our economic discussions we must remember that we can not stop with the mere acquisition of wealth. The ultimate result to be desired is not the making of money, but the making of people. Industry, thrift, and self-control are not sought because they create wealth, but because they create character. These are the prime product of the farm. We who have seen it, and lived it, we know.

It is this life that the Nation is so solicitous to maintain and improve. It dwells in the open country, among the hills and valleys and over the great plains, in the unobstructed light of the sun, and under the glimmer of the stars. It brings its inhabitants into an intimate and true relation to nature, where they can live in harmony with the Great Purpose. It has been the life of freedom and independence, of religious convictions and abiding character. In its past it has made and saved America and helped rescue the world. In its future it holds the supreme promise of human progress.

XXXI

It is not through selfishness or wastefulness or arrogance, but through self-denial, conservation, and service, that we shall build up the American spirit. This is the true constructive economy, the true faith on which our institutions rest.

CONSTRUCTIVE ECONOMY

As would be the practice in any well-managed concern, the executive heads of the various departments and bureaus of the United States Government meet twice a year for receiving a report of the results of their efforts to make the business of the Government more successful. This is primarily a meeting to consider the Federal financial operations. But it approaches that problem not from the side of the finding and the raising of revenue but from the opposite side of the conservation and the expenditure of revenue. It is an eternal challenge to which we respond, of how to secure a more efficient government with a smaller expenditure of money. It is a great test of engineering skill in the constant elimination of waste, in the making of every dollar count, and in the conserving of national energy. On the success with which we meet these requirements depends the welfare of the Government and the prosperity and happiness of the American people.

It is for these reasons that the greatest emphasis should be placed on constructive economy. Merely to reduce the expenses of the Government might not in itself be beneficial. Such action might be only the discontinuance of a wholly necessary activity. No civilized community would close its schools, abolish its courts, disband its police force, or discontinue its fire department. Such action could not be counted as gain, but as irreparable loss. The underlying spirit of economy is to secure better education, wider administration of justice, more public order, and greater se-

At the Tenth Regular Meeting of the Business Organization of the Government, Memorial Continental Hall, January 30, 1926.

curity from conflagration, all through a superior organization which will decrease the unit of cost. It is all reducible to a question of national efficiency.

Each one of you may sometimes feel that you are performing a small and ineffective part and that the expenditures in your department will make so little difference that it is not worth while to put forth much effort. Pausing long enough to remind you that in the first place the character of the manhood and womanhood which you develop will depend entirely on the amount of effort that you put forth, I pass over that consideration to the fact that though each of you may contribute a comparatively small share to the general result, yet in a concern so vast as the Government of the United States the aggregate is very large. I want to see the public service of my country make a large contribution to the character of those who are employed in it and become the most efficient instrument of organized government in the world. Before you admit that your own part is small and ineffective you should remember that the whole is equal to the sum of all the parts and take a survey of the broad plan which is gradually being framed in accordance with the system of constructive economy for the conduct of the Federal business.

It happens that this is the tenth Budget meeting. If you will look back at the situation which existed in June, 1921, only four and one-half years ago, when your first meeting was held, you will be able better to understand the tremendous results of a policy of constructive economy. At that time 5,000,000 of our people were without employment, trade and commerce were despondent, transportation was unable to finance itself, the loss of buying power on the part of the wage earner depressed the price of all agricultural products, our foreign relations were in an uncertain state, we were threatened with an inundation of alien goods and alien peoples, about $7,000,000,000 of unfunded public debt was shortly to mature. It was almost impossible to secure private credit. The burden of taxation was overwhelming.

The action of the Government was prompt and effective. It is for us to see that it remains sustained. The flood of immigration and importations was checked by legislation. Our own people began to find work. Our own goods began to find a market. Taxes were enormously reduced. Federal expenditures, which then amounted to $5,538,000,000 for that fiscal year, it is now estimated will be cut down to $3,619,000,000 for this fiscal year. That is a saving of $1,919,000,000. Our short-term obligations were so skillfully funded that instead of embarrassing business the operation actually stimulated it. The public debt then was $23,997,000,000. At the end of this fiscal year it is estimated it will be less than $20,000,000,000. This is a payment of about $4,000,000,000 and represents a yearly saving in interest of $179,000,000. Credit was extended to agriculture and transportation through the War Finance Corporation.

With the return of employment and high wages the consumption of agricultural products increased 18 per cent. Our foreign relations were adjusted in a manner which added to the peace and stability of the world. The enormous debts due to us from abroad have been steadily adjusted until but one of large importance remains. The system of foreign loans has increased foreign purchasing powers. Economies in production have decreased our domestic costs. Our exports and imports for the last year were about $9,000,000,000, the highest mark ever reached in time of peace. With our assistance the economic condition of the whole world has been very greatly improved.

To eliminate competition in armaments and prevent the friction and suspicion which inevitably arises from that practice, the Washington Conference provided treaties

which not only afford great financial relief but are very
effective in the promotion of international good will and
confidence. Before us is the prospect of another conference
which holds the promise of further advance in this most
attractive field. These accomplishments mean international peace, economic prosperity, and financial stability.

In your own peculiar field the most impressive action was
the adoption of the Budget system. With the cooperation
of the Congress, with your loyal support, and under the
forceful leadership of General Dawes, it was put into operation. In a little over two years it became apparent that
largely because of its efficient continuance under General
Lord it was possible again to reduce taxes. Such a bill was
enacted by the Congress which convened in December,
1923. Due to the same moving factors, we have been en-
abled to propose another reduction in taxes, which is now
pending before the Congress and promises to be speedily
enacted. This is your record. It is due to your individual
action. Measured in its entirety, it is not small or inconse-
quential, but tremendous in its results and of overwhelming
significance in its implications. It has been a large contributing factor to prosperity at home, and to peace, repara-
tion, and restoration abroad.

It is my belief that we should supplement these achievements, round out these accomplishments and reinforce this
same general policy of constructive economy, enlarged prosperity, and peace, by adhering to the Permanent Court of
International Justice. When accompanied with proper reservations I can see in such action no diminution of our
sovereignty, no increase in our national peril, but rather an
instrument which will add more securities to human rights
and more guaranties to international tranquility. We
have not reached these domestic results without struggle
and sacrifice and the encountering of opposition. We shall
not be able to do much good to ourselves or make much

contribution to the welfare of the world, unless we continue the same struggle and make increasing sacrifices.

To me, all these proposals for conservation and economy do not seem either selfish or provincial, but rather they reveal a spirit dedicated to the service of humanity. If these things are not important, then there are no earthly considerations that are important.

Although these accomplishments are past history and ought to be known of all men, yet it is well that they be recalled and reiterated, in order that we may better understand the general plan which not only all the people in the Government but all the people in the country are engaged in putting into effect. The penalty for achievement is always a demand for even greater achievement. In this effort for retrenchment you have not disappointed the people or the President, and it is my firm conviction that you never will. If you at times grow weary of the constant stress put on economy, you will see that something more is involved than can be measured in dollars and cents. The spirit of real constructive economy is something higher and nobler. It does not imply so much a limitation as an attempt to be free from limitation. It does not contemplate curtailing ample supplies for worthy purposes and real needs, but it is the enemy of waste and the ally of orderly procedure. It is an attempt to increase and enlarge the scope of the individual and the life of the nation.

How great a need exists to emphasize the homely fundamental virtue of government economy is seen when we contemplate the mounting tide of expenditure and indebtedness of municipal and State governments. This tendency is one of great concern. The very fact that the Federal Government has been able to cut down its expenditures, decrease its indebtedness, and reduce its taxes indicates how great is the accomplishment which you have made in behalf of the people of the Nation. These results are all monuments to you and to the Congress. It has been your work and your cooperation that has brought forth these fortunate conclusions.

Heretofore I have expressed the opinion that we can not look for further reductions in the cost of the actual transacting of the business of the Government. It is only natural that the normal growth of the Nation would produce some expansion. But constant scrutiny is necessary to prevent fossilization and decay. Careful oversight of personnel is always required. The pay roll represents the largest single item in the business of the Government. During the past calendar year this has been reduced locally by more than 5,000 names—an annual saving of $8,000,000—although when persons are dropped from one department they are always taken care of in another wherever possible.

Past experience has shown that a reduction of taxes has been followed by increased prosperity. As the volume of business increases the Federal revenue increases. If we are moderate in our expenditures, the natural increase in profits ought within the next few years to furnish us again with a surplus revenue which will permit a further tax reduction.

We were the first nation in recent years to adopt a plan to reduce our debt and put the plan into operation. We are maintaining our sinking fund and applying the payments made on our foreign loans to the retirement of our debt. As a result this Nation has to-day the best credit in the world. We have lowered our interest costs not only by reducing our debt, but by so improving our credit that we can borrow at lower rates. Since interest is 22½ per cent of our total Federal expenditures, a reduction in interest is a most fruitful field for permanent saving. If we continued this plan during the post-war depression, there is certainly little reason for changing it in these days of prosperity.

Very soon you will have your appropriations for the next fiscal year. It would be wise early to lay out a carefully prepared program in making the apportionment over the several periods of the year, as is required by the law. If all our expenditures are wisely planned and wisely made, retrenchment will take care of itself. You should not forget to lay aside an emergency fund. Something unexpected usually happens, but if it does not a real saving is made. The reserve set up in this way for the last fiscal year has an unexpended balance of $24,000,000. It is of the utmost importance to remember that constructive economy means preparation for the future. Our country is in need of internal improvements and developments. A new building bill is under way, and our great interior should be provided with river and waterway facilities. These two projects represent a capital investment on which the returns will undoubtedly justify the costs. But we should beware of increased permanent commitments.

When the Government rents privately owned buildings it pays a high rate of interest, all the taxes, and some profit. When it occupies its own buildings the interest represented is very low, and taxes and profits are eliminated. The opening up of waterways means the development of commerce, less cost for freight on raw materials, and a large saving to our agricultural regions. The extent to which these projects can be undertaken in the immediate future awaits the outcome of the pending tax bill.

What all these efforts mean would be greatly underestimated if it be thought that they begin and end with the saving of money. Considered in their entirety, they play an important part in the wonderful American experiment for the advancement of human welfare. It is not only the method by which we have built railroads, developed agriculture, created commerce, and established industry, not only the method by which we have made nearly 18,000,000 automobiles and put a telephone and a radio in so large a proportion of our homes, but it is also the method by which we have founded schools, endowed hospitals, and erected places of religious worship. It is the material groundwork on which the whole fabric of society rests. It has given to the average American a breadth of outlook, a variety of experience, and a richness of life that in former generations was entirely beyond the reach of even the most powerful princes.

All of this effort represents not merely the keeping of our money but the keeping of our faith. One of the chief dangers to the success of popular government is that it will throw away self-restraint and self-control and adopt laws which, being without sound economic foundation, bring on such a financial distress as to result in want, misery, disorder, and the dissolution of society. America has demonstrated that self-government can be so administered as fairly to protect each individual in all his rights, whether they affect his person or his property. Under constitutional authority we tax everything, but we confiscate nothing. It is not through selfishness or wastefulness or arrogance, but through self-denial, conservation, and service, that we shall build up the American spirit. This is the true constructive economy, the true faith on which our institutions rest.

Our chief of staff in the direction of all this work is General Lord. It is because of his continuing efforts and your constant cooperation that our Government service to-day is a greatly improved service. It is more efficient and better able to function. The day of administration without coordination has passed. Our country has adopted a system of ordered finance. While much of the inspiration for this great achievement is furnished by the words of General Lord, the action has been furnished by yourselves. I present him to you not as your opponent or your critic, but as your most loyal friend and your most sympathetic defender.

XXXII

Truth dissipates misunderstanding and miscon-
ception. It is the function of a free press not
only to make the truth available to everyone
within its sphere, but to cherish and develop a
public sentiment for all that is loyal to the truth.
A free and enlightened press, by this means, be-
comes one of the safeguards of liberty.

JOURNALISM IN THE NEW WORLD

THIS is the First Pan American Congress of Journalists. In the number of countries represented and in the extent of territory embraced, it is without doubt one of the most important meetings of publishers and editors that was ever held. And when it is considered that within your numbers are those who control and shape the policies of the press in almost all the Western Hemisphere, the weight and significance of your conference becomes still more impressive. It is a peculiar pleasure to extend to your Congress, which represents so many American Republics, a most cordial greeting, and to assure you that the Government and people of the United States are pleased to make an appropriate response to the honor which your presence confers.

Possibilities of broad and beneficial results lie in the very nature of the untrammeled constituency of your body. While provision was made for it under a resolution of the Fifth International Conference of American States, commonly known as the Fifth Pan American Conference, held at Santiago, Chile, in 1923, it is not an official gathering. Your members in no wise represent their respective governments. You are here in your individual capacities as the free agents of a free press of free countries, in voluntary conference to discuss ways and means of bringing the people of the western world to a better understanding and a more sympathetic accord.

Truth dissipates misunderstanding and misconception. It is the function of a free press not only to make the truth

Address before the First Pan American Congress of Journalists, Washington, D. C., April 8, 1926.

available to everyone within its sphere, but to cherish and develop a public sentiment for all that is loyal to the truth. A free and enlightened press, by this means, becomes one of the safeguards of liberty. When devoted to these ideals it is a vitally stimulating cultural force.

Since the earliest establishment of Republics in Latin America there has been a common bond between the people of those countries and our people. The strength of this bond has grown with the years. But, up to very recent times, there has been an unfortunate lack of information on the part of the general public of the United States of the aims, achievements, and progress of those regions. And, I am told, a similar condition in regard to affairs in the United States has existed among their people. Such conditions can be remedied only by the dissemination of knowledge. Various Pan American organizations have done a most valuable work in this direction. But one of the most important factors in bringing about a better understanding has been an awakening of interest among us in the news of the countries represented by our visitors; conversely has come the desire on their part to learn more of what we are doing and why we are doing it. This has resulted in the enlargement of old and the organization of new services for the interchange of news. As I understand the purpose of your conference, it is not only for the forming of friendships by personal contact, but also for the exchange of views and the discussion of conditions and problems, as they come to the editor who is striving to present to his readers a true perspective of what is taking place in his own country and in other countries.

After your deliberations in Washington you, who are our most welcome guests, will visit other parts of our country to see for yourselves the material and cultural progress we are making. Perhaps in other years our journalists will have the privilege of coming into intimate contact with your nations and of seeing for themselves the wonderful advance you have made in these directions, thus giving us both a more complete knowledge and understanding of our common aims, aspirations, and achievements.

It is most appropriate that you are meeting in this beautiful building. In a very real sense this is your home. The ideals and the purposes of the Pan American Union are those which the press of this hemisphere should seek to serve. It should promote a better understanding among the western Republics, and it should foster a spirit of sympathy, harmony, and cooperation. Your newspapers may do much to emphasize and make more effective the efforts of this organization to bring the United States and the Latin American Republics into closer bonds of mutual helpfulness.

Your visit to our country will, I trust, be beneficial to you by reason of what you may learn of our general mode of life. You will come in contact with our industries, our universities, our political and our religious institutions. This will enable you the better to interpret our ideals in your future communications to your own people. It will also provide an opportunity for our citizens to give you personal assurances of the depth and breadth of the friendship which exists here for you and your people, and the earnest desire for a continuation of those friendly relations which are the result of commercial intercourse and mutual aspirations.

It will also afford the occasion for the inhabitants of our country to learn more of what our sister Republics are and what they represent. It will give them an opportunity to recall that the early inhabitants of colonial South America established centers of culture earlier than similar agencies were established in English colonial possessions in North America. No less than eight institutions of higher learning were founded prior to the establishment in 1636 of Harvard, the oldest university in the United States. The Royal and Pontifical University of St. Paul, in Mexico, and the Greater University of St. Mark, in Lima, both were chartered by royal decree in the year 1551. These institutions were intended to equip their pupils for the priesthood, just as the first schools in North America were designed primarily to train young men for the ministry.

Printing in the New World first appeared in Latin America. The first printing press this side of the Atlantic was set up in Mexico in 1535 and the second in Lima in 1586. It was not until 1639 that the first printing press, in what is now the United States, was used in Cambridge, Mass. The dissemination of news in printed form was resorted to in South America as early as 1594. A leaflet published in Lima gave to the public the news of the capture of an English pirate. About 1620 news leaflets frequently appeared in Mexico and Lima, but publications resembling later-day newspapers in any degree were not attempted until 1772.

In any consideration of the comparative progress and achievements of Latin America and the United States we must remember that the United States had the advantage of a national existence for more than forty years before the Latin American countries had become independent. The Battle of Yorktown, which marked the end of our Revolution, was in 1781, while the decisive battle for Latin American independence was fought at Ayachucho, Peru, in 1824.

Since about 1876, these independent Republics have been expanding commercially at a rapid rate. The following are very striking figures, although prepared some years ago. In 1919, with a population under 80,000,000, the total foreign commerce of Latin American countries amounted to over $5,000,000,000. With these figures compare those of the United States in 1900, when our population was about

76,000,000 and our foreign commerce less than $2,500,-000,000.

Historians refer to the nineteenth century as distinguished by the development of the United States. Elihu Root, after his official visit, said, in 1906, "I believe that no student can help seeing that the twentieth century will be the century of phenomenal development in South America." Theodore Roosevelt made a similar statement at the time of his trip to Brazil in 1914. All that has happened since has tended to prove the correctness of these prophecies.

Too few people in this country have an adequate realization of the immensity of Latin America. Many do not know that these twenty Republics cover an area of 9,000,000 square miles, approximately three times the area of the United States; that Brazil alone is larger than the United States, and that Argentina is nearly two-thirds as large. And, I fear, the conception of our average citizen is woefully deficient as to the extent to which these Republics have developed in industry, science, and the arts, and to which they enjoy all the improvements of modern civilization, oftentimes improving these improvements.

In some measure this has been due to the lack of information in our press. Some one has remarked there was a time when readers of our newspapers here might have imagined revolutions and volcanic disturbances were the chief product of Latin America. On the other hand, the readers of Latin American papers got little idea of our national life from the accounts of train wrecks, lynchings, and divorces, which, it was said, constituted the principal news printed there about our country.

That day has passed. Since 1916, due to our increased cable facilities and the reduction of cable tolls, as well as the keen desire for more information, the amount of news exchanged between the Americas has been increased greatly, and its character is more constructive. I venture the prediction that as a result of this Congress the papers in the United States in the future will present more complete and more accurate pictures of the cultural and industrial progress of Latin America, and that the press of those Republics will give to their readers a better understanding of the ideals and purposes of the United States.

The awakening of the spirit of independence in Latin America, just as the world was turning into the nineteenth century, inspired a literature that ranks high in quality. This literary inspiration continued to be fed by the series of romantic events following independence. I can mention only a few of the many men of literary distinction whose works in time may become as well known to us as those of French, Italian, German, and English authors, as we extend the study of Latin American tongues in our schools. Among these are Domingo Faustino Sarmiento, of Argentina; Andrés Bello, of Venezuela; Rubén Darío, of Nicaragua; Jorge Isaacs, of Colombia; Ricardo Palma, of Peru; Benjamín Vicuña Mackenna, of Chile; José Enrique Rodó, of Uruguay; Juan de Dios Peza, of Mexico; Olavo Bilac, of Brazil; José María Heredia, of Cuba; and José Joaquin Olmedo, of Ecuador. You will recall many other brilliant names.

One of our writers, after calling attention to the fact that Sarmiento was a contemporary of Washington Irving, James Fenimore Cooper, Bryant, Poe, Longfellow, Emerson, Hawthorne, Lowell, Oliver Wendell Holmes, all famous writers of the United States, adds: ". . . . none exhibits Sarmiento's combination of activity and reflection, romanticism and practicality, brilliance and warmth. With the exception of Emerson it is doubtful if any of these paladins of our golden age of literature was his superior, and it was certain that none did more to uplift his country and to raise the general level of culture."

Sarmiento should be well known in this country. After serving here as minister plenipotentiary of Argentina he became its President. He was a great student of the institutions and history of the United States and wrote a biography of Abraham Lincoln. After conference with Horace Mann he established a system of education in Argentina modeled after some of those in this country.

In the field of drama Latin America has produced Juan Ruiz de Alarcon. Scholarship, poetry, fiction, criticism, and political writing all have had their exponents in the various Latin American Republics. Argentina, Brazil, Chile, Mexico, and Venezuela have national academies of art and conservatories of music. There are many who consider the Palace of Fine Arts of Santiago, Chile, as the finest of its kind on the Western Hemisphere.

The Mexican Government through all the years never has failed to encourage art. This encouragement has been put in concrete form by the establishment in recent years of the Coyoacán Art School. Music is more genuinely popular in Latin America probably than in the United States. Most cities or towns of any size have open-air concerts, and the great operatic stars have been received with proper acclaim and rewarded with large remunerations. State and municipality foster the drama and erect fine buildings in which to produce it. The Solís, of Montevideo; the National Theater of Mexico, and the Colón of Buenos Aires surpass most of our theaters in the United States in size, cost, and beauty. The best theatrical companies in Europe are obtained, and much native talent is being developed.

Latin America has its share of scientists, to which number are being added each year many graduates of the leading universities. I might mention the names of Dr. Oswaldo Cruz, municipal sanitation expert; Rodrigues, the botanist, and Lacerda, the biologist, all Brazilians; Dr. Alejandro

Alvarez, of Chile, widely known throughout the world as an authority on international law, and Dr. Luis Drago, of Argentina, who enunciated the Drago doctrine. That many in the United States may not have heard of these eminent men, simply indicates a lack of information on our part.

While popular education was not developed in Latin America so soon as in the territory originally comprising the English colonies, it has made rapid strides there since 1880. The development of normal schools has been marked. "They are proving in particular," one of our writers says, "the educational and economic salvation of Latin American womanhood * * *." Our women who take part in public affairs might learn a great deal by studying the history of the Sociedad de Beneficencia, composed of about sixty prominent women of Buenos Aires. For many years this organization has conducted most of the public philanthropies of that city, collecting and distributing benevolences on a large scale. The income of the society, I understand, amounts to more than $4,000,000 a year.

In recent years has come a profound realization that the commercial interests of Latin America and the United States have a strong natural bond. Since the World War we have enlarged that interest by vastly increasing our shipping facilities between here and various Latin American ports, by establishing branches of our banks, and by the investment of great amounts of capital. It is estimated that in 1923 United States capital invested in Latin America amounted to $3,760,000,000; in 1924, a trifle over $4,000,-000,000, and in 1925 was $4,210,000,000. In 1925 banks in the United States had some forty branches in various Latin American cities. Figures compiled by our Department of Commerce show that in 1910 our exports to Latin America, including the Guianas and all the West Indies except Porto Rico, amounted to $279,663,000 and our imports from there amounted to $408,837,000. Last year the exports were

$882,315,000 and the imports $1,041,122,000. Our exports
to the four Republics of Argentina, Brazil, Chile, and
Mexico increased from $141,615,000 in 1910 to $420,211,000
in 1925. Our imports from these countries increased in
this fifteen year period from $217,240,000 to $569,771,000. It
may be interesting to compare these 1925 figures with those
for our total foreign trade in that year, which were: Exports, $4,909,396,000; imports, $4,227,995,000. Thus we
see nearly one-fifth of all our exports went to Latin
America and practically one-fourth of our imports came
from there. While they have our mining and printing machinery, locomotives, sewing machines, cash registers,
phonographs, radio, typewriters, and other implements, we
need and have their very valuable raw products.

Their cities are developing as rapidly as our own and
some seem to have surpassed ours in the magnificence of
their buildings and in the extent of their city-planning
activities. If all our citizens here do not yet realize fully
that Latin America is as progressive as the United States;
and if some Latin Americans, as I have been told is the case,
are prone to feel that this country is interested in material
things alone, I am sure it may be explained by the lack
of that knowledge which comes from personal contact
through travel and by the mutual inadequacy of news reports of the significant facts and developments in the respective countries. With the increase of transportation
facilities between our Republics travel will increase. And
there can be no doubt you publishers and editors are constantly striving to enlarge and improve your dissemination
of vital news concerning the different people of the Western
Hemisphere.

No newspapers in the world have a higher rank than
some of those in Latin America. I understand the amount
of cable matter contained in our own press for a good
many years did not begin to compare with what was to be

found in the leading dailies of the Southern Republics. Several of these newspapers have buildings equal, if not superior, to those in our country. One newspaper in particular is notable for public service outside the mere publication of news. It maintains free legal and medical bureaus, and showrooms for the display of things intimately connected with agricultural, stock-raising, and the chemical industries. Also, it furnishes auditoriums for lectures, plays, concerts, and other gatherings. It approaches a university. The high esteem in which these pages are deservedly held throughout the world has been built up by the character of the men who have guided them. It is particularly gratifying to have present at this gathering men whose character and reputation are recognized internationally, including one who bears a name which for three generations has stood for the best in journalism.

The First Congress of Journalists was a fine idea. I hope it will achieve all that its promoters could wish. It seems to me it would be well if your gathering could be repeated periodically, possibly alternating between Latin America and the United States. Such meetings can not fail to have far-reaching consequences, not only in the preservation of the most cordial good feeling existing among our respective nations but also in the drawing together of our peoples into closer bonds of sympathetic understanding. It should result in a better comprehension that, after all, we of the Western Hemisphere are one people striving for a common purpose, animated by common ideals and bound together in a common destiny. Unto us has been bequeathed the precious heritage and the high obligation of developing and consecrating a new world to the great cause of humanity.

XXXIII

The whole system of American Government rests on the ballot box. Unless citizens perform their duties there, such a system of government is doomed to failure.

THE NEW RESPONSIBILITIES OF WOMEN

Coming to address the Thirty-fifth Continental Congress of the National Society of the Daughters of the American Revolution reminds me that I have had that privilege several times in the past. You represent one of the most distinguished patriotic orders of our Nation in cherishing the memory of the people and the record of the events of the great struggle which resulted in American independence. It is a marked honor to be invited to speak in your presence. But I do not wish to be the sole recipient of such opportunity. Perhaps you might profit by some change in the future. In a fresh view of a great period, animated by a great purpose, consecrated by a great result, you are more likely to secure a much larger inspiration.

In Massachusetts the 19th of April is known as Patriots Day. It is honored and set apart. The whole Nation is coming more and more to observe it. As the time lengthens from the occurrences of 1775, its significance becomes more apparent and its importance more real. It stands out as one of the great days in history, not because it can be said the American Revolution actually began then, but because on that occasion it became apparent that the patriots were determined to defend their rights.

The Revolutionary period has always appeared to me to be significant for three definite reasons: The people of that day had ideals for the advancement of human welfare. They kept their ideals within the bounds of what was practical, according to the results of past experience. They did

At Washington, April 19th 1926, before the Daughters of the American Revolution.

377

not hesitate to make the necessary sacrifice to establish those ideals in a workable form of political institutions. As I have examined the record of your society, I believe that it is devoted to the same principles of practical idealism enshrined in institutions by sacrifice.

This is but the natural inheritance of those who are descended from Revolutionary times. In this day, with our broadened view of the importance of women in working out the destiny of mankind, there will be none to deny that as there were fathers in our Republic so there were mothers. If they did not take part in the formal deliberations, yet by their abiding faith they inspired and encouraged the men; by their sacrifice they performed their part in the struggle out of which came our country. We read of the flaming plea of Hannah Arnett, which she made on a dreary day in December, 1776, when Lord Cornwallis, victorious at Fort Lee, held a strategic position in New Jersey. A group of the Revolutionists, weary and discouraged, were discussing the advisability of giving up the struggle. Casting aside the proprieties which forbade a woman to interfere in the counsels of men, Hannah Arnett proclaimed her faith. In eloquent words, which at once shamed and stung to action, she convinced her husband and his companions that righteousness must win. Who has not heard of Molly Pitcher, whose heroic services at the Battle of Monmouth helped the sorely tried army of George Washington! We have been told of the unselfish devotion of the women who gave their own warm garments to fashion clothing for the suffering Continental Army during that bitter winter at Valley Forge. The burdens of the war were not all borne by the men.

Such a record made it eminently fitting that in the course of time there should be founded the Daughters of the American Revolution. Starting in 1890, small in numbers but great in purpose, it is little wonder your society has grown great in membership and influence. From four chapters and 390 members at the end of the first six months, it has reached a total enrollment of more than 156,000, and a chapter roll of over 2,000. In recent years there have been periods when new members have been taken in at the rate of 1,000 a month. Truly, a powerful force for good in our country—such a body of high-minded women with such a heritage of sacrifice and devotion to an ideal! What possibilities for future service rest in such a devoted body of citizens!

I have been reading your constitution and considering the objects of your society there set forth. It declares your purpose:

"To perpetuate the memory and spirit of the men and women who achieved American independence, by the acquisition and protection of historical spots, and the erection of monuments * * *."

How well this has been carried out is known to all who have visited such spots. That it has been done is a reason for your existence. Who can measure the inspiration that may be drawn from such symbols of heroic deeds!

You have encouraged research into Revolutionary history, published the results, aided in the preservation of documents and relics, of the individual service records of soldiers and patriots. You have promoted the celebration of patriotic anniversaries. Worthy acts of service to the Nation, each and every one!

You undertake to promote institutions for the diffusion of knowledge to the end that there may be developed "the largest capacity for performing the duties of American citizens." You have added to your endeavors of this character the very practical and necessary work of helping the foreign born to understand and acquire the full benefit of living in America.

But it is the third and last, and the most important, paragraph of your declaration of purpose that arouses the keenest interest. In it you say it shall be your endeavor:

"To cherish, maintain, and extend the institutions of American freedom, to foster true patriotism and love of country, and to aid in securing for mankind all the blessings of liberty." These are principles worthy of the best support that the country can give. Yet, it is not beyond the capacity of the humblest citizen to make some contribution for their establishment. However exalted is the conception of our institutions, they are not beyond the reach of the common run of people. They are ideal, but they are practical. They rest on the every-day virtues—honesty, industry, and thrift. As the overwhelming mass of our people are thoroughly loyal to these principles, we can feel a warranted assurance that the foundations of our institutions are secure.

But while we are justified in the assumption that the heart of the people is sound, and that they are moved by worthy motives, it can not be denied that we always have and do now suffer from many minor afflictions. That would be disturbing if one did not realize that more serious maladies have been met and overcome in the past, and that there is every reason to believe that our people have sufficient character to meet the requirements of the present day.

Our Republic gives to its citizens great opportunities, and under it they have achieved greater blessings than ever came to any other people. It is exceedingly wholesome to stop and contemplate that undisputed fact from time to time. Then, it is necessary to contemplate the inescapable corollary that the enjoyment and perpetuation of these conditions necessarily lay upon our people the obligation of a corresponding service and sacrifice. Citizenship in America is not a private enterprise, but a public function. Although I have indicated that it is my firm conviction that this requirement will be met, it can not be denied that if it is not met disaster will overtake the whole fabric of our institutions.

Our very success and prosperity have brought with them their own perils. It can not be denied that in the splendor and glamour of our life the moral sense is sometimes blinded. It can not be disputed that in too many quarters there is a lack of reverence for authority and of obedience to law. Such occurrences are sporadic and produce their own remedy. When society finds that its life and property are in peril from evildoers, it is very quick to organize its forces for its own protection. That can not fail to be done in our country, for our people as a whole are thoroughly law-abiding.

It is not in violence and crime that our greatest danger lies. These evils are so perfectly apparent that they very quickly arouse the moral power of the people for their suppression. A far more serious danger lurks in the shirking of those responsibilities of citizenship, where the evil may not be so noticeable but is more insidious and likely to be more devastating.

We live in a republic. A vital principle of that form of government is representation. More and more as our population increases it becomes necessary for the people to express their will through their duly chosen delegates. If we are to maintain the principle that governments derive their just powers from the consent of the governed, if we are to have any measure of self-government, if the voice of the people is to rule, if representatives are truly to reflect the popular will, it is altogether necessary that in each election there should be a fairly full participation by all the qualified voters.

This is very far from being the case in recent years. Since 1880 there has been a marked increase in the tendency to remain away from the polls on the part of those entitled to vote. But, despite a steady decline in the vote in the five presidential elections in the period 1880-1896, there was a voting average of 80 per cent. Out of every 100 persons entitled to vote 80 went to the polls. For the last two presidential elections the average has been less than 50 per cent, and that in the face of a sincere effort on the part of numerous organizations to get out the vote. In this effort it is reported many Daughters of the American Revolution took part. From its early inception the town meeting, featuring New England life, an example of pure democracy, was generally well attended. Although representative government did not originate here, our form of representative democracy is our own product. The national election day was fixed in the Constitution, and most of the States accepted that first Tuesday after the first Monday in November as the day upon which the voters should choose their local officials. Election day in the olden times was generally considered more or less sacred—one to be devoted to the discharge of the obligations of citizenship.

In the intervening years customs and habits have changed. Opportunities for recreation have increased. Our entire mode of life has been recast through invention, the great growth of cities, and for other reasons. Undoubtedly, this has been responsible in no small measure for the widespread disregard on the part of so many of our citizens of the privilege and duty of voting. But back of these conditions there are probably some deeper and more fundamental reasons.

It was hoped that giving the vote to women would arouse a more general interest in the obligations of election day. That has not yet proved to be the case. The presidential election in 1920 was the first after the adoption of the universal suffrage amendment. There is no way to divide the total vote cast by men and women. But, after that election some rather complicated calculations were made based on the assumption that the accession of women might be presumed to double the vote. The calculators reached the conclusion that of the approximate 27,000,000 votes cast only 37 per cent represented the votes of women. Some say the percentage of feminine vote was greater in 1924. Others say it was less.

I am not disposed to accept these conclusions as altogether fair to the women. And it stands to reason that it would take some time for them to become used to exercising the privilege which had belonged to the men of this country for many generations.

It is not my purpose to draw any distinction between the men and the women as to the extent to which they take advantage of their privilege and perform their duty at the ballot box. But rather it is my idea to call your attention to the startling fact that in the last two presidential elections barely 50 per cent of those qualified to vote have done so. In the senatorial elections in off years the voting percentage is much smaller.

A published study of the senatorial vote of 1922 revealed some astonishing facts. In not a few of the States the total vote cast for senatorial candidates was less than 50 per cent of the total possible vote. In not a single case did the successful candidate secure anywhere near a majority of the total possible vote. There was one State in which the percentage was 42 and another in which it was 33. From that it ran down sharply to certain States where the candidates elected received as low as 7, 9, or 10 per cent of the total possible vote.

If we are to keep our representative form of government and to maintain the principle that the majority shall rule, it behooves us to take some drastic action to arouse the voters of this country to a greater interest in their civic duties on election day. Many remedies have been proposed, from disfranchisement to criminal action. The most practical, I believe, however, is for all bodies of men and women interested in the welfare of this country to join together under some efficient form of organization to correct this evil which has been coming on us for more than 40 years, but which within the last decade has become most acute.

Having in mind the poor showing made in the presidential election of 1920, an effort was made to get out a larger participation on election day in 1924. Such prominent bodies as the National Civic Federation, the National League of Women Voters, the American Federation of Labor, the Federal Council of Churches of Christ in America, and a large number of other organizations, business as well as civic, each in its own way, attempted to get people to the polls. Members of the Daughters of the American Revolution took part as individuals but not as an organization, I understand. When the vote was counted it was found the percentage of vote cast was very little greater in 1924 than in 1920. One of those most earnestly interested in the movement writing about it later said:

"Was it a tragedy or was it a farce—the result of the great and more or less spectacular campaign by voluntary organizations to 'Get Out the Vote'?"

Despite all this effort the percentage of those voting was barely 50. The question naturally arises, Had it not been for all this work would not the decline have reached an extraordinary and a humiliatingly low point? The very fact that there was little net increase after all the self-sacrificing and disinterested work would seem to show clearly the growing strength of the tendency to remain away from the polls on election day.

Led by our example, country after country in various parts of the world has adopted a representative form of government and extended its franchise for the election of parliamentary bodies. There was a time when America led the world in getting out the vote. It is not pleasant to find that now we have dropped far behind some of the other nations in our participation in popular elections. We are told that 82 per cent of the men and women qualified to vote went to the polls in the parliamentary elections in England and Wales in 1922. The British electorate is maintaining a voting average of 60 per cent better than ours. In Germany in 1920 the vote approximated 75 per cent of the total electorate. And it is estimated that in 1924 this was increased to 82 per cent. In 1921 in Canada, in voting for members of the lower House of Parliament, a little over 70 per cent of the voting population participated. Over a period of 21 years Australia has maintained an average of somewhat better than 70 per cent. The percentage in Italy in 1923 was 64.

The perilous aspect of this situation lies in its insidiousness. With the broadening of popular powers, the direct election of practically all public officials, and the direct nomination of most of them, there is no opportunity for an expression of the public will except at the ballot box. It is perfectly evident that all those who have selfish interests will go to the polls and will be active and energetic in securing support for their proposals and their candidates. The average voter supports what he believes to be the public interest. Unless they appear on election day that interest will go unrepresented.

As our resources increase, as the relationship between individuals becomes more intricate, the Government becomes more and more important. We do not need to fear a frontal attack upon it. Whenever the public scents that it is in danger, they will be quick enough to give it adequate support. It is only the approach of some silent and unrecognized peril that needs to give us alarm. Such a situation will develop if the Government ceases to represent the people because the public has become inarticulate. We are placing our reliance on the principle of self-government. We expect there will be mistakes, but they will be the mistakes which the people themselves make, because they control their own Government. But if the people fail to vote, a government will be developed which is not their government.

This is not a partisan question, but a patriotic question. Your society, which is organized "to cherish, maintain, and extend the institutions of American freedom," may well take a leading part in arousing public sentiment to the peril that arises when the average citizen fails to vote. The women of the country ought to be especially responsive to an appeal from you. I feel quite certain that with the men it would be almost irresistible. The American people have been especially responsive in meeting the requirements of taxation. They ought to be even more responsive in meeting the requirements of voting. The whole system of American Government rests on the ballot box. Unless citizens perform their duties there, such a system of government is doomed to failure.

XXXIV

The strength and hope of civilization lies in its power to adapt itself to changing circumstances. Development and character are not passive accomplishments. They can be secured only through action. The strengthening of the physical body, the sharpening of the senses, the quickening of the intellect, are all the result of that mighty effort which we call the struggle for existence.

TRAINING YOUTH FOR CHARACTER

THE strength and hope of civilization lies in its power to adapt itself to changing circumstances. Development and character are not passive accomplishments. They can be secured only through action. The strengthening of the physical body, the sharpening of the senses, the quickening of the intellect, are all the result of that mighty effort which we call the struggle for existence. Down through the ages it was carried on for the most part in the open, out in the fields, along the streams, and over the surface of the sea. It was there that mankind met the great struggle which has been waged with the forces of nature. We are what that struggle has made us. When the race ceases to be engaged in that great strength-giving effort the race will not be what it is now—it will change to something else. These age-old activities or their equivalent are vital to a continuation of human development. They are invaluable in the growth and training of youth.

Towns and cities and industrial life are very recent and modern acquirements. Such an environment did not contribute to the making of the race, nor was it bred in the lap of present-day luxury. It was born of adversity and nurtured by necessity. Though the environment has greatly changed, human nature has not changed. If the same natural life in the open requiring something of the same struggle, surrounded by the same elements of adversity and necessity, is gradually passing away in the experience of the great mass of the people; if the old struggle with na-

Address before the National Council of the Boy Scouts of America, Washington, D. C., May 1, 1926.

ture no longer goes on; if the usual environment has been very largely changed, it becomes exceedingly necessary that an artificial environment be created to supply the necessary process for a continuation of the development and character of the race. The cinder track must be substituted for the chase.

Art therefore has been brought in to take the place of nature. One of the great efforts in that direction is represented by the Boy Scout movement. It was founded in the United States in 1910. In September of that year the organization was given a great impetus by the visit of the man whom we are delighted to honor this evening, Sir Robert Baden-Powell. This distinguished British general is now known all over the world as the originator of this idea. That it has been introduced into almost every civilized country must be to him a constant source of great gratification. The first annual meeting was held in the East Room of the White House in February, 1911, when President Taft made an address, and each of his successors has been pleased to serve as the honorary president of the association. It has been dignified by a Federal charter granted by the Congress to the Boy Scouts of America in 1916, and thereby ranks in the popular mind with the only two other organizations which have been similarly honored, the Red Cross and the American Legion.

The Boy Scouts have been fortunate in enlisting the interest of prominent men of our country to serve as the active head of the organization. For the current year that position was held by no less a figure than the late James J. Storrow. His untimely taking off was a sad experience to all of us who knew him. I cherished him personally as a friend. I admired him for the broad public spirit that he always exhibited. Amid all the varied and exacting activities as one of our foremost business men, he yet found time to devote his thought and energy and personal attention to the advancement of this movement. His memory will constantly bring to us all that sentiment which he uttered in the New Year message that he gave to the scouts, in expressing the hope that it might bring "A more vivid realization that it is the spirit and the spiritual sides of life that count."

The more I have studied this movement, its inception, purposes, organization, and principles, the more I have been impressed. Not only is it based on the fundamental rules of right thinking and acting but it seems to embrace in its code almost every virtue needed in the personal and social life of mankind. It is a wonderful instrument for good. It is an inspiration to you whose duty and privilege it is to widen its horizon and extend its influence. If every boy in the United States between the ages of twelve and seventeen could be placed under the wholesome influences of the scout program and should live up to the scout oath and rules, we would hear fewer pessimistic words as to the future of our Nation.

The boy on becoming a scout binds himself on his honor to do his best, as the oath reads:

"1. To do my duty to God and my country, and to obey the scout law.

"2. To help other people at all times.

"3. To keep myself physically strong, mentally awake, and morally straight."

The twelve articles in these scout laws are not prohibitions, but obligations; affirmative rules of conduct. Members must promise to be trustworthy, loyal, helpful, friendly, courteous, kind, obedient, cheerful, thrifty, brave, clean, and reverent. How comprehensive this list! What a formula for developing moral and spiritual character! What an opportunity for splendid service in working to strengthen their observance by all scouts and to extend their influence to all boys eligible for membership! It would be a perfect world if everyone exemplified these virtues in daily life.

Acting under these principles, remarkable progress has been made. Since 1910, 3,000,000 boys in the United States have been scouts—one out of every seven eligible. Who can estimate the physical, mental, and spiritual force that would have been added to our national life during this period if the other six also had been scouts?

On January 1, 1926, there was an enrollment of nearly 600,000 boys, directed by 165,000 volunteer leaders and divided among 23,000 troops. Such is the field that has been cultivated. The great need now is for more leaders, inspired for service and properly equipped to carry out the program. It is estimated that 1,000,000 additional boys could be enrolled immediately if adequate leadership could be provided. We can not do too much honor to the 500,000 men who in the past sixteen years have given freely of their time and energy as scout masters and assistant scout masters. Such service is service to God and to country. The efforts to get more devoted volunteers and to find and train those fitted and willing to make this their life work is worthy of the most complete success.

Because the principles of this movement are affirmative, I believe they are sound. The boy may not be merely passive in his allegiance to righteousness. He must be an active force in his home, his church and his community. Too few people have a clear realization of the real purposes of the Boy Scouts. In the popular mind the program is arranged for play, for recreation, is designed solely to utilize the spare time of the boy in such a way that he may develop physically while engaged in pleasurable pursuits. This is but a faint conception, one almost wholly misleading. The program is a means to an end. Its fundamental object is to use modern environment in character building and training for citizenship.

Character is what a person is; it represents the aggregate of distinctive mental and moral qualities belonging to an individual or a race. Good character means a mental and moral fiber of high order, one which may be woven into the fabric of the community and State, going to make a great nation—great in the broadest meaning of that word.

The organization of the scouts is particularly suitable for a representative democracy such as ours, where our institutions rest on the theory of self-government and public functions are exercised through delegated authority. The boys are taught to practice the basic virtues and principles of right living and to act for themselves in according with such virtues and principles. They learn self-direction and self-control.

The organization is not intended to take the place of the home or religion, but to supplement and cooperate with those important factors, in our national life. We hear much talk of the decline in the influence of religion, of the loosening of the home ties, of the lack of discipline—all tending to break down reverence and respect for the laws of God and of man. Such thought as I have been able to give to the subject and such observations as have come within my experience have convinced me that there is no substitute for the influences of the home and of religion. These take hold of the innermost nature of the individual and play a very dominant part in the formation of personality and character. This most necessary and most valuable service has to be performed by the parents, or it is not performed at all. It is the root of the family life. Nothing else can ever take its place. These duties can be performed by foster parents with partial success, but any attempt on the part of the Government to function in these directions breaks down almost entirely. The Boy Scout movement can never be a success as a substitute but only as an ally of strict parental control and family life under religious influences. Parents can not shift their responsibility. If they fail to exercise proper control, nobody else can do it for them.

The last item in the scout "duodecalogue" is impressive. It declares that a scout shall be reverent. "He is reverent toward God," the paragraph reads. "He is faithful in his religious duties, and respects the convictions of others in matters of custom and religion." In the past I have declared my conviction that our Government rests upon religion; that religion is the source from which we derive our reverence for truth and justice, for equality and liberty, and for the rights of mankind. So wisely and liberally is the Boy Scout movement designed that the various religious denominations have found it a most helpful agency in arousing and maintaining interest in the work of their various societies. This has helped to emphasize in the minds of youth the importance of teaching our boys to respect the religious opinions and social customs of others.

The scout theory takes the boy at an age when he is apt to get ensnared in the complexities and false values of our latter-day life, and it turns his attention toward the simple, the natural, the genuine. It provides a program for the utilization of his spare time outside his home and school and church duties. While ofttimes recreational, it is in the best sense constructive. It aims to give a useful outlet for the abundant energies of the boy, to have valuable knowledge follow innate curiosity, to develop skill and self-reliance—the power to bring things to pass—by teaching one how to use both the hand and the head. In the city-bred boy is developed love for the country, a realization of what nature means, of its power to heal the wounds and to soothe the frayed nerves incident to modern civilization. He learns that in the woods and on the hillside, on the plain, and by the stream, he has a chance to think upon the eternal verities, to get a clarity of vision—a chance which the confusion and speed of city life too often renders difficult if not impossible of attainment. There is a very real value in implanting this idea in our boys. When they take up the burdens of manhood they may be led to return to the simple life for periods of physical, mental, and spiritual refreshment and reinvigoration.

Scouting very definitely teaches that rewards come only after achievement through personal effort and self-discipline. The boy enters as a tenderfoot. As he develops he becomes a second-class scout and then a first-class scout. Still there is before him the opportunity, in accordance with ability and hard work, to advance and get merit badges for proficiency in some seventy subjects pertaining to the arts, trades, and sciences. It is interesting to learn that in the year 1925, 195,000 merit badges were awarded as compared with 140,000 in 1924. Twenty-one such awards make the boy an "eagle scout," the highest rank. Not only does one learn to do things, but in many instances he learns what he can do best. He is guided to his life work. Vocational experts will tell you in dollars and cents what this means to society where so often much valuable time and effort is wasted by the young before they have tested, proven, and trained their individual powers.

The boy learns "to be prepared." This is the motto of the scouts. They are prepared to take their proper place in life, prepared to meet any unusual situation arising in their personal or civic relations. The scout is taught to be courageous and self-sacrificing. Individually he must do one good deed each day. He is made to understand that he is a part of organized society; that he owes an obligation to that society. Among the many activities in which the scouts have rendered public service are those for the protection of birds and wild life generally, for the conservation of natural resources, reforestation, for carrying out the "Safety first" idea. They have taken part in campaigns for church cooperation, in drives against harmful literature, and the promotion of an interest in wholesome, worthwhile reading. In many communities they have cooperated with the police and fire departments. In some instances they have studied the machinery of government by temporary and volunteer participation in the city and State administration. During the war they helped in the Liberty Loan campaigns, and more recently they have assisted in "Get-out-the-vote" movements.

All of this is exceedingly practical. It provides a method both for the training of youth and adapting him to modern life. The age-old principle of education through action and character through effort is well exemplified, but in addition the very valuable element has been added of a training for community life. It has been necessary for society to discard some of its old individualistic tendencies and promote a larger liberty and a more abundant life by cooperative effort. This theory has been developed under the principle of the division of labor, but the division of labor fails completely if any one of the divisions ceases to function.

It is well that boys should learn that lesson at an early age. Very soon they will be engaged in carrying on the work of the world. Some will enter the field of transportation, some of banking, some of industry, some of agriculture; some will be in the public service, in the police department, in the fire department, in the Post Office Department, in the health department. The public welfare, success, and prosperity of the Nation will depend upon the proper coordination of all these various efforts and upon each loyally performing the service undertaken. It will no longer do for those who have assumed the obligation to society of carrying on these different functions to say that as a body they are absolutely free and independent and responsible to no one but themselves. The public interest is greater than the interest of any one of these groups, and it is absolutely necessary that this interest be made supreme. But there is just as great a necessity on the part of the public to see that each of these groups is justly treated. Otherwise, government and society will be thrown into chaos. On each one of us rests a moral obligation to do our share of the world's work. We have no right to refuse.

The training of the Boy Scouts fits them to an early realization of this great principle and adapts them in habits and thoughts and life to its observances. We know too well what fortune overtakes those who attempt to live in opposition to these standards. They become at once rightfully and truly branded as outlaws. However much they may boast of their freedom from all restraints and their disregard of all conventionalities of society, they are immediately the recognized foes of their brethren. Their short existence is lived under greater and greater restrictions, in terror of the law, in flight from arrest, or in imprisonment. Instead of gaining freedom, they became the slaves of their own evil doing, realizing the scriptural assertion that they who sin are the servants of sin and that the wages of sin is death. The Boy Scout movement has been instituted in order that the youth, instead of falling under the domination of habits and actions that lead only to destruction, may come under the discipline of a training that leads to eternal life. They learn that they secure freedom and prosperity by observing the law.

This is but one of the many organizations that are working for good in our country. Some of them have a racial basis, some a denominational basis. All of them in their essence are patriotic and religious. Their steady growth and widening influence go very far to justify our faith in the abiding fitness of things. We can not deny that there are evil forces all about us, but a critical examination of what is going on in the world can not fail to justify the belief that wherever these powers of evil may be located, however great may be their apparent extent, they are not realities, and somewhere there is developing an even greater power of good by which they will be overcome.

We need a greater faith in the strength of right living. We need a greater faith in the power of righteousness. These are the realities which do not pass away. On these everlasting principles rests the movement of the Boy Scouts of America. It is one of the growing institutions by which our country is working out the fulfillment of an eternal promise.

XXXV

No method of procedure has ever been devised by which liberty could be divorced from local self-government. No plan of centralization has ever been adopted which did not result in bureaucracy, tyranny, inflexibility, reaction, and decline.

STATES RIGHTS AND NATIONAL UNITY

FELLOW AMERICANS:

No ONE who is interested in the early beginnings of America, or who is moved by love of our country, could come into these historic and hallowed surroundings without being conscious of a deep sense of reverence. In a land which is rich in the interesting records of the past, that portion of Virginia lying between Washington and Norfolk stands out unrivaled in important events and great names. Colonial importance, Revolutionary fame, the statesmanship of the early Republic, the great struggle for the supremacy of the Union—these epoch-making stories can not be told without relating the history of this locality and recounting the eminence of its illustrious sons. Very much of this narrative centers around the venerable town of Williamsburg and the old college of William and Mary.

Within this locality are Jamestown, where the English settlements began, and Yorktown, where English dominion ended. From Petersburg to Arlington stretches a land marked by many battle fields where the shedding of fraternal blood rededicated the Constitution. Here began the first preparation within our country for the establishment of a college. But the unfortunate interruption of hostile natives deferred the completion of the project, so that this institution ranks second in age with all our other universities. Here are the three capitals of this sovereign Commonwealth. If the work which is represented by the great names which have been associated with the growth

Address at the College of William and Mary, Williamsburg, Va., May 15, 1926.

and strength of this region were struck from the annals of our country, the richest heritage of progress and fame that ever glorified the actions of a people would sink to comparative poverty. What a wealth of distinguished figures from the time of John Smith down to the present day! I can not relate them all, these statesmen and soldiers, these founders and benefactors, who here lived and wrought with so much of enduring glory. They are represented by such stalwart characters as Patrick Henry, George Mason, Richard Henry Lee, Thomas Jefferson, and George Washington. Later came Monroe, Marshall, Madison, Randolph, and Harrison, with a long list of associates almost equally eminent in the history of our country. All Americans. It was into this region that Abraham Lincoln made his last journey from Washington.

This richest of all our historical settings made so great an appeal to me when I was approached by your two distinguished Senators, Mr. Swanson and Mr. Glass, whom I cherish as friends, honor for their devotion to their country, and esteem for the support they have often given when we have been mutually striving for sound government, bearing the invitation of your General Assembly to participate in the observance of this day, which was supported by Col. Henry W. Anderson, a lawyer who has contributed so much of his great learning and talents to the service of his country, and emphasized by my former secretary, Mr. Slemp, for many years a prominent leader in Congress, a man whose loyalty and devotion has imposed upon me so much obligation, that it seemed almost a patriotic duty to respond.

It is difficult to determine where or when the great movements in human progress had their original inception. Our life is complex and interwoven with thousands of varying motives and cross currents. One act leads to another. Yet certain actions stand out with so much prominence against the background of the past that we are justified in saying of them that at least there is an event which is one of the beginnings of a new epoch. In accordance with this standard, we are altogether warranted in asserting that 150 years ago, on the 15th of May, 1776, formal action was taken in this city by a patriotic band of loyal Virginians, in their public capacity as servants of the common cause of the American Colonies, which had a most direct influence in leading to the Declaration of Independence.

It is not necessary at this time to relate again the various events that preceded and caused the American Revolution. The people of this Commonwealth had been constantly alert in the assertion and maintenance of their constitutional rights against British encroachment. Under the lead of Samuel Adams, the Boston town meeting in May, 1764, adopted resolutions against the proposed stamp tax, but the first formal defiance of that act after its passage came from Virginia, when in May, 1765, Patrick Henry introduced a series of resolutions in the Assembly declaring that the only power of taxation lay in the people themselves, or in their chosen representatives.

Again, in May, 1769, the House of Burgesses, numbering among its membership Washington, Henry, and Jefferson, condemned the laws of Parliament taxing the Colonies and requested other Colonies to join them in this protest. When the governor took the disciplinary measure of adjourning them, they met at the Raleigh Tavern, where Washington prepared a resolution pledging themselves to continue the policy of non-importation, which was adopted. Also in March, 1773, the Virginia Assembly unanimously voted to establish a system of intercolonial committees of correspondence. As great an authority as John Fiske calls this "the most decided step toward revolution that had yet been taken by the Americans." This original suggestion appears to have come from the eminent divine Jonathan Mayhew, who suggested to James Otis that the communion of churches furnished an excellent example for a communion of Colonies. Again, late in 1772, a Boston town meeting had taken the lead in adopting a committee for correspondence for the Colony of Massachusetts, and Samuel Adams wrote to Richard Henry Lee, who had already expressed the same idea, urging a like action for Virginia. But in March, 1773, this Colony had already anticipated that course and enlarged upon it by making it an intercolonial committee. The convocation of such a body would result in the setting up of a Congress which would represent the united authority of the Colonies. Events moved rapidly, and in the closing days of 1775, incensed by his tyranny, a body of patriots, including John Marshall, drove Lord Dunmore, the governor, out of Norfolk, a place of 9,000 inhabitants, and took possession. In retaliation the governor set fire to the town by shells from the harbor on New Year's Day, and it was consumed.

Confirming my statement that it is difficult to date and locate the exact beginning of any event, we find that on the 22nd of April the people of Cumberland County adopted a resolution prepared by Carter Henry Harrison instructing their delegates to the Virginia Convention, which was to meet in this town in May, "positively to declare for an independency" and to "promote in our convention an instruction to our delegates now sitting in Continental Congress to do the same." A like sentiment was being unofficially, though publicly, expressed in other counties. On the 20th of April Lee wrote from the Congress in Philadelphia to Henry to propose in the coming convention a separation of the Colonies from Great Britain.

It was on the 6th of May, 1776, that there assembled at Williamsburg a convention which was to become historic. It was presided over by Edmund Pendleton, who had op-

STATES RIGHTS AND NATIONAL UNITY 405

posed the stamp act resolutions of Patrick Henry, but eleven
years and the wanton cruelty of the royal governor had
made a great change in the public opinion of the Colony,
and he had become a loyal supporter of independence. He
now joined with Patrick Henry and Meriwether Smith in
drafting resolutions to be prosposed by Thomas Nelson,
which refer to our country as "America," and after setting
out the grievances that it had endured and "appealing to
the Searcher of Hearts for the sincerity of former declarations" and a discussion in which Mason and Madison, to
be known to future fame, took part, on the 15th of May,
1776, it was

"Resolved unanimously, That the delegates appointed to
represent this Colony in General Congress be instructed to
propose to that respectable body to declare the United
Colonies free and independent States, absolved from all
allegiance to, or dependence upon, the Crown or Parliament of Great Britain; and that they give the assent of
this Colony to such declaration, and to whatever measures
may be thought proper and necessary by the Congress for
forming foreign alliances, and a confederation of the Colonies, at such time, and in the manner, as to them shall
seem best: *Provided,* That the power of forming government for, and the regulation of the internal concerns of
each Colony, be left to respective colonial legislatures.

Resolved unanimously, That a committee be appointed
to prepare a declaration of rights, and such a plan of government as will be most likely to maintain peace and order
in this Colony and secure substantial and equal liberty
to the people."

The import of these resolutions was well understood in
this locality. The event was marked that evening by a
celebration, the ringing of bells, and the firing of guns.
The British flag went down at the statehouse never to rise

again, and in its place was flown the crosses and stripes, the temporary emblem of a new government.

These resolutions coming by the action of the duly constituted representatives of the largest of the Colonies were of an importance that can not be described as anything less than decisive in the movement for independence. Other localities held the same opinions, but this action of the Old Dominion was needed to make such opinions effective. Richard Henry Lee now had the assurance of the support of his constituents. On the 7th of June he moved the Congress—

"That these United States are, and of right ought to be, free and independent States; that they are absolved from all allegiance to the British Crown, and that all political connection between them and the State of Great Britain is, and ought to be, totally dissolved; that it is expedient forthwith to take the most effectual measures for forming foreign alliances; that a plan of confederation be prepared and transmitted to the respective Colonies for their consideration and approbation."

This motion was at once seconded by John Adams, of Massachusetts. In this great crisis the Pilgrim and the Cavalier stood side by side united in the common cause of human liberty under constitutional law.

The excellence of the official documents of the Revolutionary period has often been remarked. It was such as to draw praise from the foremost British statesmen. In that respect the Virginia resolution of May 15 left little to be desired. They are characterized by a most admirable restraint, clear and logical in their presentation of facts, and clothed in appropriate language. They have a dignity and strength that are compelling and a courage and reserve that are convincing. They were composed by no ordinary men. Such a document could only be produced by character and culture. The influences which had flowed from the eighty-odd years of existence of William and Mary College can not be separated from the form and substance of these resolutions. Into their making went all that was best of some of her most distinguished sons.

What purpose had planted these institutions of learning in the American wilderness? What raised up Harvard, that it might become the teacher of Otis and Hancock and the Adamses? What nourished William and Mary, that it might furnish inspiration to Bland, to Wythe, to Nelson, and to Jefferson? These two seminaries had a common benefactor in the famous Robert Boyle. And when the wanton ravages of war reduced this once flourishing institution that had spoken so boldly in the cause of liberty to a state that left little but the vibrant tones of the college bell and the fervent prayers of a devout President, it was a distinguished son of Harvard, Senator Hoar, who plead her just cause with such eloquence in the Halls of Congress that a dilatory Government at last made restitution for a part of the damage done, that this seat of learning might be restored to take its active place again as a citadel of truth and liberty and righteousness. No one can contemplate these events without a deep realization that those who participated in them were guided by an inspired vision.

It has not been the experience of history that political ideals spring into full development all at once. They are the process of the discipline of a long and severe training and constant and continued study. The Virginia resolutions in the fewest possible words map out a course of action and lay down the fundamental principles by which America has since sought to guide and direct its political life. The members of the convention, however, would not have argued that they were embarking upon a new theory of political relationship with so much assurance as they would have contended that they were adapting well-established theories of constitutional law to their own condition.

They declared for complete independence. They abjured both the Crown and the Parliament of Great Britain. Much emphasis has been placed on our political independence. It has become one of our most fundamental traditions of government, and rightly so. In our domestic affairs our sovereignty rises to its most complete state. We tolerate no outside interference. But as the devout Mayhew had seen the communion of colonies in the communion of churches, so these resolutions, even though unconsciously, recognized a communion of nations when they authorized the forming of foreign alliances. They could not escape the conclusion that as the individual derives his liberty from an observance of the law, so nations derive their independence and perpetuate their sovereignty from an observance of that comity by which they are all bound. As modern developments have brought the nations closer and closer together, this conclusion has become more and more unavoidable. While the rights of the citizen have been in no wise diminished, the rights of humanity have been very greatly increased. Our country holds to political and economic independence, but it holds to cooperation and combination in the administration of justice.

The resolutions did not fail to recognize the principle of nationality. It was the "United Colonies" that they proposed should be declared independent, and it distinctly authorized "a Confederation of the Colonies." This was an early and authoritative statement of the theory that this is all one country bound up in a common interest, destined to the experience of a common fortune. It was the expression of a desire for a yet unformulated plan for a Federal Government. How great a part Virginia was to play in the final adoption of such a Government was by this action already indicated. When that great test came some years later it was the known wish of the great Washington, aided by the superb reasoning powers of Marshall, notwithstanding the direct opposition of Henry, that caused Virginia to ratify the Federal Constitution at a time which was again decisive in the formation of the Union. For a second time the action of this great Commonwealth was the determining factor in the destiny of America.

It is impossible to lay too much emphasis upon the necessity of making all our political action of the Federal Government harmonize with the principle of national unity. For many years now this course has been greatly impeded from the fact that those who substantially think alike have so oftentimes been unable to act alike. Our country ought to be done with all sectional divisions and all actions based upon geographical lines. Washington warned us against that danger in his Farewell Address. Experience has time and again demonstrated the soundness of his advice and the breadth of his wisdom. It would be difficult to suggest anything more likely to enhance the progress of our country than united political action in all parts of the Nation in accord with the advice of Washington for the support and maintenance of those principles of sound economics and stable constitutional government in which they so substantially agree. All sections have the same community of interests, both in theory and in fact, and they ought to have a community in political action. We can not deny that we are all Americans. To attempt to proceed upon any other theory can only end in disaster. No policy can ever be a success which does not contemplate this as one country.

The principle that those who think alike ought to be able to act alike wherever they happen to live should be supplemented by another rule for the continuation of the contentment and tranquillity of our Republic. The general acceptance of our institutions proceeds on the theory that they have been adopted by the action of a majority. It is obvious that if those who hold to the same ideals of

government fail to agree the chances very strongly favor
a rule by a minority. But there is another element of recent development. Direct primaries and direct elections
bring to bear upon the political fortunes of public officials
the greatly disproportionate influence of organized minorities. Artificial propaganda, paid agitators, selfish interests, all impinge upon members of legislative bodies to force
them to represent special elements rather than the great
body of their constituency. When they are successful minority rule is established, and the result is an extravagance
on the part of the Government which is ruinous to the
people and a multiplicity of regulations and restrictions for
the conduct of all kinds of necessary business, which becomes little less than oppressive. Not only is this one
country, but we must keep all its different parts in harmony
by refusing to adopt legislation which is not for the general
welfare.

The resolutions did not stop here. Had they done so,
they would have been very far from comprehending and
expressing the necessities of the American people. They
went on to provide that "the regulation of the internal
concerns of each colony be left to respective colonial legislatures." This was a plain declaration of the unassailable
fact that the States are the sheet anchors of our institutions. If the Federal Government should go out of existence, the common run of people would not detect the difference in the affairs of their daily life for a considerable
length of time. But if the authority of the States were
struck down disorder approaching chaos would be upon
us within twenty-four hours. No method of procedure has
ever been devised by which liberty could be divorced from
local self-government. No plan of centralization has ever
been adopted which did not result in bureaucracy, tyranny,
inflexibility, reaction, and decline. Of all forms of government, those administered by bureaus are about the least

satisfactory to an enlightened and progressive people. Being irresponsible they become autocratic, and being autocratic they resist all development. Unless bureaucracy is constantly resisted it breaks down representative government and overwhelms democracy. It is the one element in our institutions that sets up the pretense of having authority over everybody and being responsible to nobody.

While we ought to glory in the Union and remember that it is the source from which the States derive their chief title to fame, we must also recognize that the national administration is not and can not be adjusted to the needs of local government. It is too far away to be informed of local needs, too inaccessible to be responsive to local conditions. The States should not be induced by coercion or by favor to surrender the management of their own affairs. The Federal Government ought to resist the tendency to be loaded up with duties which the States should perform. It does not follow that because something ought to be done the National Government ought to do it. But, on the other hand, when the great body of public opinion of the Nation requires action the States ought to understand that unless they are responsive to such sentiment the national authority will be compelled to intervene. The doctrine of State rights is not a privilege to continue in wrong-doing but a privilege to be free from interference in well-doing. This Nation is bent on progress. It has determined on the policy of meting out justice between man and man. It has decided to extend the blessing of an enlightened humanity. Unless the States meet these requirements, the National Government reluctantly will be crowded into the position of enlarging its own authority at their expense. I want to see the policy adopted by the States of discharging their public functions so faithfully that instead of an extension on the part of the Federal Government there can be a contraction.

These principles of independence, of the integrity of the Union, and of local self-government have not diminished in their importance since they were so clearly recognized and faithfully declared in the Virginia convention of 150 years ago. We may wonder at their need of constant restatement, reiteration, and defense. But the fact is that the principles of government have the same need to be fortified, reinforced, and supported that characterize the principles of religion. After enumerating many of the spiritual ideals, the Scriptures enjoin us to "think on these things." If we are to maintain the ideals of government, it is likewise necessary that we "think on these things." It is for this purpose that educational institutions exist and important anniversaries are observed.

Each generation has its problems. The days of the Revolution had theirs, and we have ours. They were making an advance in the art of government which, while it has been broadened in its application, has not changed and does not seem likely to change from the fundamental principles which they established. We are making our advance and our contribution to the betterment of the economic condition and the broader realization of the humanities in the life of the world. They were mostly bent on seeing what they could put into the Government; we are mostly bent on seeing what we can get out of it. They broke the power of Parliament because its actions did not represent, were not benefiting the American public. They established institutions guaranteed under a reign of law where liberty and justice and the public welfare would be supreme. Amid all the contentions of the present day nothing is more important to secure the continuation of what they wrought than a constant and vigilant resistance to the domination of selfish and private interests in the affairs of government in order that liberty and justice may still be secure and the public welfare may still be supreme.

XXXVI

Great men are the product of a great people.

JOHN ERICSSON

It is one of the glories of our country that we all have the privilege of being Americans. Some of us were born here of an ancestry that has lived here for generations. Others of us were born abroad and brought here at a tender age, or have come to these shores as a result of mature choice. But when once our feet have touched this soil, when once we have made this land our home, wherever our place of birth, whatever our race, we are all blended in one common country. All artificial distinctions of lineage and rank are cast aside. We all rejoice in the title of Americans. But this is not done by discarding the teachings and beliefs or the character which have contributed to the strength and progress of the peoples from which our various strains derived their origin, but rather from the acceptance of all their good qualities and their adaptation to the requirements of our institutions. None of those who come here are required to leave any good qualities behind, but they are rather required to strengthen and fortify them and supplement them with such additional good qualities as they find among us.

While it is eminently proper for us to glory in our origin and to cherish with pride the contributions which our race has made to the common progress of humanity, we can not put too much emphasis on the fact that in this country we are all bound together in a common destiny. We must all be united as one people. This principle works both ways. As we do not recognize any inferior races, so

At the dedication of the statue of John Ericsson at Washington, May 29, 1926.

we do not recognize any superior races. We all stand on an equality of rights and of opportunity, each deriving just honor from his own worth and accomplishments. It is not, then, for the purpose of setting one people above another that we assemble here to-day to do reverence to the memory of a great son of Sweden, but rather to glory in the name of John Ericsson and his race as a preeminent example of the superb contribution which has been made by many different nationalities to the cause of our country. We honor him most of all because we can truly say he was a great American.

Great men are the product of a great people. The are the result of many generations of effort, toil, and discipline. They do not stand by themselves; they are more than an individual. They are the incarnation of the spirit of a people. We should fail in our understanding of Ericsson unless we first understand the Swedish people both as they have developed in the land of their origin and as they have matured in the land of their adoption.

Sweden is a country where existence has not been easy. Lying up under the Arctic Circle, its climate is tinged with frost, its landscape is rugged, its soil yields grudgingly to the husbandman, so that down through the centuries its people have been inured to hardship. These external conditions have contributed to the strength, the greatness, and the character of that little nation which even now numbers scarcely 6,000,000 people. Independence, courage, resourcefulness have marked the race since we read of them in Tacitus and Ptolemy. The meagerness of their soil drove them to the sea; their natural characteristic drove them to adventure. Their sea rovers touched all known shores and ventured far into the unknown, making conquests that have had a broad influence upon succeeding European history. At an early period they were converted to the Christian faith and their natural independence made them early responsive to the Protestant Reformation, in which their most famous king, Gustavus Adolphus, "The Lion of the North," was one of the most militant figures in the movement for a greater religious freedom. It was under this great leader that plans were first matured to establish a colony in this country for purposes of trade and in order that the natives, as was set out in the charter, might be "made more civilized and taught morality and the Christian religion * * * besides the further propagation of the Holy Gospel."

While it was under a new charter that a Swedish colony finally reached the Delaware in 1638, they never lost sight of their original purpose, but among other requests kept calling on the mother country for ministers, Bibles, and Psalm books. Forty-one clergymen came to America prior to 1779. One of the historians of this early settlement asserts that these colonists laid the basis for a religious structure, built the first flour mills, the first ships, the first brick-yards, and made the first roads, while they introduced horticulture and scientific forestry into this Delaware region.

It was not until after 1843, when the restrictions on leaving their own country were removed, that the large movement of Swedish immigrants began, which with their descendants are now estimated at nearly 2,000,000 people. Stretching into our Northwestern States they have cut down the forests and brought the wide prairies under cultivation over an area of more than 10,000,000 acres. The building of nearly 2,000 churches and nearly as many schools stands to their credit. They have established about twenty higher institutions of learning; set up a large number of charitable organizations and more than a thousand societies for public welfare and mutual benefit; written thousands of books and published hundreds of newspapers, among which are some of the leading journals of the country. Always as soon as they have provided shelter for themselves they have turned to build places of religious worship and founded institutions of higher learning with the original purpose of training clergymen and teachers. Augustana College, Gustavus Adolphus College, and Bethany College are seminaries of learning which stand to their credit.

Though few in numbers during the period of our Revolutionary War, they supported the Colonial cause and it has been said that King Gustavus III, writing to a friend, declared "If I were not King I would proceed to America and offer my sword on behalf of the brave Colonies." One of the signers of the Declaration of Independence was John Morten or Mortenson, and it has been claimed that Betsy Ross was of Swedish descent. No less than fourteen Swedish officers served our cause either in the Army or in the French fleet which took part in the Revolutionary campaigns. After the close of the war the Swedish minister at Paris called upon our representative, Benjamin Franklin, and offered to negotiate a treaty of commerce and amity, thus making Sweden the first European power which voluntarily and without solicitation tendered its friendship to the young Republic. This treaty was ratified by Congress in July, 1783. The title of "President of the United States in Congress Assembled" was first held by John Hanson, of Maryland, in 1781.

As these Americans of Swedish blood have increased in numbers and taken up the duties of citizenship, they have been prominent in all ranks of public life. They have been distinguished in the public service of the States, filling many of the offices from the governorship down. I shall name but one of the public officials of the Swedish race who have served our country so faithfully as representative of the great legion whose names spring to our thoughts, a learned lawyer, blessed with great ability, possessed of high character, a seasoned parliamentarian with a record of prominent leadership in the legislature of his own State and in the Congress of the United States, a man endowed with the old Norse spirit, a true American, the senior Senator from Washington, Irvine L. Lenroot. Others of the race have sat in the National House and Senate and been prominent at the bar and on the bench. Their painters were among the earliest and have produced pictures of great merit; but of all the arts they have been most proficient in music. Inspired by Jenny Lind and Christina Nilsson they have as a people given great attention to vocal music, maintaining famous choral clubs and producing noted opera singers, displaying also a high degree of talent as composers.

When Lincoln began his great struggle for the integrity of the Union this strain was becoming increasingly numerous, and Dr. Amandus Johnson declares that 16½ per cent of all Americans of Swedish blood volunteered for service in the Federal Army. Among those who reached a high command were General Stolbrand and Rear Admiral Dahlgren, while the rank and file maintained the record of fame for the fighting qualities which from time immemorial have characterized the race. Such is the background and greatness of the Swedish people in the country of their origin and in America that gave to the world John Ericsson. They have been characterized by that courage which is the foundation of industry and thrift, that endurance which is the foundation of military achievement, that devotion to the home which is the foundation of patriotism, and that reverence for religion which is the foundation of moral power. They are representative of the process which has been going on for centuries in many quarters of the globe to develop a strain of pioneers ready to make their contribution to the enlightened civilization of America.

The life of this great man is the classic story of the immigrant, the early struggle with adversity, the home in a new country, the final success. Born in the Province of Vermland in 1803, at the age of seventeen he entered the army. But the urge for a wider opportunity for his talents possessed him, and at twenty-three he went to England. He entered an engineering firm and always preferred to be considered an engineer rather than an inventor. The development of power interested him, and within a year his fertile mind had begun improvements of far-reaching extent upon boilers and engines. With that boundless energy which was to characterize him through life he soon designed the fire engine and developed the screw propeller for marine use. It was this new invention which brought him to America in 1839. His hopes to interest the Federal Government in this method of navigation were not immediately realized, but he began constructing propeller boats on the Great Lakes and started a fleet on the canal between Baltimore and Philadelphia, which caused the railroad to cut its fare in two, and where the boat service still keeps the name of the Ericsson Line. He was soon building a small steamboat, called the *Princeton,* which was the first man-of-war equipped with a screw propeller and with machinery below the water line out of reach of shot. In 1876 he described this vessel as "the foundation of the present steam marine of the whole world. She revolutionized naval vessels." President Tyler and his Cabinet made a trial trip down the Potomac on this boat, which, although marred by a fatal accident caused by the bursting of a gun, demonstrated the desirability and success of this type of warship.

It was therefore no novice but a seasoned and practical shipbuilder who responded when the Secretary of the Navy, alarmed at reports of a Confederate ironclad, advertised for armored ships. This great mechanical genius wrote to President Lincoln offering to "construct a vessel for the destruction of the hostile fleet in Norfolk and for scouring southern rivers and inlets of all craft protected by southern batteries." He further declared:

"Attachment to the Union alone impels me to offer my services at this frightful crisis—my life if need be—in the great cause which Providence has caused you to defend. * * * It is not for me, sir, to remind you of the immense moral effect that will result. * * * Nor need I allude to the effect in Europe, if you demonstrate that you can effectively drive hostile fleets away from our shores."

This offer was accepted, and as a result a strange new craft, sometimes described as a cheese box on a raft, steamed into Hampton Roads late after dark on the day of March 8, 1862. It arrived none too soon, for that morning the Confederate ironclad *Virginia*, reconstructed from the *Merrimac*, began a work of destruction among 16 Federal vessels, carrying 298 guns, located at that point. The *Cumberland*, with 24 guns, was battered to pieces, losing 117 of its 300 men. The *Congress*, with 15 guns, was grounded and set afire, and the *Roanoke* and *Minnesota* were badly damaged and run ashore.

The result was consternation among the Federal authorities. A Cabinet member is said to have exclaimed that a shell from this new engine of destruction might be expected to fly into the White House at any time. In the South expectations were entertained of a complete destruction of the northern ships, the raising of the blockades, the capture of Washington and other cities, recognition of the Confederacy by Europe, and ultimate victory.

When the ironclad *Merrimac* went out on the morning of March 9 to complete its work of destruction it was at once surprised and challenged by this new and extraordinary naval innovation. Speaking before the Naval Institute in 1876, Admiral Luce said that the *Monitor* "exhibited in a singular manner the old Norse element in the American Navy." He pointed out that it was Ericsson "who built her," Dahlgren "who armed her," and Worden "who fought her." And well might he add:

"How the ancient Skalds would have struck their wild harps in hearing such names in heroic verse. How they would have written them in immortal runes."

After a battle lasting four hours in which the *Monitor* suffered no material damage, except from one shell which hit the observation opening in the pilot house, temporarily blinding Lieutenant Worden, the commanding officer, the *Merrimac*, later reported to have been badly crippled, withdrew, never to venture out again to meet her conqueror.

The old spirit of the Vikings, becoming American, had again triumphed in a victory no less decisive of future events than when it had hovered over the banner of William the Conqueror. It did for the Union cause on the sea what the Battle of Gettysburg later was to do for it on land. If some of the European countries had any serious thought of joining with the South, such intentions were speedily abandoned. That engagement revealed that in the future all wooden navies would be of little avail. The London Times stated that the day before this momentous battle England had 149 first-class warships. The day after she had but two, and they were iron-plated only amidships Naval warfare had been revolutionized. The great genius of Ericsson had brought about a new era in naval construction. Naval authorities now recognize the armored vessel which he sent into action as "the germ of the modern battleship," and behold in "the modern dreadnought the glorified *Monitor*."

Great as were these achievements, they are scarcely greater than those which marked the engineering and inventive abilities of this great man, which were to benefit the industry, commerce, and transportation of the country. He was a lover of peace, not war. He was devoted to justice and freedom and was moved by an abiding love of

America, of which he had become a citizen in 1848. He had a peculiar horror of slavery. In 1882 he wrote to a United States Senator:

"Nothing could induce me to accept any remuneration from the United States for the *Monitor* once presented by me as my contribution to the glorious Union cause, the triumph of which freed 4,000,000 bondsmen."

Ericsson continued his labors in his profession with great diligence, even into his eighty-sixth year, when he passed away at his home in New York City on the 8th of March, 1889, the anniversary of the arrival of the *Monitor* in Hampton Roads. At the request of the Royal United Kingdoms of Sweden and Norway, all that was mortal of the great engineer was restored to his native land during the following year. Although he had not returned during his lifetime, he always remembered with the keenest affection the people of his native land. The high estimate he placed upon their character led him at one time to say:

"It is with true satisfaction I now recall to memory the time when I associated and exchanged thoughts with the energetic youth of Norrland. Without disparaging other nations, I must say that the perseverance, sense of right, and clear heads of these youths place them far beyond the young men of the working class in the other countries. I estimate the Swedish vigor and innate good sense as beyond that of other nations."

The high opinion he held of them was no less than the high opinion they held of him. Because of the fidelity and generosity which he had exhibited toward Sweden and Norway, and his helpful service to the United Kingdoms, a captain of the Swedish Navy wrote to him: "If there is in heaven a special dwelling place for patriots, your place will certainly be in the State Apartments."

He was borne to his last resting place with appropriate

honors by the cruiser *Baltimore* under the command of Admiral Schley. Desiring to give expression to the cordial and fraternal ties that united a kindred people, the President of the United States caused to be issued the following order:

"In recognition of this feeling and of the debt that we owe to Sweden for the gift of Ericsson, whose genius rendered us the highest service in a moment of grave peril and anxiety, it is directed that at this other moment, when we give back his body to his native country, the flag of Sweden shall be saluted by the squadron."

Crowned with honor by the land of his birth and the land of his adoption, he sleeps among the mountains he had loved so well as a boy. But his memory abides here.

Both nations unite again to-day in dedicating another memorial to the memory of this illustrious man. His Royal Highness, Crown Prince Gustaf Adolf, and Her Royal Highness, Crown Princess Louise, have most graciously come from Sweden to be present on this occasion and join with us in paying tribute to a patriot who belongs to two countries. It is significant that as Ericsson when he was a young soldier had the friendship and favor of the Crown Prince of that day, so his memory has the marked honor of the Crown Prince of to-day.

This memorial by which we rededicate America to the spirit which Ericsson represented stands most fittingly by the bank of the river on which floated the first craft with which he undertook to benefit this Government, in the shadow of the majestic temple which has been reared to the fame of the immortal Lincoln, whose cause he served, and within sight of the lofty monument that recalls the name of Washington, whose country he helped to save. As the ceaseless throng of our citizens of various races shall come and go, as they enter and leave our Capital City in the years to come, as they look upon their monuments and upon his and recall that though he and they differed in blood and race they were yet bound together by the tie that surpasses race and blood in the communion of a common spirit, and as they pause and contemplate that communion, may they not fail to say in their hearts, "Of such is the greatness of America."

XXXVII

It is one of the glories of our country that so long as we remain faithful to the cause of justice and truth and liberty, this action will continue. We have waged no wars to determine a succession, establish a dynasty, or glorify a reigning house. Our military operations have been for the service of the cause of humanity. The principles on which they have been fought have more and more come to be accepted as the ultimate standards of the world. They have been of an enduring substance, which is not weakened but only strengthened by the passage of time and the contemplation of reason.

WAYS TO PEACE

Fellow Americans:

This Nation approaches no ceremony with such universal sanction as that which is held in commemoration over the graves of those who have performed military duty. In our respect for the living and our reverence for the dead, in the unbounded treasure which we have poured out in bounties, in the continual requiem services which we have held, America at least has demonstrated that republics are not ungrateful. It is one of the glories of our country that so long as we remain faithful to the cause of justice and truth and liberty, this action will continue. We have waged no wars to determine a succession, establish a dynasty, or glorify a reigning house. Our military operations have been for the service of the cause of humanity. The principles on which they have been fought have more and more come to be accepted as the ultimate standards of the world. They have been of an enduring substance, which is not weakened but only strengthened by the passage of time and the contemplation of reason.

Our experience in that respect ought not to lead us too hastily to assume that we have been therefore better than other people, but certainly we have been more fortunate. We came on the stage at a later time, so that this country had presented to it, already attained, a civilization that other countries had secured only as a result of a long and painful struggle. Of the various races of which we are composed, substantially all have a history for making warfare which is oftentimes hard to justify, as they have come up through various degrees of development. They bore

At Arlington May 31, 1926.

this burden in ages past in order that this country might be freed from it.   Under the circumstances it behooves us to look on their record of advance through great difficulties with much compassion and be thankful that we have been spared from a like experience, and out of our compassion and our thankfulness constantly to remember that because of greater advantages and opportunities we are charged with superior duties and obligations.   Perhaps no country on earth has greater responsibilities than America.

Notwithstanding all the honor which this country has bestowed upon the living and all the reverence that has marked its attitude toward the dead who have served us in a military capacity, we are not a warlike Nation.   As a people we have not sought military glory.   Because of our fortunate circumstances, such wars as we have waged have been for the purpose of securing conditions under which peace would be more permanent, liberty would be more secure, and justice would be more certain.   It was this principle that peculiarly characterized the forces who acknowledged as their commander in chief Abraham Lincoln.

While this day was legally established many years ago as an occasion to be devoted to the memory of our country's dead, it can not but each year refresh the sentiment of respect and honor in which our country holds their living comrades.   Of those great armies that maintained the long struggle from 1861 to 1865, which ranked in size with any the world had ever before seen, but a few shattered ranks now remain.   The old valor yet lives.   The old devotion to country, the old loyalty to the flag remain.   But the youth and physical vigor which caused them to be characterized as the boys in blue are gone from these heroes of a former generation.

But the spirit which they so nobly represented two generations ago has not departed from the land.   It was resurgent in the days of 1898 and in 1917, and finds a lineal succession in the three branches which make up the land and sea forces of the present day and in the public opinion of the people. Our country has never had a better-equipped Army or a more efficient Navy in time of peace than it has at the present time. The Air Service is being perfected, better quarters are being provided, and our whole Military Establishment is being made worthy of the power and dignity of this great Nation. We realize that national security and national defense can not be safely neglected. To do so is to put in peril our domestic tranquillity and jeopardize our respect and standing among the other nations.

Yet the American forces are distinctly the forces of peace. They are the guaranties of that order and tranquillity in this part of the world, which is alike beneficial to us and all the other nations. Every one knows that we covet no territory, we entertain no imperialistic designs, we harbor no enmity toward any other people. We seek no revenge, we nurse no grievances, we have inflicted no injuries, and we fear no enemies. Our ways are the ways of peace.

We are attempting to make our contribution to the peace of the world, not in any sensational or spectacular way but by the application of practical, workable, seasoned methods and an appeal to the common sense of mankind. We do not rely upon the threat of force in our international relations or in our attempt to maintain our position in the world. We have seen force tried, but the more people study its results the more they must be convinced that on the whole it has failed. Conditions sometimes arise where it seems that an appeal to arms is inevitable, but such conflicts decide very little. In the end it is necessary to make an appeal to reason, and until adjustments are reached by covenants which harmonize with the prevailing sense of justice a final solution has not been found.

Ever since the last great conflict the world has been putting a renewed emphasis, not on preparation to succeed in war, but on an attempt by preventing war to succeed in peace. This movement has the full and complete approbation of the American Government and the American people. While we have been unwilling to interfere in the political relationship of other countries and have consistently refrained from intervening except when our help has been sought and we have felt that it could be effectively given, we have signified our willingness to become associated with other nations in a practical plan for promoting international justice through the World Court. Such a tribunal furnishes a method of the adjustment of international differences in accordance with our treaty rights and under the generally accepted rules of international law. When questions arise which all parties agree ought to be adjudicated but which do not yield to the ordinary methods of diplomacy, here is a forum to which the parties may voluntarily repair in the consciousness that their dignity suffers no diminution and that their cause will be determined impartially, according to the law and the evidence. That is a sensible, direct, efficient, and practical method of adjusting differences which can not fail to appeal to the intelligence of the American people.

But while we put our trust not on force but on a reign of law and the administration of justice, yet we know that the maintenance of peace can not but to a large extent be dependent upon our sentiments and desires. In spite of all the treaties we may make and all the tribunals we may establish, unless we maintain a public opinion devoted to peace we can not escape the ravages of war. A determination to do right will be more effective than all our treaties and courts, all our armies and fleets. A peaceful people will have peace, but a warlike people can not escape war.

Peace has an economic foundation to which too little

attention has been given. No student can doubt that it was
to a large extent the economic condition of Europe that
drove those overburdened countries headlong into the
World War. They were engaged in maintaining competitive armaments. If one country laid the keel of one warship, some other country considered it necessary to lay the
keel of two warships. If one country enrolled a regiment,
some other country enrolled three regiments. Whole
peoples were armed and drilled and trained to the detriment of their industrial life, and charged and taxed and
assessed until the burden could no longer be borne. Nations
cracked under the load and sought relief from the intoler-
able pressure by pillaging each other. It was to avoid a
repetition of such a catastrophe that our Government proposed and brought to a successful conclusion the Washington Conference for the Limitation of Naval Armaments.
We have been altogether desirous of an extension of this
principle and for that purpose have sent our delegates to a
preliminary conference of nations now sitting at Geneva.
Out of that conference we expect some practical results.
We believe that other nations ought to join with us in laying aside their suspicions and hatreds sufficiently to agree
among themselves upon methods of mutual relief from the
necessity of the maintenance of great land and sea forces.
This can not be done if we constantly have in mind the
resort to war for the redress of wrongs and the enforcement of rights. Europe has the League of Nations. That
ought to be able to provide those countries with certain
political guaranties which our country does not require.
Besides this there is the World Court, which can certainly
be used for the determination of all justiciable disputes.
We should not underestimate the difficulties of European
nations, nor fail to extend to them the highest degree of
patience and the most sympathetic consideration. But we
can not fail to assert our conviction that they are in great

need of further limitation of armaments and our determination to lend them every assistance in the solution of their problems. We have entered the conference with the utmost good faith on our part and in the sincere belief that it represents the utmost good faith on their part. We want to see the problems that are there presented stripped of all technicalities and met and solved in a way that will secure practical results. We stand ready to give our support to every effort that is made in that direction.

While we are thus desirous of the economic welfare of other countries in part because of its relation to world peace, we ought to remember that our own Government owes a great duty to the American people in this direction. It is for this reason in part that I have insisted upon a policy of constructive economy in the national administration. If we can make the circumstances of the people easy, if we can relieve them of the burden of heavy taxation, we shall have contributed to that contentment and peace of mind which will go far to render them immune from any envious inclination toward other countries. If the people prosper in their business, they will be the less likely to resort to the irritating methods of competition in foreign trade out of which arise mutual misunderstandings and animosities. They will not be driven to the employment of sharp practices in order to support and maintain their own position. Being amply supplied with their own resources, they will not be so inclined to turn covetous eyes toward the resources of other nations.

Such a condition will likewise give opportunity to devote our surplus wealth, not to the payment of high taxes, but to the financing of the needs of other nations. Our country has already through private sources recognized the requirements in this direction and has made large advances to foreign governments and foreign enterprises for the purpose of reestablishing their public credit and their private industry.

By such action we have not only discharged an obligation to humanity, but have likewise profited in our trade relations and established a community of interests which can not but be an added security for the maintenance of peace. In so far as we can confirm other people in the possession of profitable industry, without injuring ourselves, we shall have removed from them that economic pressure productive of those dissensions, discords, and hostilities which are a fruitful source of war.

It has been in accordance with these principles that we have made generous settlements of our foreign debts. The little sentiment of "live and let live" expresses a great truth. It has been thought wise to extend the payment of our debts over a long period of years, with a very low rate of interest, in order to relieve foreign peoples of the burden of economic pressure beyond their capacity to bear. An adjustment has now been made of all these major obligations, and they have all but one been mutually ratified. The moral principle of the payment of international debts has been preserved. Every dollar that we have advanced to these countries they have promised to repay with some interest. Our National Treasury is not in the banking business. We did not make these loans as a banking enterprise. We made them to a very large extent as an incident to the prosecution of the war. We have not sought to adjust them on a purely banking basis. We have taken into consideration all the circumstances and the elements that attended the original transaction and all the results that will probably flow from their settlement. They have been liquidated on this broad moral and humanitarian basis. We believe that the adjustments which have been made will be mutually beneficial to the trade relations of the countries involved and that out of these economic benefits there will be derived additional guaranties to the stability and peace of the world.

But if we are to maintain our position of understanding and good will with the nations abroad, we must continue to maintain the same sentiments at home. We are situated differently in this respect from any other country. All the other great powers have a comparatively homogeneous population, close kindred in race and blood and speech, and commonly little divided in religious beliefs. Our great Nation is made up of the strong and virile pioneering stock of nearly all the countries of the world. We have a variety of race and language and religious belief. If any of these different peoples fall into disfavor among us, there comes a quick reaction against the rest of us from the relatives and friends in their place of origin which affects the public sentiment of that country, even though it may not be actually expressed in the official actions of their Government. Such misunderstandings interfere with our friendly relations, are harmful to our trade, and retard the general progress of civilization. We all subscribe to the principle of religious liberty and toleration and equality of rights. This principle is in accordance with the fundamental law of the land. It is the very spirit of the American Constitution. We all recognize and admit that it ought to be put into practical operation. We know that every argument of right and reason requires such action. Yet in time of stress and public agitation we have too great a tendency to disregard this policy and indulge in race hatred, religious intolerance, and disregard of equal rights. Such sentiments are bound to react upon those who harbor them. Instead of being a benefit they are a positive injury. We do not have to examine history very far before we see whole countries that have been blighted, whole civilizations that have been shattered by a spirit of intolerance. They are destructive of order and progress at home and a danger to peace and good will abroad. No better example exists of toleration than that which is exhibited by those who wore the blue toward those who wore the gray. Our condition to-day is not merely that of one people under one flag, but of a thoroughly united people who have seen bitterness and enmity which once threatened to sever them pass away, and a spirit of kindness and good will reign over them all.

The success with which we have met in all of these undertakings is a matter of universal knowledge. We are at peace with all the world. Those of this generation who passed through the World War have had an experience which will always cause them to realize what an infinite blessing peace is. We are in an era of unbounded prosperity. The financial condition of our National Government is beginning to be more easy to be borne. While many other nations and many localities within our own country are struggling with a burden of increased debts and rising taxes, which makes them seek for new sources from which by further taxation they can secure new revenues, we have made large progress toward paying off our national debt, have greatly reduced our national taxes, and been able to relieve the people by abandoning altogether many sources of national revenue. We are not required to look altogether to the future for our rewards and find in our lot nothing but sacrifices for the present. Now, here, to-day, we are all able to enjoy those benefits which come from universal peace and nation-wide prosperity.

As these old soldiers, the living descendants of the spirit of Washington that made our country, go down toward the setting sun, representing the spirit of Lincoln, who saved our country, they will have the satisfaction of knowing that they are leaving behind them the same spirit, still undaunted, still ready to maintain in the future a more abiding peace and a more abounding prosperity, under which America can continue to work for the salvation of the world.

XXXVIII

In its main features the Declaration of Independence is a great spiritual document. It is a declaration not of material but of spiritual conceptions. Equality, liberty, popular sovereignty, the rights of man—these are not elements which we can see and touch. They are ideals. They have their source and their roots in the religious convictions. They belong to the unseen world. Unless the faith of the American people in these religious convictions is to endure, the principles of our Declaration will perish. We can not continue to enjoy the result if we neglect and abandon the cause.

THE INSPIRATION OF THE DECLARATION

WE meet to celebrate the birthday of America. The coming of a new life always excites our interest. Although we know in the case of the individual that it has been an infinite repetition reaching back beyond our vision, that only makes it the more wonderful. But how our interest and wonder increase when we behold the miracle of the birth of a new nation. It is to pay our tribute of reverence and respect to those who participated in such a mighty event that we annually observe the fourth day of July. Whatever may have been the impression created by the news which went out from this city on that summer day in 1776, there can be no doubt as to the estimate which is now placed upon it. At the end of 150 years the four corners of the earth unite in coming to Philadelphia as to a holy shrine in grateful acknowledgement of a service so great, which a few inspired men here rendered to humanity, that it is still the preeminent support of free government throughout the world.

Although a century and a half measured in comparison with the length of human experience is but a short time, yet measured in the life of governments and nations it ranks as a very respectable period. Certainly enough time has elapsed to demonstrate with a great deal of thoroughness the value of our institutions and their dependability as rules for the regulation of human conduct and the advancement of civilization. They have been in existence long enough to become very well seasoned. They have met, and met successfully, the test of experience.

At Philadelphia, July 5, 1926, celebrating the one hundred and fiftieth anniversary of the Declaration of Independence.

441

It is not so much then for the purpose of undertaking to proclaim new theories and principles that this annual celebration is maintained, but rather to reaffirm and reestablish those old theories and principles which time and the unerring logic of events have demonstrated to be sound. Amid all the clash of conflicting interests, amid all the welter of partisan politics, every American can turn for solace and consolation to the Declaration of Independence and the Constitution of the United States with the assurance and confidence that those two great charters of freedom and justice remain firm and unshaken. Whatever perils appear, whatever dangers threaten, the Nation remains secure in the knowledge that the ultimate application of the law of the land will provide an adequate defense and protection.

It is little wonder that people at home and abroad consider Independence Hall as hallowed ground and revere the Liberty Bell as a sacred relic. That pile of bricks and mortar, that mass of metal, might appear to the uninstructed as only the outgrown meeting place and the shattered bell of a former time, useless now because of more modern conveniences, but to those who know they have become consecrated by the use which men have made of them. They have long been identified with a great cause. They are the framework of a spiritual event. The world looks upon them, because of their associations of one hundred and fifty years ago, as it looks upon the Holy Land because of what took place there nineteen hundred years ago. Through use for a righteous purpose they have become sanctified.

It is not here necessary to examine in detail the causes which led to the American Revolution. In their immediate occasion they were largely economic. The colonists objected to the navigation laws which interfered with their trade, they denied the power of Parliament to impose taxes

which they were obliged to pay, and they therefore resisted
the royal governors and the royal forces which were sent to
secure obedience to these laws. But the conviction is inescapable that a new civilization had come, a new spirit
had arisen on this side of the Atlantic more advanced and
more developed in its regard for the rights of the individual
than that which characterized the Old World. Life in a
new and open country had aspirations which could not be
realized in any subordinate position. A separate establishment was ultimately inevitable. It had been decreed by
the very laws of human nature. Man everywhere has
an unconquerable desire to be the master of his own
destiny.

We are obliged to conclude that the Declaration of Independence represented the movement of a people. It was not,
of course, a movement from the top. Revolutions do not
come from that direction. It was not without the support of
many of the most respectable people in the Colonies, who
were entitled to all the consideration that is given to breeding, education, and possessions. It had the support of another element of great significance and importance to which
I shall later refer. But the preponderance of all those who
occupied a position which took on the aspect of aristocracy
did not approve of the Revolution and held toward it an
attitude either of neutrality or open hostility. It was in
no sense a rising of the oppressed and downtrodden. It
brought no scum to the surface, for the reason that colonial
society had developed no scum. The great body of the
people were accustomed to privations, but they were free
from depravity. If they had poverty, it was not of the
hopeless kind that afflicts great cities, but the inspiring kind
that marks the spirit of the pioneer. The American Revolution represented the informed and mature convictions of
a great mass of independent, liberty-loving, God-fearing

people who knew their rights, and possessed the courage to dare to maintain them.

The Continental Congress was not only composed of great men, but it represented a great people. While its members did not fail to exercise a remarkable leadership, they were equally observant of their representative capacity. They were industrious in encouraging their constituents to instruct them to support independence. But until such instructions were given they were inclined to withhold action.

While North Carolina has the honor of first authorizing its delegates to concur with other Colonies in declaring independence, it was quickly followed by South Carolina and Georgia, which also gave general instructions broad enough to include such action. But the first instructions which unconditionally directed its delegates to declare for independence came from the great Commonwealth of Virginia. These were immediately followed by Rhode Island and Massachusetts, while the other Colonies, with the exception of New York, soon adopted a like course.

This obedience of the delegates to the wishes of their constituents, which in some cases caused them to modify their previous positions, is a matter of great significance. It reveals an orderly process of government in the first place; but more than that, it demonstrates that the Declaration of Independence was the result of the seasoned and deliberate thought of the dominant portion of the people of the Colonies. Adopted after long discussion and as the result of the duly authorized expression of the preponderance of public opinion, it did not partake of dark intrigue or hidden conspiracy. It was well advised. It had about it nothing of the lawless and disordered nature of a riotous insurrection. It was maintained on a plane which rises above the ordinary conception of rebellion. It was in no sense a radical movement but took on the dignity of a resistance to illegal usurpations. It was conservative and represented the action of the colonists to maintain their constitutional rights which from time immemorial had been guaranteed to them under the law of the land.

When we come to examine the action of the Continental Congress in adopting the Declaration of Independence in the light of what was set out in that great document and in the light of succeeding events, we can not escape the conclusion that it had a much broader and deeper significance than a mere secession of territory and the establishment of a new nation. Events of that nature have been taking place since the dawn of history. One empire after another has arisen, only to crumble away as its constituent parts separated from each other and set up independent governments of their own. Such actions long ago became commonplace. They have occurred too often to hold the attention of the world and command the admiration and reverence of humanity. There is something beyond the establishment of a new nation, great as that event would be, in the Declaration of Independence which has ever since caused it to be regarded as one of the great charters that not only was to liberate America but was everywhere to ennoble humanity.

It was not because it was proposed to establish a new nation, but because it was proposed to establish a nation on new principles, that July 4, 1776, has come to be regarded as one of the greatest days in history. Great ideas do not burst upon the world unannounced. They are reached by a gradual development over a length of time usually proportionate to their importance. This is especially true of the principles laid down in the Declaration of Independence. Three very definite propositions were set out in its preamble regarding the nature of mankind and therefore of government. These were the doctrine that all men are created equal, that they are endowed with certain inalienable rights, and that therefore the source of the just powers of government must be derived from the consent of the governed.

If no one is to be accounted as born into a superior station, if there is to be no ruling class, and if all possess rights which can neither be bartered away nor taken from them by any earthly power, it follows as a matter of course that the practical authority of the Government has to rest on the consent of the governed. While these principles were not altogether new in political action, and were very far from new in political speculation, they had never been assembled before and declared in such a combination. But remarkable as this may be, it is not the chief distinction of the Declaration of Independence. The importance of political speculation is not to be under-estimated, as I shall presently disclose. Until the idea is developed and the plan made there can be no action.

It was the fact that our Declaration of Independence containing these immortal truths was the political action of a duly authorized and constituted representative public body in its sovereign capacity, supported by the force of general opinion and by the armies of Washington already in the field, which makes it the most important civil document in the world. It was not only the principles declared, but the fact that therewith a new nation was born which was to be founded upon those principles and which from that time forth in its development has actually maintained those principles, that makes this pronouncement an incomparable event in the history of government. It was an assertion that a people had arisen determined to make every necessary sacrifice for the support of these truths and by their practical application bring the War of Independence to a successful conclusion and adopt the Constitution of the United States with all that it has meant to civilization.

The idea that the people have a right to choose their own rulers was not new in political history. It was the foundation of every popular attempt to depose an undesirable king. This right was set out with a good deal of detail by the Dutch when as early as July 26, 1581, they declared their independence of Philip of Spain. In their long struggle with the Stuarts the British people asserted the same principles, which finally culminated in the Bill of Rights deposing the last of that house and placing William and Mary on the throne. In each of these cases sovereignty through divine right was displaced by sovereignty through the consent of the people. Running through the same documents, though expressed in different terms, is the clear inference of inalienable rights. But we should search these charters in vain for an assertion of the doctrine of equality. This principle had not before appeared as an official political declaration of any nation. It was profoundly revolutionary. It is one of the corner stones of American institutions.

But if these truths to which the declaration refers have not before been adopted in their combined entirety by national authority, it is a fact that they had been long pondered and often expressed in political speculation. It is generally assumed that French thought had some effect upon our public mind during Revolutionary days. This may have been true. But the principles of our declaration had been under discussion in the Colonies for nearly two generations before the advent of the French political philosophy that characterized the middle of the eighteenth century. In fact, they come from an earlier date. A very positive echo of what the Dutch had done in 1581, and what the English were preparing to do, appears in the assertion of the Rev. Thomas Hooker of Connecticut as early as 1638, when he said in a sermon before the General Court that—

"The foundation of authority is laid in the free consent of the people.

"The choice of public magistrates belongs unto the people by God's own allowance."

This doctrine found wide acceptance among the nonconformist clergy who later made up the Congregational Church. The great apostle of this movement was the Rev. John Wise, of Massachusetts. He was one of the leaders of the revolt against the royal governor Andros in 1687, for which he suffered imprisonment. He was a liberal in ecclesiastical controversies. He appears to have been familiar with the writings of the political scientist, Samuel Pufendorf, who was born in Saxony in 1632. Wise published a treatise, entitled "The Church's Quarrel Espoused," in 1710, which was amplified in another publication in 1717. In it he dealt with the principles of civil government. His works were reprinted in 1772 and have been declared to have been nothing less than a textbook of liberty for our Revolutionary fathers.

While the written word was the foundation, it is apparent that the spoken word was the vehicle for convincing the people. This came with great force and wide range from the successors of Hooker and Wise. It was carried on with a missionary spirit which did not fail to reach the Scotch-Irish of North Carolina, showing its influence by significantly making that Colony the first to give instructions to its delegates looking to independence. This preaching reached the neighborhood of Thomas Jefferson, who acknowledged that his "best ideas of democracy" had been secured at church meetings.

That these ideas were prevalent in Virginia is further revealed by the Declaration of Rights, which was prepared by George Mason and presented to the general assembly on May 27, 1776. This document asserted popular sovereignty and inherent natural rights, but confined the doctrine of equality to the assertion that "All men are created equally free and independent." It can scarcely be imagined that Jefferson was unacquainted with what had been done in his own Commonwealth of Virginia when he took up the task of drafting the Declaration of Independence. But these thoughts can very largely be traced back to what John Wise was writing in 1710. He said, "Every man must be acknowledged equal to every man." Again, "The end of all good government is to cultivate humanity and promote the happiness of all and the good of every man in all his rights, his life, liberty, estate, honor, and so forth * * *."

And again, "For as they have a power every man in his natural state, so upon combination they can and do bequeath this power to others and settle it according as their united discretion shall determine." And still again, "Democracy is Christ's government in church and state." Here was the doctrine of equality, popular sovereignty, and the substance of the theory of inalienable rights clearly asserted by Wise at the opening of the eighteenth century, just as we have the principle of the consent of the governed stated by Hooker as early as 1638.

When we take all these circumstances into consideration, it is but natural that the first paragraph of the Declaration of Independence should open with a reference to Nature's God and should close in the final paragraphs with an appeal to the Supreme Judge of the world and an assertion of a firm reliance on Divine Providence. Coming from these sources, having as it did this background, it is no wonder that Samuel Adams could say "The people seem to recognize this resolution as though it were a decree promulgated from heaven."

No one can examine this record and escape the conclusion that in the great outline of its principles the Declaration was the result of the religious teachings of the preceding period. The profound philosophy which Jonathan Edwards applied to theology, the popular preaching of George Whitefield, had aroused the thought and stirred the people of the Colonies in preparation for this great event. No doubt the speculations which had been going on in England, and especially on the Continent, lent their influence to the general sentiment of the times. Of course, the world is always influenced by all the experience and all the thought of the past. But when we come to a contemplation of the immediate conception of the principles of human relationship which went into the Declaration of Independence we are not required to extend our search beyond our own shores. They are found in the texts, the sermons, and the writings of the early colonial clergy who were earnestly undertaking to instruct their congregations in the great mystery of how to live. They preached equality because they believed in the fatherhood of God and the brotherhood of man. They justified freedom by the text that we are all created in the divine image, all partakers of the divine spirit.

Placing every man on a plane where he acknowledged no superiors, where no one possessed any right to rule over him, he must inevitably choose his own rulers through a system of self-government. This was their theory of democracy. In those days such doctrines would scarcely have been permitted to flourish and spread in any other country. This was the purpose which the fathers cherished. In order that they might have freedom to express these thoughts and opportunity to put them into action, whole congregations with their pastors had migrated to the colonies. These great truths were in the air that our people breathed. Whatever else we may say of it, the Declaration of Independence was profoundly American.

If this apprehension of the facts be correct, and the documentary evidence would appear to verify it, then certain conclusions are bound to follow. A spring will cease to flow if its source be dried up; a tree will wither if its roots be destroyed. In its main features the Declaration of Independence is a great spiritual document. It is a declaration not of material but of spiritual conceptions. Equality, liberty, popular sovereignty, the rights of man— these are not elements which we can see and touch. They are ideals. They have their source and their roots in the religious convictions. They belong to the unseen world. Unless the faith of the American people in these religious convictions is to endure, the principles of our Declaration will perish. We can not continue to enjoy the result if we neglect and abandon the cause.

We are too prone to overlook another conclusion. Governments do not make ideals, but ideals make governments. This is both historically and logically true. Of course the government can help to sustain ideals and can create institutions through which they can be the better observed, but their source by their very nature is in the people. The people have to bear their own responsibilities. There is no method by which that burden can be shifted to the government. It is not the enactment, but the observance of laws, that creates the character of a nation.

About the Declaration there is a finality that is exceedingly restful. It is often asserted that the world has made a great deal of progress since 1776, that we have had new thoughts and new experiences which have given us a great advance over the people of that day, and that we may therefore very well discard their conclusions for something more modern. But that reasoning can not be applied to this great charter. If all men are created equal, that is final. If they are endowed with inalienable rights, that is final. If governments derive their just powers from the consent of the governed, that is final. No advance, no progress can be made beyond these propositions. If anyone wishes to deny their truth or their soundness, the only direction in which he can proceed historically is not forward, but backward toward the time when there was no equality, no rights of the individual, no rule of the people. Those who wish to proceed in that direction can not lay claim to progress. They are reactionary. Their ideas are not more modern, but more ancient, than those of the Revolutionary fathers.

In the development of its institutions America can fairly claim that it has remained true to the principles which were declared 150 years ago. In all the essentials we have achieved an equality which was never possessed by any other people. Even in the less important matter of material possessions we have secured a wider and wider distribution of wealth. The rights of the individual are held sacred and protected by constitutional guaranties, which even the Government itself is bound not to violate. If there is any one thing among us that is established beyond question, it is self-government—the right of the people to rule. If there is any failure in respect to any of these principles, it is because there is a failure on the part of individuals to observe them. We hold that the duly authorized expression of the will of the people has a divine sanction. But even in that we come back to the theory of John Wise that "Democracy is Christ's government * * *." The ultimate sanction of law rests on the righteous authority of the Almighty.

On an occasion like this a great temptation exists to present evidence of the practical success of our form of democratic republic at home and the ever-broadening acceptance it is securing abroad. Although these things are well known, their frequent consideration is an encouragement and an inspiration. But it is not results and effects so much as sources and causes that I believe it is even more necessary constantly to contemplate. Ours is a government of the people. It represents their will. Its officers may sometimes go astray, but that is not a reason for criticizing the principles of our institutions. The real heart of the American Government depends upon the heart of the people. It is from that source that we must look for all genuine reform. It is to that cause that we must ascribe all our results.

It was in the contemplation of these truths that the fathers made their declaration and adopted their Constitution. It was to establish a free government, which must not be permitted to degenerate into the unrestrained authority of a mere majority or the unbridled weight of a mere influential few. They undertook the balance these interests against each other and provide the three separate independent branches, the executive, the legislative, and the judicial departments of the Government, with checks against each other in order that neither one might encroach upon the other. These are our guaranties of liberty. As a result of these methods enterprise has been duly protected from confiscation, the people have been free from oppression, and there has been an ever-broadening and deepening of the humanities of life.

Under a system of popular government there will always be those who will seek for political preferment by clamoring for reform. While there is very little of this which is not sincere, there is a large portion that is not well informed. In my opinion very little of just criticism can attach to the theories and principles of our institutions. There is far more danger of harm than there is hope of good in any radical changes. We do need a better understanding and comprehension of them and a better knowledge of the foundations of government in general. Our forefathers came to certain conclusions and decided upon certain courses of action which have been a great blessing to the world. Before we can understand their conclusions we must go back and review the course which they followed. We must think the thoughts which they thought. Their intellectual life centered around the meeting-house. They were intent upon religious worship. While there were always among them men of deep learning, and later those who had comparatively large possessions, the mind of the people was not so much engrossd in how much they knew, or how much they had, as in how they were going to live. While scantily provided with other literature, there was a wide acquaintance with the Scriptures. Over a period as great as that which measures the existence of our independence they were subject to this discipline not only in their religious life and educational training, but also in their political thought. They were a people who came under the influence of a great spiritual development and acquired a great moral power.

No other theory is adequate to explain or comprehend the Declaration of Independence. It is the product of the spiritual insight of the people. We live in an age of science and of abounding accumulation of material things. These did not create our Declaration. Our Declaration created them. The things of the spirit come first. Unless we cling to that, all our material prosperity, overwhelming though it may appear, will turn to a barren sceptre in our grasp. If we are to maintain the great heritage which has been bequeathed to us, we must be like-minded as the fathers who created it. We must not sink into a pagan materialism. We must cultivate the reverence which they had for the things that are holy. We must follow the spiritual and moral leadership which they showed. We must keep replenished, that they may glow with a more compelling flame, the altar fires before which they worshipped.

INDEX

Absolutism, 183, 184.

Adams, John, 54, 154, 274, 275, 306, 406.

Adams, Samuel, 403, 404; quoted, 449.

Africa, 32.

Aggrandizement, military, 24.

Agriculture, 203, 280-282, 335 ff.; coöperative movement in, 347-349.

Agriculture, Department of, 348, 350.

Alarcon, Juan Ruiz de, 371.

Alvarez, Dr. Alejandro, 372.

America, national unity of, 15, 16, 22, 23, 26, 250, 409; early beginnings of, 54-56; services of, to Europe, 99, 100, 144, 163-165; 193, 197-199, 300, 327 ff.; variety of racial elements in, 159 ff., 250, 297, 436; reasons for migration to, 161; spiritual unification in, 209 ff.; the melting pot, 250; contribution of, to financial stability of the world, 328, 329, 435.

American Expeditionary Forces, First Division of, 135 ff.; war record of, 136-138.

American ideals, 53-55, 77, 83, 85, 96-98, 108-112, 142, 194-196, 205, 300, 331, 454.

American Legion, the, 287 ff., 390.

American principles, 51 ff., 67 ff., 97, 98, 106 ff., 144, 145, 175, 204, 231, 260, 293, 306, 309, 380, 436, 447, 452, 453.

Americanism, 194, 195, 298-301, 415.

Amundsen, 252.

Anarchy, 110.

Anderson, Colonel Henry W., 402.

Andros, 448.

Anniversaries, commemoration of, 249.

Antæus, the Giant, 67.

Appropriations Committees, the, 46.

Arbitration, international, 24-26, 196, 432; voluntary and compulsory labor, 81.

Argentina, 305, 308, 369.

Arlington National Cemetery, 16, 19, 221, 429.

Armaments, Conference for Limitation of, 77, 357, 433.

Armaments, limitation of, 24, 196, 241, 243, 292, 293, 433; competitive, 292, 433.

Armenia, 329.

Army, maintenance of an adequate, 24, 84.

Army, United States, 291.

Arnett, Hannah, 378.

Artigas, 306.

Asbury, Bishop Francis, 149 ff.

"Association, The," 118, 119.

Atheists, 68.

Athletics, 7, 9.

Australia, 326, 385.

Austria, 99, 327, 329.

Authority, 106, 107.

Baden-Powell, Sir Robert, 390.

Baltimore, the, 424.

Baseball, 9; professional, 131; the Washington Team, 129 ff.

Belgium, 328.

Bello, Andrés, 370.

Bible, the, in the Colonies, 212, 213, 218, 454.

Bilac, Olavo, 370.

Bill of Rights, British, 447.

Blake, Tiany, 153.

Bolivar, 306.

Boston port bill, the, 272.

455

34741

DATE

DEC 05 2014

GAYLORD